Communication an
Editor: Jeremy T

The international ne

In the same series

Journalists at work
Jeremy Tunstall

The making of a TV series
Philip Elliott
(published by Hastings House USA)

The political impact of mass media
Colin Seymour-Ure

The manufacture of news
Stan Cohen and Jock Young (editors)

Children in front of the small screen
Grant Noble

The Fleet Street disaster
Graham Cleverley

The silent watchdog
David Murphy

The media are American
Jeremy Tunstall
(published by Columbia University Press USA)

Putting reality together
Philip Schlesinger

The sociology of rock
Simon Frith

*Newspaper history: from the 17th century
to the present day*
George Boyce, James Curran, Pauline Wingate (editors)

Deciding what's news
Herbert J. Gans
(published by Pantheon Books USA)

*This book is the thirteenth volume in a series
edited by Jeremy Tunstall and devoted to
explorations of the interrelationships between
society and all forms of communication media.*

OLIVER BOYD-BARRETT

The international news agencies

CONSTABLE
London

SAGE Publications
Beverly Hills, California

First published in Great Britain 1980
by Constable and Company Ltd
10 Orange Street London WC2H 7EG

Hardback ISBN 0 09 463400 9
Paperback ISBN 0 09 463480 7

Published in the United States of America 1980
by Sage Publications Inc
275 South Beverly Drive
Beverly Hills California 90212
Hardback ISBN 0–8039–1511 X
Paperback ISBN 0–8039–1512 8
Library of Congress Catalog Card No. 80–51779

Copyright © 1980 by Oliver Boyd-Barrett
All rights reserved. No part of this
book may be reproduced or utilized in
any form or by any means, electronic,
or mechanical, including photocopying,
recording, or by any information
storage and retrieval system, without
permission in writing from the
publisher.
Set in Monotype Times 10pt
Printed in Great Britain by The Anchor Press Ltd
and bound by Wm Brendon & Son Ltd
both of Tiptree, Essex

for Leah, Audrey, Jack and Irene

Contents

Preface	11
Introduction	13
The agency continuum	14
The 'Big Four': as the paramount news sources	15
The 'Big Four': a unique blend	22
1 Business begins at home	31
Ownership and control	31
Revenue and expenditure	36
Clients	40
Manpower and bureaux	43
Service variety	50
(i) Range	50
(ii) Technology	52
(iii) Direct and indirect distribution	54
(iv) Languages	59
Regionalization of news services	60
Agency-client relations	67
2 Structure and process	73
Editorial controls	74
Centralization of editorial control	79
The bureau system	85
Bureau scope, size and composition	88
At work: in the office	95
Travel	96
News sources	96

Wordage	97
Markets	97
Competition	98
Foward planning	99
Selection criteria	99
Freedom to report	100
News content	103
Conclusion	111
3 Wholesale news and market control: Domestic	112
Reuters	112
The Reuters–PA alliance	113
Domestic and external competition	114
Relations with the Establishment	117
New ownership structure	119
Post-1945 market competition	120
Development of the finance market	121
Havas/AFP	122
Master of clients	122
Government ally	125
Domestic competition	125
Agence France Presse: the reaction	126
AP and UPI	130
Early conflicts: the metropolitan interest	130
Exclusivity	133
A.M. and P.M.	134
Print and broadcasting	137
Market trends, 1970s	139
The 'supplementaries'	144
The political factor	148
4 Wholesale news and market control: Foreign	152
Factors that determine the location of major bureaux	152
Distinctive features in the development of world markets	155
New agencies in the Old World	157

Contents

Eastern Europe 161
Old agencies in the New World 165
Backyard empires: South America 171
Backyard empires: Africa and the Middle East 177
'From Bombay to Yokohama' 180
Japan: Asian prize 185
Towards the Asian vernacular 189

5 *National news agencies: the unstable nexus* 192
The growth and resource distribution of national agencies 193
News flow as news exchange 195
The satellite agencies 198
World agency promotion of new satellites 201
General character of the agency nexus 204
Resistance and alternatives 209
Shifting centres of resistance 211

6 *New markets, new methods, conflict and risk* 218
The economic news services: Reuters 221
Intensification of competition 231
Wirephoto to newsfilm 234
The newsfilm agencies 238
Communications 242
Other 'spin-offs' 243
Diversification 245

Conclusion 247
Postscript 252
Notes and references 253
Bibliography of major sources 263
Index 275

List of tables

1. Full-time editorial strength in thirty countries for one American agency in the early 1970s. (*Source*: Interview data 1971–5) — 48
2. Sales to non-aligned countries by three news agencies. (*Source*: Pinch, E. T.) — 56
3. APME Committees, 1977 — 70
4. Twenty-eight countries in which agency bureaux were visited or which supplied questionnaire evidence, 1972–4 — 86
5. Selected instances of bureaux with multi-nation responsibilities in the early 1970s — 89
6. AP employees engaged in international news handling in Latin American bureaux, 1971. (*Source*: Hester, A., 1974) — 91
7. Morning and evening strength of major US agencies, 1934–1974. (*Sources*: Schwarzlose, 1966, and Boyd-Barrett, 1976) — 137
8. Market penetration by US news agencies to US daily newspapers, 1966–78. (Various sources) — 140
9. Leading supplementary agencies in order of their percentages of total daily newspapers subscriptions to supplementaries. (*Sources*: Schwarzlose, 1966 and figures computed from the *Editor and Publisher Yearbook* 1974) — 145

Preface

The decade 1970–80 was an extremely eventful one in the world of news agencies. Events moved more rapidly than the process of research could safely record and interpret them. To monitor, simultaneously, all relevant information from all parts of the globe, all of the time, proved impossible. Inevitably, therefore, the different chapters of this book do not all converge on one identical date of completion. Very broadly it is possible to say that the book covers the development of the major western news agencies up to the late 1970s. The original research was made possible by a grant from the Leverhulme Trust, 1971–5. Professor Jeremy Tunstall originally conceived the idea of a news agency project, and his application to the Leverhulme Trust generated the research. But I am especially indebted to Professor Tunstall for his constructive criticism along the route from thesis to book. He will probably not forgive me for saying that his ability to fuse the tradition of speculative academic enquiry with the relentless pursuit of fact has been an important example for many of us who work in the growing field of media sociology. The very large number of agency executives and correspondents and other media journalists in many different countries who were generous with their time will understand if I do not record my individual thanks to them all. An earlier draft of the manuscript was sent to senior executives in each of the agencies in September 1979, but no comments had been received from three of the agencies by the time this book went to press early in February 1980. I am grateful to Reuters for drawing attention to several points of detail. Dr Michael Palmer conducted several interviews for the original project in Paris and Brussels, and his extensive work on the French agency, AFP, is reported in a separate French-language study of the agencies in collaboration with the author (*Le Trafic des Nouvelles*, Paris, Alain Moreau). Hazel Grayson contributed in a major way to the content analysis for the original research. In such a complex field, however, it is more than ever necessary for me to accept full responsibility for the completed work. Leah, my wife, joined me on the way, and it is with her patient support and cheerful company that this book came to be written.

Introduction

Compared with newspapers and broadcasting, the major world news agencies had enjoyed a period of relative obscurity in the public consciousness until three events in the mid-1970s beamed a sometimes hostile spotlight in their general direction. The non-aligned nations, at the Fourth Non-Aligned Summit in Algiers, 1973, endorsed a recommendation for the establishment of a Non-Aligned News Agencies Pool, to help compensate for perceived shortcomings in the existing system of international news supply for developing countries. A similar concern helped inspire draft declarations discussed at the General Conference of UNESCO in 1976 and in 1978 which, had they been accepted in their original forms, would have endorsed the control by governments of all news moving in and out of their territories. Acting on the mandate of the 1976 UNESCO General Conference, UNESCO's Director-General Amadou Mahtar M'Bow set up an International Commission for the Study of Communication Problems whose world brief included a consideration of international news and the role of the major world news agencies.

Common to each of these events, in so far as each pertained to the world news agencies, was a focus on the *relationship* between these agencies and the national news media of the developing countries. Moreover the sympathetic thrust of this focus was very much informed by a concern for the interests of the developing countries. These events, therefore, however laudatory or inevitable their choice of issue so far as the news agencies were concerned, had adopted a partial framework of analysis.

But given that any analysis of international news supply must include the world news agencies, it is important that these agencies be seen not only in relation to the media of developing countries but also to those of the developed world. The major world agencies face imposing problems even in these more affluent markets. It is certainly in the interests of developed countries, and very probably of developing countries as well, to initiate a full review of such problems, and relate these to the global situation. While in the developing world there is a move towards establishing supplemental news services to the 'Big Four', western media analysts must begin to wonder whether the existing total global market is large enough to sustain even the 'Big Four' in their present form indefinitely, and what arrangement, if any, could possibly replace them.

The agency continuum

The 'Big Four' are the major western-based news agencies: two American agencies, Associated Press (AP) and United Press International (UPI), the British agency Reuters, and the French agency Agence France Presse (AFP). Differences between news agencies can be conceptualized as representing different points on a continuum, which itself is made up of several dimensions. The world agencies, for example, not only collect news from most countries and territories of the world, but also distribute news to most countries and territories.

This is why, despite their national affiliations, these agencies (with some important qualifications) can be described as 'world' agencies. These are the agencies with which this book is primarily concerned. The Russian TASS is often considered to be the communist version of a 'world' agency. There are some other agencies with extensive international representation and distribution, such as DPA[1]* of West Germany, Kyodo of Japan, Tanjug of Yugoslavia, ADN of East Germany, EFE of Spain. Yet they are commonly regarded as intermediate between the 'world' agencies and the average 'national' agency. The scale of their international operations is smaller; their activity is more highly concentrated in a few specific geographic areas. Their foremost concern is the news requirement of their own domestic markets. They individually serve far fewer overseas clients on a contractual basis than any of the 'Big Four'. These intermediate agencies also subscribe to the services of the world agencies, whereas the western-based world agencies do not subscribe to one another's international services.[2]

The 1970s saw the development of what can be called the 'international intermediate' category, agencies without a specific national base or involving the cooperation of many different national agencies, and generally catering for the news requirements of specific regions or certain categories of country: these include the Non-Aligned News Agencies Pool; CANA, the Caribbean news agency; and ASIN, a Latin American and Caribbean news exchange pool established in 1979. Then at a further jump down the continuum is the 'national' agency, which typically does not have more than a handful of foreign correspondents, does not engage in foreign distribution

* References begin on p. 253.

(although it will often exchange its service with other agencies, including a partial exchange with a world agency) and functions solely for the benefit of its domestic market. In some countries the primary function of a national news agency is simply to distribute news from the 'Big Four' to local media or government departments. At the bottom of the hierarchy or continuum is a wide variety of generally smaller organizations which may specialize in certain kinds of news, such as economics, photo, sports, or news features, or in certain geographic regions of a country, or in certain kinds of client. A few of these, like the syndicated services of some of the large US newspaper dailies, serve sizeable international markets.

The 'Big Four': as the paramount news sources

Possibly less than two dozen newspapers around the entire world could make a reasonable claim to independence in the gathering of a comprehensive international news file. Most of these are situated in a small handful of countries: e.g. the US, the UK, Japan, West Germany, France. The others are wholly or at least heavily dependent on the world agencies for their fare of news about other countries, either directly, or indirectly by subscribing to national news agency selections from world agency files, by monitoring radio broadcasts, many of which will have also derived initially from world agency news reports, or both. Even those media which might seem to have the resources to survive without the agencies do in fact subscribe to them and at high cost. The more extensive the international news-gathering operations of any individual 'retail' news medium, in fact, the greater the range of news agency services to which, as a general rule, it subscribes.

The services of the 'Big Four' agencies eventually affect, to a greater or lesser degree, a total world daily newspaper circulation in excess of 450m. and a world broadcast audience well in excess of 1,283m. persons.[3] The extent of media dependence on the world agencies has been documented in dozens of academic and professional studies over the past quarter century. Dependence takes a variety of forms. The most visible is the quantitative extent to which media around the world depend on the world agencies not only for general world news but also for news of their own geopolitical regions and – in the case of the US, France and one or two other countries – for their national news as well. To take some recent examples:

(1) An analysis of the coverage of three international crises in the 1960s by four Norwegian papers showed that 87% of the examined news items came from the same four agencies.[4]

(2) Content analysis of leading newspapers in five countries (India, Kenya, Lebanon, Japan, and Norway) in monthly periods of 1961 and 1968 found that 'at least half' of international news items came from AP, UPI, Reuters and AFP, not including non-credited 'Big Four' reports which had been filtered through the national news agencies.[5]

(3) A study of Third World news coverage of fourteen Asian newspapers in 1977 found that a little over three-quarters of all non-local Third World news came from the 'Big Four'.[6]

(4) A study of reciprocal coverage of the US and Canada showed that the world agencies accounted for over 70% of US news in Canadian newspapers and over 80% of Canadian news in US newspapers.[7]

The US and Western Europe are the world's most well-endowed regions for media facilities. In 1971 they accounted for 62% of the world's daily newspapers (excluding China).[8] It is their circulation revenue and volume of advertising which helps provide the resources for extensive foreign news-gathering. Yet in the US by far the most important sources of domestic and international news for most dailies are AP and UPI. Increasingly, US dailies leave even local State House news to the agencies. The London Fleet Street press is particularly well endowed with its own foreign correspondents. Yet all national papers subscribe to Reuters (and either AP or UPI or both) while most provincial dailies rely on an edited service of Reuters and AP news from the UK's national agency, the Press Association (PA). Though the world agencies may be less visible to the public on the pages of the UK press than in most other countries, their importance as initial spot-news tipsters, providing 'wholesale' input for editorial reprocessing is enormous. In most other parts of the world, where individual media rarely have substantial alternative sources of their own and where there is insufficient community wealth to support large, collectively-owned world news agencies, the scope for western-based world agency influence is potentially all the greater. Japan is almost the only non-western and non-communist country which could claim to be self-sufficient in terms of international news-gathering resources, though its principal national agency, Kyodo, does subscribe to the 'Big Four' agencies. Likewise TASS and Xinhua,[9] which use 'Big Four' agency reports in compiling their international news services for Russia and China respectively.

The agencies do not supply newspapers merely with general news, and they do not merely serve newspapers. Each of the western agencies has a specialist economic news service. Most important of these are Reuters Economic Services (RES), and Associated Press–Dow Jones, which is run in conjunction with North America's leading domestic economic news agency. Both these services are distributed internationally, not only to media clients but also to non-media clients like banks, brokers, and commercial houses. Well over 80% of Reuters' revenue now comes from such sources. The American agencies, AP and UPI, have newsphoto services unequalled by the European agencies or any other institution. AP, UPI and Reuters all provide various forms of communication and technical assistance to other media via the sharing of communications networks and consultancy services for smaller news agencies. UPI and Reuters, through their involvement with UPITN and Visnews respectively, are leading providers of international newsfilm for television. And all the major agencies sell to radio and television stations. Increasingly, they sell to data-banks.

It is difficult to quantify the contribution of the agencies to broadcast media, but what evidence there is suggests it is at least as substantial as their press contribution. There are four major kinds of world agency service for broadcast stations: specially tailored teleprinter services; audio 'voicecasts'; printed news and news pictures for CATV; and television newsfilm. Many of the smaller radio stations in the United States use agency teleprinter services directly. These are the 'rip and read' radio news programmes. The anchorman rips off the news as it comes in on the printer and reads it out over the airwaves. Larger stations have their own news editorial staff, but the agencies remain by far the most important single source of international and non-local news stories. A 1974 US study, for instance, found that even for local area news, agencies accounted for 59% of incoming stories to the 29 radio stations studied, of which 45% were used for broadcast purposes. As in radio, so in television; for example:

> As do the other networks, NBC* bases the bulk of its news service on the world-wide facilities of the AP, UP and Reuters.[10]

A case study of two American affiliate television stations found that information from some sources, especially from the news agencies, was accepted without secondary checking:

* It has been estimated that 70–80% of the stories read on camera by television news commentators are gleaned from the wire services. Moreover, US television network bureaux overseas are heavily dependent on the wire services for decisions on which stories to film (Larson, J.F., 1979). The combined dependence on print and film news agencies can be even higher for developing countries. In a study of leading Nigerian broadcast media, the combined influences of Reuters, AP, AFP and Visnews as sources of all foreign stories amounted to 85% (Golding and Eliott, 1979).

Wire services are staffed by professional journalists who are assumed to check on their stories before 'sending' them over the wires. Since most of the reported stories are too far removed to be verified by local newsmen, stories sent by wire services are assumed to be 'institutionally verified'.[11]

Analysis of US television network coverage of a three month period of the Vietnam war concluded that 'most TV news reports from Vietnam consisted of a few sentences rewritten from AP and UPI dispatches and read aloud on the camera by anchormen in "visual" variations of the nightly radio news of previous decades',[12] but wire services were seldom directly credited.

In Britain, the news agencies were identified as the most important basic news sources for BBC Television News in a 1974 BBC Television documentary.[13] And between November 1976 and October 1977 Visnews and UPITN (involving Reuters and UPI respectively) accounted for 40% of all items input to the Eurovision network of television news exchange,[14] an extremely important source of world news for European television networks. The film agencies are of even greater importance to very many television stations in the developing world.

There is no strong evidence to suggest that over time the quantitative importance of the 'Big Four' agencies has diminished. Many western media in the 1970s have cut back on their own full-time foreign correspondents,[15] and are potentially more reliant on the 'Big Four' in consequence. There has been an increase in supplementary services such as the *New York Times News Service* (NYTNS), but these often concentrate on background, feature-type material rather than spot-news coverage, and their services are generally far less comprehensive. It may be that especially in developing countries the growth of 'intermediate' agency services, regional news agencies (e.g. CANA, although CANA distributes Reuters world service), or regional news exchanges (e.g. NANAP) have slightly reduced the overall dependence upon the world agencies. Client media however invariably prefer to concentrate most of their attention on a few comprehensive services rather than attempt to blend together stories from an extremely heterogeneous diversity of much more limited services.

The supply of news received via exchange arrangements is of greatly varying quality and often arrives late. Even in the case of Tanjug, the central coordinating agency for the NANA pool, reports from other members of the pool and other national agencies in 1977 accounted for approximately 40% of world news input and 21% of output, while the 'Big Four' supplied 52% of input and 37% of output.[16] Moreover a 1977 study of media editors in Bangladesh and Sri Lanka found that they distrusted NANA news sent from Tanjug on the grounds that the government sources of much NANA news reduced its value; the 'development' service, DepthNews, organized by the Press Foundation of Asia had no subscribers at all in these two countries.[17]

The agencies as agenda-setters

The agencies exercise several important 'agenda-setting' functions. Historically, they have been one of the most formative influences in the development of the very concept 'news' in the western world. They aimed to satisfy the news appetite of as many daily retail media as possible, regardless of political persuasion, so they promoted the idea of 'impartiality' as a valued journalistic objective.[18] They relied on telegraphic communications because the speed with which they delivered news (especially economic news for financiers and investors etc.) was as important as the news itself. And because the telegraph was costly, they excelled at terse and precise expression. Amongst their potential media clients they focused their attention on the established daily press and helped to confirm its supremacy amongst print news media. Because they supplied the same news to clients whose individual circumstances varied they constructed a product that was at once standardized and yet flexible: 'the inverted pyramid' became the basic principle of all news reporting.[19] The standardized nature of the product helped bring about a substantial measure of uniformity in professional theory and practice far beyond the confines of their initial markets.

In this way the news agencies have played an 'agenda-setting' function by influencing the very concept of 'news'. On a day-to-day basis there are four other distinct agenda-setting functions. The first of these, as we have seen, is exercised in their provision of a substantial proportion of the general and international news presented by 'retail' media.

A second more subtle influence which it is often alleged the agencies exercise is upon the judgements which client media make about the relative weight or importance of different kinds of news. Most, but not all, the relevant academic analyses are of US newspaper usage of AP and UPI. In his study of sixteen telegraph editors[20] in a US newspaper sample, Geiber[21] found that the news agencies had become 'the recommender of news to the wire editor and thus the real selector of telegraph news. The wire editor evaluated the news according to what the AP sent him.' Studies of one such editor, 'Mr Gates', in two periods, 1949 and 1966, largely supported this view. The attention which Mr Gates gave to various categories of news closely reflected the space allocated to the categories on the wire services he received.[22] Liebes (1966)[23] found that agency 'budget' statements, announcing the outstanding stories which they were due to send in the near future, were decisive factors in the planning of 25% of the telegraph editors in his sample. However, Stempel (1959),[24] in a study of six small Michigan evening papers all receiving UPI, found that only 8 out of a weekly total of 764 wire stories were used by *all* the papers. There was 31% agreement on the use of articles. The papers also differed from the wire and between themselves in the content balance of the stories they chose. The implication of Stempel's study would appear to be that the degree of correspondence between agencies and newspapers in the selection of specific stories is not commensurate with the degree of correspondence found in other studies between the agencies and the newspapers in the relative emphases given to general content categories. Where there is high correspondence between the agencies and the media in terms of content balance, it is difficult to determine whether it is the agencies which influence the clients more, or the clients who make their preference known to the agencies. Certainly there is an element of both, while clients are also influenced by one another, and by their reading publics. But where the agencies are initial sources of a majority of news items, as is often or usually the case in the supply of non-local news for many news media, they are plausibly the dominant partners in this mutual 'agenda-setting' process. This may be especially so in international news, where there are fewer corroborative sources, and where high agency–client correspondence in story selection is found even in those world regions known for their intense concern about over-dependence on the 'Big Four' and the need for alternative sources. Schramm found what he described as a 'remarkable' correspondence between the overall content balance of the 'Big Four' wires and fourteen Asian newspaper clients in the supply of non-local Third World news:

> One seldom obtains correlations like that from research involving human elements and large numbers ... The practical significance is that either the newspapers are following to an extraordinary degree the news agenda set by the wires or the wires are meeting to an extraordinary degree the tastes of the newspapers, or the newspapers are following the lead of the wires, whether they like it or not, because they have no way of changing it and no suitable alternatives.[25]

Given that the Asian newspaper market is of relatively little revenue importance to the agencies, that these newspapers have few other equally comprehensive resources to draw on, and that Asian media executives frequently attack 'Big Four' agency news provision for taking insufficient account of their needs, the *prima facie* evidence in favour of Schramm's third interpretation is impressive. As in Stempel's study, however, there were great variations between the wires and their client papers and between each member of these two categories on individual stories: for example, in the total length of stories, the particular choice of stories from any given country or category of news, and the style of coverage, etc. This suggests that correspondence between agencies and clients on the overall structure of the news package is greater than correspondence on individual items, and this again may be a function of the sheer volume of news which agencies provide and from which editors must choose.

The most striking feature of the agencies' 'agenda-setting' role is the influence they exercise on the approach of client media to their *own* news-gathering. It affects the evaluation which news editors place on the work of their own correspondents:

> No less important, an AP or UPI story, coming off the news tickers before anything else, heavily influenced big-league editors and producers on the 'tilt' of a given event, even if they later received contrary evidence, or a contrary account, from their own staff men. Indeed, there were often complaints from newsmen abroad that nothing *became* news until AP picked it up.[26]

Agenda-setting affects the way in which client media deploy their own scarce news-gathering resources, with the news agencies, the 'umbilical cords' as Tuchman has called them, binding the media together into a 'news net':

> News media send reporters to occurrences they have learned of through wire service accounts. They send a reporter to develop the local angle at a national event for which there is wire-service coverage. By complementing the wire services, they reaffirm the sagacity of the wire services' initial identification of the occurrence. Additionally, they fan their reporters through institutions in the same pattern used by the wire services.[27]

In the US the agencies further influence client reporting by issuing 'day books' which list the major events due to happen that day in each major city. This helps media plan their own news coverage, and, since the agencies (especially AP) take stories from client media in the US, it helps secure the kind of local and national news the agencies want. On a world-wide basis the agencies (but especially the US agencies) keep each other and themselves 'in line' by closely monitoring the play given to their stories in those client media which subscribe to more than one agency service. More indirectly, the agencies shape client media news-gathering through their involvement in consultancy and training programmes (especially for newly developing national agencies). In the 1970s Reuters, for example, depended for almost all of its news from some Black African countries on national agencies which it had helped to establish. Most surreptitiously of all, perhaps, the agencies influenced client media news-gathering practices through the sheer force of example, represented through the constant exposure of sub-editors around the world to news-agency 'style', although the agencies might themselves often wish that for the benefit of world news flow such influence was even greater.

Agency influence extends beyond client media and affects decision-making in many important walks of life. In economic services, for instance, Reuters' money-market Monitor Service effectively becomes a market-place in itself. More significantly, the agencies are possibly the single most important international news sources for government departments. Three times during the 1961 Cuban missile crisis a news-agency dispatch was the first source of information for Washington on Moscow developments.[28] A 1974 study[29] of news sources in European diplomacy concluded that

> The role of the wire services deserves special mention. At every major Foreign Office and at many Embassies, one finds wire service tickers clacking out news. The printouts are examined frequently (at one Foreign Office every 15 minutes) by officials designated for this task, and are distributed to other officials with particular geographical and functional responsibilities. These reports may cause cables to be dispatched, they may affect a decision that is being made, or they may lead to the preparation of an explanatory statement . . . A member of the Foreign Office of a major European power described how the wire service had entered into one decision. 'Recently the Prime Minister asked for a briefing (on a developing crisis) at 11:00 in the morning. I stayed with the ticker until 10:55 and then rushed over to the P.M.'s office with my arm full of paper. Literally all we had on it was from the agencies.' The same P.M. frequently asked for 8:00 a.m. briefings on reports received from the wire service during the night.

The 'Big Four': a unique blend

It is too easy to lump the 'Big Four' together as a composite entity at whose door the problems of imbalance in international news flow can be conveniently be laid. Certainly the 'Big Four' share important similarities, but it is the particular combination of similarities and differences which largely explains why they have survived as world agencies as long as they have; it is in some respects a fragile combination, and its viability has very important implications for the media of both the developed and the developing world.

To begin with, each of the 'Big Four' can claim *long heritage* as international news merchants. AFP, as direct successor to Havas, which was established in 1835, is the oldest of the surviving world agencies. AP's birth can be established as 1848: Reuters as 1851; UPI started as UPA in 1907, and had indirect links with an older organization, also called UP, going back to 1882. (UPA became UPI when in 1959 it purchased the Hearst-owned International News Service (INS) dating from 1909.) Long heritage indicates a considerable accumulation and continuity of experience, and while it may also sometimes imply organizational rigidity, the post-war adaptability of all the agencies suggests that this does not apply or no longer applies.

The major European agencies were based in *imperial* capitals. Their expansion outside Europe was intimately associated with the territorial colonialism of the late nineteenth century. Significantly, the third most important of the nineteenth-century agencies was Wolff of Prussia, founded in 1849. Even after unification Germany was the least adventurous in the 'scramble for colonies'. Nor did Wolff survive as a major agency after World War I. As imperial agencies Reuters and Havas benefited in access to communications, news-sources and clients. Given the relatively modest territorial ambitions of the United States, the North American agencies were eventually to capitalize on the anti-imperial international image of their base country in breaking what many considered to be the stranglehold of the European agency cartel. Thus they greatly diversified sources of world news and established what for a long time represented the minimum tolerable level of potential source plurality from the viewpoint of clients outside the communist block. In practice, however, the original cartel established by Reuters, Havas and Wolff, in which AP was for many decades a participating member, together with the natural American 'zones of influence' reflecting the shift in the balance of power towards the USA, left a permament legacy in the division of world markets which served to avoid what for the agencies might have proved excessive international competition.

The 'Big Four' agencies appeared among the world's most *advanced nations*, precisely where the demand for international as well as national news had almost fully matured. Fully matured for three reasons: the growth of international trade and investment required a constant source of reliable hard data about international economic affairs; trade and empire required a constant supply of information affecting political alliances and military security; population mobility as a result of international trade and empire helped create a popular demand for news of these places among relatives at home and established a general climate of international awareness. Especially important was the fact that in these countries, Britain, France and above all the United States, news media flourished in conditions which, relative to most other countries, even European, were extremely sympathetic. News media were here allowed to cater for mass markets, relatively uninhibited by political restraint, and with their large circulations they attracted advertisers.

These *domestic* markets of the major agencies therefore represented tremendous wealth, and have remained by far the most important sources of wealth for the American and French agencies ever since. In France the importance of domestic media (excluding State clients) as compared with foreign media is less than in the case of the US agencies, while for Reuters with its huge non-media market, overseas wealth has grown to represent over 80% of its revenue. In terms of the general viability of the 'Big Four' this important difference means that Reuters and perhaps even AFP may have had greater motivation to respond to international news requirements. It also means that as Britain and France have declined as global political actors, their strong agencies may seem to some as having the merit at least of not being *too* closely associated with the super-powers. While the US agencies have also sought to cater for the special needs of many of the major international markets, the importance to many countries of having an American source of American news is a further strength and one which by virtue of its internal specialisms and divisions of effort has also helped maintain the 'Big Four' system intact.

All four agencies began as *non-government* agencies. Reuters, in the inter-war years, cultivated a cosy relationship with British imperial interests, which did not, however, profit it financially in any important respect. Any hint of government collusion has long since disappeared, although it is still sometimes inaccurately alleged to continue. From early in its history Havas received a government subvention to help meet the cost of news-gathering, and its successor, AFP, is heavily dependent on government assistance in the form of service subscriptions by central and local government departments. But by comparison with many national agencies the French agency-government relationship is at arm's length.

The general non-government character of the 'Big Four' has

operated as an extremely effective buoy in international markets where much of the potential competition is from government-backed agencies. Attempts to deflate the buoy by ascribing ideological motives, and by identifying correspondencies between the agencies and the political aspirations of their domestic governments, have always been easy to make, if somewhat more difficult to substantiate. This constitutes an area of vulnerability for the 'Big Four', but its impact is limited by the generally more substantial evidence against the agencies of the accusing nations. French government assistance to AFP, meanwhile, may have encouraged that agency to provide more generously for the specific client needs of media and governments in many ex-French colonial territories, and its record in the supply of region-specific African news, for instance, is especially good.

In their relationship with clients the agencies have universally operated on a *contractual basis*, involving the exchange of a world service for cash or cash plus the national news service of a subscribing agency. In some instances the cash required may be less than cost, but the cash element places the agencies in a different category from those news services which, for propaganda or public relations reasons, some government-backed agencies may distribute free, and from those news services which are exchanged between national agencies. The cash relationship might seem to place an implicit obligation on the world agencies to supply a service of a higher standard than those in the other categories. While clients and agencies may dispute what that standard should be, it would seem that the cash relationship does represent a lever of some kind. But a single client, especially in a developing country, may feel that the very extent of its dependence weakens its bargaining power: its sole recourse being its power to change from one 'Big Four' agency to another.

Management of the world agencies allows scope for *client media participation*, reflected in their respective ownership structures. AP is a cooperative of daily US newspapers; Reuters is owned by four daily press associations; a majority of media representatives sit on AFP's general council; while UPI is also owned by media interests. Agencies differ in the actual intensity and manner of media client participation, but their ties with media are important constraints on their freedom to adopt policies or explore new business possibilities which would seem to conflict with traditional media interests or tarnish in any way their reputation for disinterested objectivity. However, such influence is not always sufficiently uniform nor concerted to inhibit innovations which may be essential for agency survival and whose consequences for traditional media client interests are ambiguous or uncertain. Moreover, media participation tends to be concentrated in the domestic markets of the agencies.

Diversification of services has been an important feature of agency development, both within media markets and in non-media markets, such as banking or education, but again the agencies differ in the extent and especially in the manner of such diversification. In general, diversification has functioned to supplement the relatively poor returns that are characteristic of traditional agency services to media, thus helping indirectly to maintain more diversity of such services than the real state of the traditional newspaper market probably would have allowed. Since the manner and speed of diversification has differed, the intensity of inter-agency competition in the newer markets has to some extent been contained. But clearly, similar organizations are likely to see the same kind of possibilities for market extension, so that in the longer term the trend may simply be to duplicate the problem of excessive competition relative to possible returns.

By and large, the agencies produce a *similar kind of product*. The similarity is evident, above all, in their focus on 'spot news', that is, news of events which are in the process of happening or which have happened within the current product-cycle of agencies' clients, although different sets of clients will be in different stages of their product-cycle at any given time. The temporal dimension of an agency's definition of what constitutes an 'event', therefore, is even slighter than that of, say, a daily newspaper or even a broadcast organization. This factor alone, together with the constant organizational pressure exerted by emergent 'new' events, precludes even that extent of backgrounding, analysis and commentary which is characteristic of many of the wide-circulation dailies, and even more so of weekly news media. A typical extent to which background is given is the identification of the prominent actors of the story by name and position etc., and the pegging of the story by reference to the immediately preceding event of which client media are likely to have an organizational memory.

In addition to 'spot news' however, some agencies have also increased the proportion of their wires given over to background, feature and commentary journalism, especially in periods of relatively slack output, although this kind of journalism in the agencies' case may strike the observer as relatively low-key in tone by comparison with the commentary of many client media. Nevertheless, the concession to 'commentary' journalism helps serve clients' increasing appetite for pre-packaged news analysis and also provides a suitable occasion for by-lined articles to slake the thirst of some agency journalists for the 'star' syndrome characteristic of much newspaper journalism. Client media may be more likely to print by-lines for these more 'personal' forms of journalism.

'Spot news' is generally not the product of a formed ideological vision, one which is consciously moulded to accord with a predefined 'correct' interpretation. However, like any human activity, it does and must inevitably represent the expression of certain social interests, in this case as mediated by (often conflicting) client media and *their* respective relationships to governments, readers and advertisers, as well as certain interests of the agencies themselves. Thus it is certainly available for sociological study as an expression of a social ideology. But it is by and large distinct from the tautological use of 'news' coverage to directly support and confirm established and formally articulated dominant ideological orthodoxies as, for instance, is expected of some of the socialist agencies and agencies of some of the 'developing' countries. Ideology for the western-based world agencies emerges from (1) whatever professional and sociopolitical consensus can be attributed to the journalistic communities of the agencies' base countries ('consensus' signalling either agreement on specific values or agreement as to what the issues of conflict should be), together with (2) the 'routinized' handling of organizational and task constraints in the light of experience for the purpose of organizational and individual survival.

Product similarity extends beyond the 'spot-news' emphasis to aspects of the form and substance of the services provided, namely, the approximate weights given to broad categories of news, particular stories covered, geographical regions represented etc. But 'similarity' is far from being complete: differences of emphasis and style within the broad pattern of conformity are very symptomatic of differences between the agencies – for example, in terms of which markets are their most important, the distribution of their respective news-gathering resources, differences in the extent to which editorial operations are centralized, differences of length and style of writing, and even differences of quality in the output of individual bureau teams.

The broad business climate in which the agencies operate is clearly perceived by them as a *competitive* one, and this spirit of competition is experienced at every level of their separate organizations. Nevertheless the intensity of competition is not uniform: where in some cases it seems that four organizations are competing, in other instances it seems that the competition has been effectively reduced to two, or even on occasion that only one agency has cornered a particular market. And on certain issues, in certain international forums, the agencies cooperate. It is not unknown even at bureau level that, just as other journalists from rival organizations will occasionally offer mutual assistance or trade information, agency journalists sometimes do likewise. For a time in agency history there was a structure of considerable and overt collusion which although now dismantled has had a continuing influence. A degree of cooperation beyond the mere provision of services is also evident between agencies and certain clients or client groupings; and ambiguous competitor–colleague relationships are to be found in individual relationships between the agencies and smaller 'rivals'.

The agencies have a geographically more diffused clientele than any other comparable organizations in the news business; their product-cycle, if not continuous, is at least shorter than any other media organization's, and their product, because of the 'spot-news' emphasis and because of the competition, is highly perishable. They have therefore developed extensive and complex systems of communication for news-gathering and news-dissemination. They have been *innovators* in adapting existing communications to their own task requirements; increasingly they have become innovators in communication technology per se, and in the design of associated transmission and reception hardware. They have developed communications expertise associated with nation-wide and international systems of news-handling with which few, if any, other media organizations could compete. Because of their size they benefit from economies of scale, benefits which can then be made available to client media (through what, for example, might be termed the effective 'sub-leasing' of communications facilities). But the important point is that in the communications business the world agencies are leaders, innovators and traders on a scale which would make it very difficult indeed for newcomers to emulate.

Seen from a distance, in the abstract, for the benefit perhaps of academic and political delegates at UNESCO conferences, it is easy to lump the world agencies together and attribute to them common motives and common behaviour. Closer inspection reveals not only that there are significant differences but that the precise blend of similarities and differences is the key to their survival. And it is most important to recognize that the question of their survival is a very real one. The basic raw material in which they deal is cheap, by comparison with, say, mineral extraction. It doesn't take many people to mine it, though the 'marginal' cost of getting more than a tolerable basic service of 'routine' news may be surprisingly high. This factor, coupled with the relatively low prices at which news has traditionally been retailed in the important western markets, has led to an in-built minimum pricing tendency. If they try to do much more than just cover costs in their pricing policies for media they are in trouble. In the non-profitable Third World markets higher prices could not be paid anyway, while in the industrial markets the relatively low establishment costs would encourage competition, especially in the form of new media cooperatives making do with existing staff or with only slight additions to substitute for the world services for as long as it took to get the high prices down again. But so long as the existing world agencies adopt a minimalist pricing structure, together with their advantages of tradition and their carefully balanced network of similarities and differences, there is little scope for new candidates. Certainly there is no profit incentive, since the world's most affluent media markets are precisely those which enjoy the closest relationship with, and best services from, the existing world agencies, and do not share the same political and/or content balance concerns of, say, some of the leading national agencies of the developing countries. An ideological incentive exists, particularly in the Third World, but so far the political and economic resources have not sufficiently matured to realize a truly world-wide and credible substitute. But for the existing world agencies the low pricing policy is the source of a constant vulnerability to such factors as deteriorating profit-margins in retail news dissemination or circumstances which require prolonged and substantial increases in news-coverage costs Quite apart from any real concern they have that there might be emergent new competition, in the form, say, of regional news exchanges (but the evidence suggests this does not concern them unduly), they might well feel they could operate more securely with even less competition amongst themselves. But experience has shown that the affluent western media markets regard news-agency cartels with considerable suspicion. While many European countries are accustomed to having dominant national agencies which are the most important sources of processed world-agency news for many news media, they place high value on the availability of competing world news agencies and would be unhappy with a monopoly news supplier. Moreover a monopoly news supplier, being more visible, would very likely be much more vulnerable than the existing 'Big Four' to charges of direct or indirect political and ideological tendencies, and would have a more difficult task in proving that it served all media clients with equal concern.

In the meantime, diversification has been one response to the problem of how to escape the consequences of a fragile market, but there may be restraints on the extent to which news agencies can diversify without affecting their credibility as news agencies. Thus, the world agencies are caught in a tight vice in their efforts to avoid the problems of excessive competition in traditional media markets on the one hand and, on the other, the problems of news monopoly or oligopoly, and of conflicts of interest that can arise from diversification.

Several practical issues follow from these considerations. For example: since the agencies are mainly or partly controlled by Western media groups which also subscribe to agency services, owners as well as media clients may resist domestic tariff increases on media services, even though agency costs sometimes represent only a small fraction of overall costs for the media client. What are the implications for tariffs on non-media services? In some cases, owner-organizations are associated with important non-media interests (e.g. oil interests associated with some UK media groups). Is a conflict of interest conceivable here? In the case of Reuters, there is the question of whether its highly successful diversification into economic news services for non-media clients can be sustained indefinitely against the competition from other agencies or other sources. In the case of the US agencies, especially, there is the question of the eventual impact of new markets, like those of cable television or data-banks. How far do the requirements for new technological investment detract from or even assist in the more basic endeavour to ensure adequate resourcing for general news-gathering?

1
Business begins at home

Paradoxically, the single most important feature of the world agencies is their fundamentally *national* character. This is immediately apparent upon examination of their ownership, control, revenues, resources and range of services. To a large extent it is a logical consequence of their dual role as both national and world news agencies, except that Reuters, alone of the 'Big Four', does not operate a national agency for its home market, and is far less dependent on domestic revenue. (Reuters is, however, part-owned by the national UK agency, the Press Association.) The close tie that each world agency maintains with its respective home market is certainly inevitable, and in some respects desirable, as succeeding chapters will demonstrate.

Ownership and control

There are also three other striking features in the pattern of ownership and control of the world agencies. Agency ownership is distinctively but not exclusively linked with daily newspapers, above all other media forms. And while these hybrid newspaper owner-clients play an important *formal* role at the apex of each agency's management system, there is a clear tendency for organizational control to rest with the full-time salaried employees. And thirdly, there is generally no question of profit-distribution.

All three features characterize Associated Press, the leading agency of the USA. AP is incorporated as a nonprofit cooperative under the Membership Corporations Law of New York State. Of its two categories of membership, regular and associate, only regular members (which must be newspapers) have voting rights. A person or corporation owning several newspapers therefore is eligible for as many votes as there are newspapers. Regular members may also purchase bonds issued by the corporation, and by waiving any claim to interest on such bonds they become entitled to votes in the election of AP's directors. The number of votes is proportionate to the number of bonds held, subject to an established ceiling. Regular membership was extended to Canadian newspapers in 1971.

Associate membership is open to broadcast organizations, to foreign subscribers and to US newspapers which do not want regular membership. It means relatively little in terms of organizational influence and control, except that associate members may attend and be heard at general meetings. Not until 1976 did AP's regular membership give full recognition to the growing importance of AP's broadcast client-associate members, by increasing the number of directors from eighteen to twenty-one, to allow AP associate broadcast members three representatives on the Board. Of course, many of AP's regular members also had broadcast interests, and AP broadcasters have had their own separate annual conventions since 1971.

A 1965 study[1] of AP concluded that even the influence of regular members was in practice rather limited. The power to vote in the election of directors was the main inspiration for publishers to maintain regular membership. The composition of AP's boards over the years had consequently tended to reflect the interests of the larger, more affluent, members, those most likely to have many bondholder votes. The role of the directors was also limited since organizational power had drifted away from the board to the general manager (later called president) which it appointed, and to the agency's administration. In practice, one of the principal concerns of the directors in more recent years has been the rate at which subscription increases have been set.

Nevertheless, AP's executives are very aware of their special relationship of accountability to the agency's members. Occasionally, the 'climate' at AP may feel as close to a branch of the civil service as to a newspaper office; which is rather different from the tradition of America's second major agency, United Press International, UPI, up to 1979. UPI was not a cooperative; nor was it a public body of any kind, and it issued no formal annual report (although annual 'progress' reports were inaugurated in 1973). The controlling interest was held by the US newspaper group, E. W. Scripps Co. E. W. Scripps also controlled Scripps-Howard Newspapers, one of the larger US newspaper chains; United Media Enterprises (incorporating a number of important syndicated news and feature services); Scripps-Howard Supply Co. Inc. (dealing in newsprint); Allied Newspapers Inc. (handling advertising for Scripps-Howard Newspapers); and Scripps-Howard Broadcasting Co., licensee of a number of radio and television stations. A minority 5% interest in UPI was held by the Hearst newspaper group, which had controlled International News Service (INS), America's third major agency, until it was incorporated with UP to form UPI in 1958. A major shake-up in UPI's ownership structure was heralded in August 1979, when

Scripps-Howard Co. offered to sell shares in UPI to newspaper or broadcasting companies in blocks of 3% or less (*cf.* Ch. 3 and Postscript: the offer was withdrawn in February 1980).

Management at UPI may sometimes seem less orthodox by comparison with AP; its climate hitherto more coloured by the spirit of free enterprise (although UPI had not returned a dividend to stockholders for over 20 years in 1977).[2] While it has less to show in the way of formal public records, its employees, in this author's experience, are seemingly more open, often less cautious, sharing with the news service itself an image of brashness which does not always work in its favour, but which still reflects the populist and eccentric character of its founder, E. W. Scripps. What of its relationship with the parent company up to 1979? The original E. W. Scripps had 'paid little attention to the detailed operation of UP'. He had 'brought the new UP into being, he gave it initial direction, and then left it for someone else to run.'[3] In 1967 E. W. Scripps Co. told the Senate Judiciary Committee's Subcommittee on antitrust and monopoly that it could not transfer UPI profits to its newspapers, but that it could lend money to its subsidiaries, an important facility in the light of UPI deficits in the 1970s.[4] Furthermore, an *Editor and Publisher* report[5] of US Justice Department hearings of an application by the loss-making Scripps-owned *Cincinnati Post* to merge with the *Cincinnati Enquirer*, in 1978, revealed that before 1975 when UPI rates were standardized, the *Post* had paid 50% more than the post-1975 standardized rates. Scripps' financial vice-president Lawrence A. Leser was reported as saying that Scripps papers had paid more for news services provided by Scripps-owned companies. Despite the agency's special relationship with E. W. Scripps Co., and possibly in anticipation of the need to broaden the ownership base, UPI sought to encourage client participation in policy-making with the formation in 1973 of a UPI Newspaper Advisory Board, voted into existence at the EDICON conference of UPI client editors and publishers, and of a Broadcast Advisory Board in 1976.

While ownership of Reuters is primarily in the hands of the principal daily newspapers associations of the UK, representing the national and provincial daily press, it does not feature all the characteristics of a cooperative such as AP. It is a limited liability company, incorporated under the Companies Act (UK). The UK Press Associations and Newspaper Publishers' Association have approximately equal shares of the capital, amounting to some 88% of the total; some 12% is held by the Australian Associated Press, representing Australian daily newspapers, and the New Zealand Press Association, representing the dailies of New Zealand. The Australian and New Zealand directors each year attend several of the monthly board meetings in London, as well as the half-yearly meetings of the Company's Pacific Board for discussion of area-related issues. Real control of the organization rests largely with the managing director, appointed by the board, and his staff. This is possibly even more the case than with AP, since the owners have been steadily less important, proportionately, as sources of revenue. This means that by comparison with the other agencies of the 'Big Four', the domestic media have had to bear rather less of the pressure of inflationary subscription rates than might otherwise have been predicted.

Of the four world agencies, AFP is the only one to which its own country's government has a direct channel of influence in policy-making. The agency is a public organization formally directed by an administrative council which elects a chairman and managing director for a renewable period of three years and retains the power to suspend him. The budget is approved by the council, which otherwise delegates a major part of its powers to the managing director. In this respect therefore the administrative council is similar in function to the respective boards of Reuters and AP. It is unlike these other agencies in that its legal status was conferred directly by parliament, which in 1957[6] established the composition of the administrative council. Although the majority of the fifteen-man council is made up of media representatives (eight newspaper directors and two representatives of the state broadcasting system) there are also three representatives of the public service clients (designated respectively by the prime minister, the minister of foreign affairs, and the minister of finance), and two representatives of the agency's own staff, of whom one must be a journalist. Above the administrative council, moreover, there is a higher council to ensure that the agency's fundamental obligations are complied with. These obligations require for example that the agency should be objective and independent, that it should be a world news agency, and that its resources should be used solely for the purpose of providing a *news* service (which might therefore seem to limit the possibilities for diversification). The higher council's eight-man body includes, in addition to four media representatives, one member of parliament who is automatically president of the council, and one magistrate from the supreme court of appeal. While the body has rarely been formally convened it represents a formidable legal safeguard by virtue of its powers to impose its requirements, suspend decisions of the lower council and fire the lower council's president. There is also a financial commission whose three-man body includes two members of the court of accounts and an accountant appointed by the minister of finance. This checks that the accounts are correct and that the budget is balanced. It has reserve powers of complete access to agency records and can require the appointment of a provisional administrator.

The potential for political influence in the affairs of AFP would seem to rest primarily with the government representatives of the administrative council and its two higher councils and, second, on the importance of government departments and prefectures as clients of the agency's services, whose subscriptions provide well over half the agency's revenues. Direct and indirect political pressures have sometimes been alleged with respect to the appointment and reappointment of director-generals. Such pressures were perhaps customary when the agency's status was merely provisional. Jean Marin's period of office, however, lasted from 1954 to 1975. Then, in 1975 under pressure from parliament which refused to approve the agency's budget, and from the government representatives on the council, who refused to accept the requested increases in subscriptions, the council refused to reappoint Marin. And when Marin's successor Claude Roussel, completed his term there were further complaints of pressure. This time, the editor of *Le Monde*, Hubert Beuve-Monde, resigned from the board in protest against alleged interference by the communications minister in attempting to secure the election of the new managing director, Robert Bouzinac. When Bouzinac was succeeded in 1979 by Henri Pigeat, union representatives again complained of political pressure. Pigeat had been AFP's deputy managing director for three years, but his previous background was almost entirely in government service and he was a former director of the government's information service. A principal source of political interference, however, concerns the conflict between conservative users, fearful of rising costs, and the expansionary administration, anxious to secure AFP's place as a world agency. The intensity of world events in the late 1970s may have diminished this source of conflict. Suggestions that political influence has affected AFP coverage, especially of domestic French as opposed to international affairs have sometimes been made but are difficult to substantiate. Increased conflict between militant journalist unions and the administration have increased the frequency of such allegations. Of course it would hardly be surprising to find that AFP erred on the side of caution in the handling of stories of an exceptionally sensitive and political character, and if so it would hardly differ in this respect from many other western media organizations which have similar 'public' status. And while such status can be a constraint, it can also be an important safeguard against actions or policies which could damage the agency's credibility in other ways – for instance, the statutory requirement that resources be used solely for the purpose of gathering and disseminating news would seem to preclude anything akin to the involvement of its predecessor (Havas) in financial advertising and government propaganda.

The overall tendency among the world agencies towards a divorce of ownership from control has the merit that it increases the influence of the practising journalist in management. And this could tend to reduce the possibility of excessive expediency in management responses to short-term financial, political and other constraints arising from the market structure. Broadcast users tend to be under-represented in terms of ownership and control, but since the spot-news needs of broadcast users tend to be less comprehensive than those of the press, and since in the case of the European agencies the broadcast users include giant 'public' bodies, it could be that under-representation actually helps to sustain the priority for comprehensiveness and to protect the agencies against direct political interference.

Revenue and expenditure

It is not simply ties of ownership therefore that make it possible to describe the world agencies as fundamentally national organizations. Of possibly greater importance is the relative wealth of their domestic markets, on which in all cases their initial establishment was based, and on which in three cases they have continued to depend very heavily. And in all four cases, overseas revenue and expenditure is concentrated in the more affluent world markets. But of particular importance is the fact that only one of the 'Big Four' claimed to be operating its *foreign* media services at a profit in the late 1970s. UPI claimed to spend more on foreign operations than it recouped in revenue; Reuters' foreign services were profitable mainly because of the agency's economic services for non-media clients; and AFP's foreign operations were possible only on account of the high subscriptions paid by government clients at home. Even AP's rosier media position was qualified by the contribution (extent unknown) of the sale of AP–Dow Jones economic news to non-media clients. Of course, it is difficult to assess what differences, if any, different accounting procedures might have made. How is it possible to relate costs of foreign news-gathering to revenues taken from foreign clients when the extent of foreign news-gathering is also related to each agency's competitiveness on its respective domestic market, a difficulty which is compounded by the intimate links between costs for general and economic news services, special services for broadcast clients etc.? But the accumulation of evidence suggests that the 'Big Four' are quite serious in their public assessment of the value to them of revenue from their foreign media services.

Compared with other industries, even with other large media organizations, the agencies have not been exceptionally big spenders. Operating budgets for the US agencies in 1977 were $100,000,000 and $75,000,000 for AP[7] and UPI[8] respectively. AP made an overall profit on its foreign services[9] but foreign subscribers probably accounted for only about 20% of its budget.[10] Foreign clientele in the 1970s have accounted for only a quarter of UPI's annual revenue[11] but absorbed 33% of its operating costs in 1977.[12] While there are questions about the comparability of accounting practices between the agencies and about the reliability of published figures and recorded statements, the above figures suggest that despite the difference in AP's favour between the total budgets of the two US agencies, it may be that UPI spent up to 25% more on foreign services than AP in the mid-1970s. That there are problems with the available figures, however, is suggested by data on resource distribution in a later section.

The most active overseas regional markets for both US agencies in the post-war period have been Western Europe and South America. Figures provided by Righter[13] indicate that in an average week of 1977, UPI's European division (incorporating Africa and the Middle East) accounted for 18% of operating costs, but recouped only 12% of revenue – a discrepancy accounted for by the very poor revenue position of UPI in Africa. South America has generated greater revenue proportionate to cost; it was an important foreign growth area for AP in the 1960s and 1970s, while for UPI in 1977 it accounted for 4% of revenue, 5% of costs. But clearly Third World areas have been of relatively little revenue importance in the post-war era. For instance, in a 1956 IPI survey a UP source was quoted as saying that only 3–4% of total revenue came from Asian clients,[14] while in 1977 this region still accounted for only 4% of UPI revenue (but 7% of cost).[15] An AP Tokyo bureau chief in the 1950s estimated that only 3% of his agency's total income was derived from the Asian service.[16] The percentages estimated by both the AP and UPI sources for the IPI survey mainly reflected the considerable importance of the Japanese market in Asia. Perhaps the most telling assessment of the Third World's revenue importance for the US agencies was made by AP's president, Keith Fuller, when he told an IPI Assembly in 1978 that

> AP's total gross revenue from the lesser-developed countries is less than 1% of our income. Our coverage costs in those areas exceed our revenues many times over.[17]

He did not, however, specify which countries he classified as 'lesser-developed'. The implication was that low as the revenue percentages might be for non-western geographical regions they were much lower when some of the wealthier countries in these regions were excluded. AP's vice-president, Stan Swinton, has estimated that it costs AP fifteen times more to cover the Third World than it receives in revenue from the Third World.[18]

Reuters, unlike the other three agencies, has no domestic arm as such, although the proportion of its revenue coming from the UK might still be considered high for just one country. Most of its revenue in the last few decades has come from overseas, and in absolute terms its overseas trade (including the economic services) was greater in the late 1970s than that of any other agency, but as with the other agencies this trade was concentrated in the more affluent of the international markets. The bulk of its trade, however, is in economic news services for non-media clients.

The rate of growth achieved by Reuters in the 1970s was remarkable. Whereas in 1972 its turnover was less than half AP's budget, by 1977 the two agencies had very similar total expenditures, at the $100,000,000 mark.* As much as 84% of Reuters' trading revenue came from overseas compared with AP's 20%. But of course it did not operate a national news agency. This task is undertaken by the UK Press Association, part-owner of Reuters, which distributes a selection of international news from Reuters and from AP to the provincial daily newspapers in addition to its range of domestic news services. Reuters distributes its service of world news (non-UK) direct to the national press and broadcast organizations in London, to the Press Association's London head office (the same address as Reuters') and to a few of the London offices of the larger provincial dailies. It distributes financial and economic news services to clients throughout the country. While Reuters maintains a UK news desk in London to feed UK news into its services for international clients, its special relationship with the PA reduces the importance of the UK market as a cost and as a revenue factor. This market could not, in any case, support Reuters as a non-government world news agency, and it is significant that the proportion of total revenue to be earned from overseas has steadily increased and that note of this trend has been made in almost all annual reports since 1961. In the period 1966–77, the percentage increased from 73% to 84%. A rough calculation on the basis of the available (and problematic) figures, assuming an approximate relationship between expenditure and revenue, suggests that by 1977 Reuters' total overseas expenditure may have been in the order of $60 million

*cf. Postscript.

more than the total foreign expenditure of either American agency. However, since 82%[19] of Reuters' revenue derives from its economic services for non-media clients, this apparent lead is nowhere near as important as far as the general news for foreign media clients is concerned. But because the overheads and costs associated with Reuters' general and economic news services are so intimately interlinked it is impossible to suggest even an approximate comparative estimate, beyond saying that there is no reason to expect excessive divergencies between Reuters and each of the American agencies in their respective expenditures on general news for foreign clients, in any analysis of the 1970s situation.

While Reuters' domestic base is a small one relative to the other world agencies, in revenue terms, revenue sources are highly concentrated in affluent markets. There is a sense in which the UK together with continental Europe serves as Reuters real 'base' – in 1972, for instance, this area accounted for 59% of total revenue, followed by North America (17%), Asia (11%), Africa (7%), the Middle East (3%) and South America (3%).[20] By 1976, the UK and continental Europe accounted for 63%, North America for 19% while the three Third World regions together accounted for only 18%. The trend in the 1970s, therefore, largely reflecting the location of major economic news markets, was towards a proportionate increase of business in the affluent markets and a proportionate decline elsewhere. It will be seen that South America is of lesser proportionate interest to Reuters than it is for the US agencies, while Reuters' involvement in Asia and Africa is greater.

AFP, like the two American agencies, depends on its domestic market for the bulk of its revenue. Its total budget however, is a great deal smaller than that of the other major agencies, standing at $43,000,000 in 1976 (when the next highest was UPI's at $67 million). And most of the domestic revenue comes from state clients. The importance of government-derived revenue has increased during the 1970s as the inevitable consequence of the agency's determined attempt to compete on equal terms on world markets and to sustain its dominant domestic market position, which in turn have required it to seek large increases in subscriptions from domestic clients. In the early 1970s foreign markets accounted for only 17–18% of the total budget, although the agency spent 60% more on foreign coverage than it received in foreign revenue. Of the domestic revenue, 79% (or 64% of the total) came from the state sector (including the state-run broadcasting organizations). But if the state sector was excluded, the French media were only a little more important in revenue terms than the foreign media clients, and this was reflected in the scale of AFP's overseas services. In the late 1970s the trend has been towards a slightly greater dependence on government clients (65% of revenue in 1978)[21] at the expense of a proportionate decline in the significance of the agency's overseas clients, threatening to reverse a previous trend in the 1950s and 1960s for the importance of overseas clients to increase in revenue terms. Like Reuters, AFP's most important involvement in foreign markets is with the rest of continental Europe. Proportionate to its income, however, AFP's involvement in Africa is probably greater than that of any other agency, and in absolute terms is certainly greater than that of the American agencies. In South America, but not in Asia, AFP has maintained a more visible presence than Reuters.

The relative importance of domestic markets as revenue sources reflects, amongst many factors, domestic client willingness and ability to pay for services which combine national and international news, which they regard as sympathetic to their news interests. In Paris in 1974, for instance, the 360,000 circulation paper *Le Monde* was charged a monthly fee of 42,000 French francs for the AFP national and world service, but for the world services of the other global agencies it paid only 4,200 for UPI, 6,790 for AP and 7,840 for Reuters (which generally charges more than the American agencies, depending less than they on domestic market income).[22] An average 260,000 circulation paper in the US would have paid approximately $200,000 for the whole year in 1974 for one of the American wire services,[23] roughly ten times as much as the world service of AP cost *Le Monde*. A 200,000-circulation Norwegian paper paid approximately $34,000 for the AP world service, almost a sixth of that paid by the US daily for a domestic plus world service. A smaller 100,000-circulation Norwegian daily paid approximately $18,000 for AP, less than a tenth of the US paper, and obtained an edited version of Reuters and AFP through the Norwegian national agency for approximately $77,000.[24] Reuters, which distributes only the world service in its 'domestic' market, the UK, also charges more for this than the other global agencies charge UK media. In the case of one of the popular UK national dailies, for instance, the Reuters subscription in 1975 was almost four times greater than that paid to the more expensive of the two American agencies (£30,000 as against £8,175).[25]

Clients

The domestic markets are exceptionally wealthy markets for three of the world agencies (less so for Reuters), because these are amongst the most media-saturated markets in the world. Each domestic market accounts for a large percentage of the total number of clients served by its agency, although up until the mid-1970s at least there were some signs that overall the proportion of foreign clients was increasing.

In the case of the US agencies in the late 1970s, foreign clients represented between a third and a half of UPI's and AP's respective client totals. On the domestic market AP served more newspapers than UPI and UPI served more broadcast outlets. The major growth area on the domestic market in terms of client numbers was in services to radio and television media, and these alone accounted for approximately 20% of AP's total revenue[26] and a substantially higher proportion of UPI's revenue by the late 1970s.[27]

On the US market, by the end of 1977 AP served 1,320 newspaper members (news and photo services) and 3,400 broadcasters.[28] Reflecting the relatively constant numbers of daily newspapers in the previous two decades, growth of newspaper members had risen only 4% from a 1957 total of 1,256. But the extent of growth in numbers of broadcast outlets was 15% in the period 1966–77 alone, a little less than the extent of growth in the total membership from 8,500 in 1966 to around 10,000 by 1977. The proportion of foreign clients in this period remained fairly constant at around 50% of AP's total clientele. It is not known how many of the foreign clients of the US agencies are in fact non-media clients, private or governmental. UPI, at the end of 1977, served 1,134 newspapers and 'other publications' (news and photo) on the US market[29] and 3,699 broadcasters. As with AP the major area of domestic outlet growth has been in broadcasting. There has been a substantial 68% growth of foreign clients served directly by UPI from 1,336 in 1964 to 2,246, so that the proportion of foreign clients to UPI's total clientele has increased sharply from 23% to 32% in 1977.* But this actually represents a return to the situation in the early 1950s[30] before the UP–INS merger and UPI's subsequent efforts to strengthen its position on the domestic market in competition with AP. Almost 70% of UPI's foreign outlets in 1964 were reported by one source to be newspaper and broadcast organizations within the agency's Europe–Middle East–Africa division controlled from London, and most of these were in fact European.[31] If so then it is very likely that in proportionate terms there are now rather more UPI clients in South America and Asia.

While the proportion of foreign outlets for the US agencies has remained relatively constant overall, it is significant that their

* An *Editor and Publisher* report, September 29th, 1979, in the context of explaining the E. W. Scripps Co. offer of partnerships in UPI, gives a global figure of UPI clientele of 5,900, which suggests a shortfall of 1,179 on 1977 figures.

absolute numbers have greatly increased. Between 1939 and 1977, for instance, UPI's foreign clientele increased almost fivefold from 486 to 2,246.

Relatively few of Reuters' direct media clients are located in the UK, since most UK provincial media clients are served by the PA. Overseas, Reuters claims to distribute its news services in more countries and territories than either American agency. Whereas in 1977 AP and UPI services went to 108 and 92 countries respectively, AFP services went to 129 and Reuters to 150 countries,[32] further evidence therefore of a somewhat greater international orientation of the European agencies, especially Reuters. But just as Reuters' revenue base tends to be continental Europe, which in conjunction with the UK accounts for over half of the total trading revenue, this same area accounts for a substantial majority of media clients. For instance, in 1969 Reuters distributed directly or indirectly to 3,154 newspapers around the world: 52% of these, or 1,640, were located in Europe.[33] Its economic news sales tend towards a further concentration on the more affluent world markets, especially in Europe and North America.

AFP is more similar to Reuters than the American agencies in the distribution of client numbers, since although most of its revenue comes from French government clients, the total *number* of domestic clients is far less than the total number of foreign clients. In 1972, 550 overseas clients were recorded for AFP services, and these had increased to 1,300 by 1978. As with other major agencies these included many national agencies which in turn distributed edited versions of AFP services to their own media and non-media outlets. Excluding government subscribers there were 345 clients for the primary AFP services in France, so that the home market accounted for some 21% of the client total.

The agencies may not attach much revenue importance to all their foreign media markets, but they are certainly proud of the numbers of foreign clients. Even where client numbers are not revealed, the number of countries to which the services are distributed are in all cases carefully accounted for. Such numbers testify to the agencies' claim to being world-wide organizations, to their provision of 'impartial' news which is acceptable to diverse nations, interests, races and creeds. While the revenues may not exceed estimations of cost, the agencies would probably be worse off if they could *not* sell to foreign media, since they have to station news-gathering personnel in as many countries as possible anyhow. More important, if they did not sell overseas, their right to gather news from foreign countries would be even less acceptable to many countries than it has been in the 1970s. So while the number of foreign clients and the revenue they produce may not always seem economically viable in the pages of their accounts there are clearly important invisible revenues from such foreign operations, without which the agencies would not as easily cope in the affluent markets to whose news demands they must be receptive in order to survive.

Manpower and bureaux

Concentration of ownership, revenue and clients within national or at least geopolitical boundaries must inevitably influence the distribution of agency resources in favour of privileged markets. The logic of the market dictates that the best services are provided for those who can afford to pay for them. While the less affluent markets are apt to become obsessed by the apparently disadvantaged position in which they are placed, there are also certain benefits for them. They are assured of a more than adequate service of news about those more developed countries with whose affairs, rightly or wrongly, they themselves are intimately associated (although the weight of such coverage is less than often supposed). Moreover, innovations of service or technology which emerge originally in response to perceived interest in the developed markets do often eventually percolate through to at least some of the less important markets.

Published information on agency resources is notoriously difficult to interpret: much depends, for example, on what each agency defines as a 'bureau' or 'journalist', and definitions are infrequently supplied. Different sources are often contradictory. The overall picture was cleared only slightly with the publication of agency monographs in the working papers of UNESCO's International Commission for the Study of Communications Problems.

Available figures on manpower should be treated with caution. AP told the ICSCP that its full-time foreign correspondents numbered 559, of whom 81 were Americans,* figures almost identical to those supplied in an independent 1975 study.[35] If Harris's[36] figure for AP's total full-time 'staffer' (presumably journalist) strength of 2,500 is correct, then a credible 22% of AP's full-time journalistic staff were posted abroad in the late 1970s. UPI told ICSCP that of its total full-time 'staff' (presumably journalists) of 1,823, 578 (32%) worked abroad. But this is considerably higher than Kleisch's 1975 figure of 242 UPI foreign correspondents, of whom 67 were American. The Reuters ICSCP monograph (not supplied by Reuters itself) gave it a full-time staff of 2,000, of which 350 were said to be full-time

* The number of American nationals may have declined considerably in recent years. Quoting data from 1950s sources, Robinson (1977, p. 70), claimed there were 275 AP foreign correspondents of US nationality.

correspondents, and 200 were London editors. The 1977 Annual Report states that there were 2,377 employees altogether (all categories), and that the weekly average number in the UK was 944. AFP gave a figure of 803 total journalistic staff, of whom 80 were posted in the French provinces. Together with Harris's figure of 400 journalists in AFP's Paris office this would suggest 323 foreign correspondents (40% of the total). This is similar to a 1972-based and AFP-generated figure of 339.[37] The broad pattern then is that each agency employs between 240–559 correspondents overseas, in addition to considerable assistance from 'stringers', part-timers and freelancers. How many of the correspondents are in fact newsgatherers rather than news-processors is not known, but this author's visit to over eighty agency bureaux in the early 1970s suggests that there are rarely more than a handful of actual news-gatherers in any given bureau, and frequently fewer than this. The figures clearly show the concentration of manpower in domestic markets in the cases of AP, UPI and AFP. Among these three the proportion of foreign correspondents seems highest in the case of AFP, appropriately so in view of France's smaller size. If the ICSCP figures for UPI are truly comparative with those for AP this would reinforce the evidence which suggests that UPI may have attempted to compensate for a second place on the domestic market by concentrating a greater proportion of its total resources on foreign services. The apparent similarity of numbers of foreign correspondents fielded by Reuters and by AFP highlights the importance of AFP's dependence on government-generated revenue if Reuters, with double the turnover, relies on the same number of correspondents. But Righter (1978) gives unsourced totals of 529 full-time Reuters correspondents and of an AFP 'network' of 171. The higher figures for the American agencies may reflect the tendency, for AP especially, to engage in point-of-distribution translation in Europe, the Middle East and Asia. Since UPI does less of this than AP, Kleisch's figure may, after all, be the more accurate.

There are few available figures which detail the breakdown of agency non-domestic manpower across the world. A 1976[38] source for AFP shows that of the 339 overseas editorial staff claimed by the agency in 1972, 26% were based in Europe, 25% in Asia, 17% in Africa, 14% in South America, 7% in North America, 12% in the Middle East. These figures are probably exceptional among the agencies in favour of Third World weighting.

The importance of the US domestic market for the American agencies is again reflected in the number and proportion of domestic bureaux. A 'bureau' is an office manned by at least one full-time agency journalist. In 1977 AP maintained 112 domestic bureaux to

62 foreign bureaux. Domestic bureaux represented 64% of the total, a slight fall from the 66% recorded in 1965.[39] UPI informed ICSCP in 1977 that it maintained 96 bureaux in the US and 81 abroad.[40] This would put UPI's domestic bureaux at 54% of the total. Since a 1972 directory[41] listed 100 UPI domestic bureaux, there appears to have been a 4% reduction in the 1972–7 period. A 1976 source[42] suggests that UPI's definition of a bureau may be more liberal than AP's, but that even a stricter count of foreign bureaux (65) showed that the agency's domestic bureaux represented 59–60% of the total, a smaller proportion than AP's.* This might again indicate a greater proportionate emphasis on foreign operations, or a tendency to smaller overseas bureaux.

According to the ICSCP Reuters monograph,[43] the agency maintained offices in 60 countries in 1977, very similar to AP's foreign commitment, since Reuters had only one 'domestic' bureau in London. The AFP figures given to ICSCP claimed 13 French provincial bureaux and 108 foreign bureaux, of which 71 were staffed by 'head office journalists'. A 1977 source[44] recorded 17 provincial bureaux and 94 overseas bureaux for AFP. A 1976 source[45] recorded that in 1973 there were 12 principal AFP bureaux in France and 5 smaller ones and that overseas there were 82 principal bureaux (presumably staffed by 'head office journalists') and 27 of 'secondary' importance, probably manned by stringers. If the 1973 figures were correct there is an indication of a reduction of AFP overseas representation (fulltime) in the 1973–7 period. But it would seem on the available data that AFP maintained a larger number of bureaux than the other agencies (at least 70 on the strict definition), partly accounted for by the very much greater AFP expenditure on foreign coverage than foreign revenue obtained, expenditure made possible by French government clients. AFP bureaux, however, are very often smaller in size than those of other 'Big Four' agencies in certain countries.

Distribution of overseas bureaux between the major world regions reveals also an imbalance in favour of certain regions, only partially explicable by differences in the number of countries per region. Of AP's non-US bureaux in 1971 almost half (25) were based in Europe and the others were distributed in Asia (16), Central and South America (13), Africa (5), Australasia (1).[46] Of 65 principal UPI foreign bureaux listed in the 1974 *Editor and Publisher Yearbook*,[47]

---

* More recent figures quoted in *Editor and Publisher*, September 29th, 1979, give the number of UPI's US bureaux as 99 domestic news bureaux and 40 picture bureaux (the latter are invariably accommodated alongside news bureaux), and approximately 62 news and picture bureaux overseas. A further *Editor and Publisher* report, October 13th, 1979, in coverage of the 1979 UPI Edicon conference gives details of plans for six further UPI bureaux in the US.

a third (21) were based in Europe, a quarter each in Asia (17) and South America (15), with 7 in Africa and the Middle East, 1 in Australasia and 4 in Canada.

Clearly, Africa is under-represented, while Europe tends to be over-represented. AFP on the other hand gives special attention to Africa, the least lucrative world market, but one with which France retains important cultural, political and economic links. Of AFP's 71 principal foreign bureaux in 1977, over a third (25) were in Africa and the Middle East, a quarter in Europe (18), 12 in Central and South America, 10 in Asia, 5 in North America and 1 in Australasia.[48] Figures from Reuters were not available but from other sources it is known that its representation in Africa was numerically and proportionately higher than that of the US agencies, but lower in South America.

Measurement by numbers of bureaux is necessarily crude, since bureaux may vary in size from one to one hundred persons. The relative sizes of domestic and foreign bureaux constitute a further indication of the importance of domestic markets, especially in the case of the US agencies. The bureau size of a middle-ranking domestic AP bureau compares quite favourably with the bureau size of an average overseas bureau. Take for instance the AP bureau in Philadelphia in 1972, one of AP's ten 'hub' bureaux in the United States, responsible for the dissemination of regional news within the area covered by the 'hub', and one of three AP bureaux in Pennsylvania alone. This bureau employed twenty-two full-time journalist staffers, including photographers and excluding technicians. UPI's Philadelphia bureau was the agency's second most important bureau in the state, since the main bureau was in the state capital of Pittsburgh. Yet even the Philadelphia bureau housed a full-time staff of eight reporters, two maintenance men, one photographer, and two operators. In Austria, on the other hand, AP in 1974 had a journalist staff of three, of whom one was a photographer, and UPI had a staff of six journalists, of whom five were engaged mainly on translation work for a German language service. For Holland, AP had a journalistic staff of three, UPI had two. In Italy there were thirteen journalist staff for AP and ten for UPI. The population of Philadelphia in 1973 was estimated to be under two million.[49] For the American agencies this city was considered rather more important, measured in manpower resources, than Austria (population in 1969 of over 7 million), and Holland (population in 1970 nearly 13 million), and about as important as Italy (population in 1969 over 53 million).[50]

Similar disparities in size can be found between AFP's provincial bureaux and many of its overseas bureaux. In 1972, AFP maintained bureaux in each of thirteen French metropolitan regions. The largest,

Marseilles, had more clients than any other province, with thirteen newspapers, two ORTF stations and three regional prefectures. This bureau was manned by a regional director, six journalists and six technicians. Lyon, with eleven newspaper clients and staffed by six journalists as well as support staff, was second largest. Each of the regions had a regional director and between two and six full-time journalists. There were two for Clermont-Ferrand, three each for Lille, Nice and Le Havre, four each for Metz, Rennes and Toulouse. These figures compared quite favourably with some of the middle-ranking AFP European bureaux (generally better staffed than non-European bureaux). The Madrid bureau, additionally important as a source of news for AFP's South American clients, had a staff of four editorial men in addition to a director and auxiliary staff. In Vienna, the journalist staff consisted of one director and three editors. Athens had an editorial staff of three.

There are many curious differences of bureau size between foreign bureaux (cf. Table 1), and there is a tendency for some of the more affluent markets to attract larger bureaux. But there are factors other than economic which help explain the location and size of overseas bureaux and later chapters will explore these. What evidence there is does suggest fairly heavy concentration by the global agencies on the developed world in their total distribution of resources, rather less in the case of AFP than the others. The extent of concentration, however, is probably less than that of their largest domestic clients who field their own corps of foreign correspondents. This suggests that agencies and clients share similar priorities but that clients are especially dependent on the agencies for news of what they might consider the more 'peripheral' world regions. For instance, in 1976 over four-fifths of all UK national daily newspaper correspondents were based in North America and Western Europe, and there were no full-time 'staffer' correspondents at all at that time in the USSR and Eastern Europe, South America or Australasia/Oceania. (This pattern was offset to some extent in the distribution of stringers.[51]) In 1975, over half (51%) of all full-time overseas US correspondents working for American media were based in Europe (23% covered Asia, 16% Central and South America, 8% the Middle East and 2% Africa).[52] Even Japanese correspondents were heavily concentrated in the US and Western Europe. Of 333 correspondents listed in the 1972 *Japanese Press Directory*, for instance, 112 were based in the US, and 107 in Europe.[53] Foreign correspondents representing media of the developed countries tend in any case to dominate the foreign reporting of almost all countries, suggesting that alternative patterns of distribution to that of the western media are not very strong. A survey of foreign correspondents in eight countries in the

Table 1
Full-time editorial strength in thirty countries for one American agency in the early 1970s

	City	Country	Population 1971 (000,000)	Agency editorial staff
1	London	United Kingdom	53	40
2	Paris	France	51	26
3	Rio de Janeiro/São Paulo/Brasilia	Brazil	93	21
4	Tokyo	Japan	105	16
5	Beirut	Lebanon	3	15
6	Saigon	S. Vietnam	18	14
7	Rome	Italy	53	13
8	Buenos Aires	Argentina	23	11
9	Cairo	Egypt	34	9
10	Hong Kong	Hong Kong	4	8
11	Vienna	Austria	7	6
12	Bangkok	Thailand	35	6
13	Brussels	Belgium	10	5
14	Djakarta	Indonesia	125	3
15	Manila	Philippines	37	3
16	Taipei	Taiwan	15	3
17	Hague	Netherlands	15	3
18	Athens	Greece	9	3
19	Moscow	USSR	242	3
20	Bogotá	Columbia	20	3
21	Canberra	Australia	13	2
22	Seoul	Korea	31	2
23	Phnom Penh	Cambodia	7	2
24	Singapore	Singapore	2	2
25	Dacca	Bangladesh	65	2
26	Kuala Lumpur	Malaysia	10	1
27	Oslo	Norway	4	1
28	Copenhagen	Denmark	5	1
29	Nairobi	Kenya	11	1
30	Prague	Czechoslovakia	14	1

Source: Interview data 1971–5.

early 1970s (Belgium, Finland, Greece, Hong Kong, India, Israel, Kenya and Spain) found that American, West German and UK media dominated. In India, three-quarters of a total of 92 came from the US, UK, USSR, Japan, West Germany and France.[54] A 1978 study of foreign correspondents in the US found that Western European media accounted for almost 50% of the 949 accredited correspondents. Six national groups accounted for 50% of the total: West Germany (120), Japan (101), Britain (94), France (68), Israel (23), Australia (36) and Switzerland (28).[55]

A further sense in which it may be said that the world agencies are fundamentally national in character, and which characterizes all the agencies, including Reuters, concerns the extent to which the agencies are controlled by nationals of each agency's base or home country. While there is clearly scope for foreign nationals to climb high and while such scope may be increasing, it remains the case that the agencies are basically controlled by home-base nationals. It is true that the vast majority of jobs in overseas bureaux are held by locally recruited nationals. But the majority of top jobs, chief correspondents and managers, and editors on central bureau desks, are held by Americans, British and French. The author's 1976 study found that of 145 agency bureau chiefs around the world about which data were collected, 67% were nationals of their agency's home country and a further 9% were nationals of another agency's home country (e.g. a French national working for an American or British agency), or white Commonwealth nationals (usually Australian), and 24% were locally recruited from the countries covered by the bureaux.[56] There were no remarkable differences between the agencies. Many of the bureaux in the charge of locally-recruited bureaux chiefs were small one-journalist bureaux which might transmit their stories to regional offices for clearance before being placed on the main distribution circuits. However, this study over-represented the larger bureaux. It is also possible that the numbers of local bureau chiefs have increased since then, perhaps in an effort to economize on salary costs and expenses. And in the case of the American agencies there has been a clear tendency to appoint local nationals as bureau chiefs in South American countries since the 1960s. UPI, in its 1978 report to ICSCP, claimed that the entire staff of its Latin American desk in New York was Latin American, as were one of the two top staff in every UPI bureau in that region (i.e. 50%), and that more than half the bureau managers in Asia were Asian[57] (but sometimes 'bureau managers' are basically administrators, and not chief correspondents). In general, it is still safest to conclude that real power in the 'Big Four' rests primarily in the hands of home-base nationals.

Service variety

(i) Range

In a number of ways the domestic markets of the world agencies are more favourably served than their foreign markets, and this is partly the inevitable function of differences in the strength of market demands and capacity for payment. Of the most important services offered by AP to its US members and clients in the mid-1970s (and the UPI range of services was similar), the 'A' and 'B' national trunk wires perhaps ranked highest. The national 'A' wire carried priority national and international news. The 'B' wire carried news of lower priority, as well as articles, features and types of relatively 'timeless' material, some of which might be destined for certain localities only or even for specific clients. In addition to these there were state or regional wires mainly carrying local general, sports and economic news. Specially prepared broadcast wires catered for broadcasters, carrying a lower volume of news and at much shorter cycles than the main press wires. There were also voice commentaries for broadcasters, news services for cable television, an economic wire for media clients mainly carrying stock-market news, and an automatic transmission news-photo service for newspapers. Such services could be received in a variety of different ways. For the smaller clients there was a single wire (the 'Interbureau' wire) which carried the main ingredients of international, national and state news, compiled in Chicago and added to at state or 'hub' level. In 1975, this IB wire served approximately 1,000 of the 1,300 members, and IB subscribers received some 60% of the news and feature services carried on the trunk wire.[58] Most clients of the print services could receive them in teletypesetter form, which meant they could transmit agency material into newspaper columns without the need for further manual typesetting on their part. Already in 1975 a few clients received the high-speed news delivery services, AP's 'Datastream' (UPI's system is 'DataNews'), and their numbers grew rapidly in the late 1970s. Clients could also receive the other syndicated services via AP wires. Distribution was almost entirely by cable – in the late 1970s satellite distribution for certain radio clients was introduced and the possibility of widespread national satellite distribution examined.

Foreign clients of the US agencies did not generally enjoy the same range of services. For many there was only a single trunk wire to choose from (but of course US agency foreign services for the most part distribute only international news: i.e. they do not generally act as national agencies in the non-domestic markets). In a great many places, often as a result of government policies in foreign markets, foreign clients received only the particular selection of world agency news compiled by editors of their national news agency. The news-photo services were generally available, but in most areas there were no specially-tailored services for broadcast clients.

In the case of AFP it is also true that in its capacity as joint domestic–world agency, its French clients were provided with a wider variety of facilities than many overseas clients. Many overseas 'retail' media clients, for instance, cannot receive the AFP service direct; and there is more scope for the feed-in of local news within the domestic market.

The difference in the range of services provided between domestic and foreign markets is evident also in the variety of news provided and the ways in which it is packaged *within* the news services. AP, for instance, unlike UPI, maintains a 'special assignments' team in Washington, which works on longer-term projects that require the kind of 'digging' and 'investigative reporting' that is not common on ordinary news beats of the wire services. It tended in the sixties and early seventies at least to concentrate on Washington or federal stories of primarily domestic significance, not geared to foreign market interests and often not even transmitted overseas. An important feature of this team was that it was clearly a risk venture, tolerable only because of the overall strength of the US domestic market. The general manager, Wes Gallagher, on whose initiative the team was established in 1965, claimed research support in his 1967 address for the thesis that 'members want more enterprise reporting and less police-blotter type of coverage', and that as a result 'AP has concentrated increasingly on trends, or reporting of social change and its effect on society and the individual's way of life'.[59] But the appetite for 'heavy' special assignment coverage was limited. Many papers did not even notice the stories going out over the wires. Smaller papers were less likely to want such material, while the larger papers were sometimes deterred by the knowledge that the stories were for the general AP membership, not exclusively offered to selected media.

The team itself was frustrated by the constraints of market appetite. Seymour Hersh walked out on the team after the AP slashed one of his pieces on biological warfare from 10,000 to 1,700 words (but a decade earlier even 1,000 words might have seemed generous). In 1969, the same year that the team won the Worth Bingham Prize for 'a steady stream of reports spotlighting corruption, waste, bureaucratic bungling and other government practices ill-serving the public interest',[60] AP president Paul Miller told the AP Managing Editors' Association (APME) that lengthy 'specials' from AP were not getting the play in the newspapers for which AP had hoped.[61] Nevertheless the team survived, although its size had declined from a dozen in 1972 to only four in 1976.

In other, lighter, areas however the trend towards more feature-type coverage was very pronounced for both American agencies. AP fostered the growth of what it called 'enterprise' reporting, with its own editor in New York and a bank of 'specialists', largely based in New York, covering fields such as race relations, consumer interests, science, aerospace, education, religion, urban affairs, auto-racing, golf etc. A nation-wide 'task-force' of writers and photographers was put on call for work on enterprise reporting. And in general news-coverage there was greater emphasis on news of the 'round-up' overview type to meet a perceived change of demand from client members.

There are few such 'specialists' outside the US in the distribution of agency personnel. The term 'specialist' is rarely used at all overseas, where every correspondent can be called on at any time for any kind of coverage (as he can be at home too, but the likelihood and the need is greater overseas). But there are generally one or two journalists in the largest foreign bureaux who do spend most of their time working within a specific area. In London's AP bureau in the mid-1970s there was a diplomatic correspondent and a sports specialist. Diplomacy and sport were the fields which most frequently attracted specialist attention during the period of the author's original study of agency foreign bureaux. Economic reporting for AP overseas is increasingly coupled with AP–Dow Jones, and in the case of UPI economics was another frequently encountered specialist interest at least until the economic news link-up between UPI and Commodity News Service (CNS). The majority of bureaux, however, do not have specialists in this sense. Nor can they usually exercise the option of calling in a specialist from some other bureau in the same way that regional bureaux in the US can request the services of a specialist from the New York Head Office. However, there has developed a handful of élite senior news agency reporters known as 'roving correspondents' who can drift in and out of major news centres for feature-type coverage or for a fresh angle on a developing major story.

(ii) Technology

A further area of discrepancy between services for foreign markets and services for domestic markets in the mid-1970s was in technology. Quality of transmission and reception varied tremendously in the mid-1970s. Originally the principal mode of agency communication was the telegraphic cable, and foreign clients were concentrated in those parts of the world linked by cable. Between the world wars the supremacy of cable was challenged by radio-teletype. The European agencies were particularly interested in the exploitation of radio, since their clients were still at that time the more dispersed around the globe. Radio was cheaper and it allowed for volume expansion. The US agencies also transmitted some services by radio, but maintained a strong preference for cable, especially on the domestic market. And after World War Two all the agencies established cable networks in Europe, relying heavily on radio-teletype transmissions for non-western markets. The introduction of multiplexing (multiplying the number of communication channels possible per cable) in the early 1960s heralded a new era for cable transmission, greatly increasing the potential news volume in those areas served by cable, while satellites overcame many of the atmospheric and sunspot interferences suffered by normal radio transmissions. By the late 1970s satellite transmission of world agency services had become widespread for distribution to much but not all of Latin America, and Asia, but a lot less so for Africa. This meant that many of the poorest Third World countries still relied entirely on radio transmissions, which were frequently garbled, and which could necessitate several repeats of each dispatch. Local distribution to many of the smaller clients in Third World countries which could not afford teleprinter reception was still by printed messenger-delivered bulletins prepared by local agency bureaux.

These considerations apply to the distribution of news services. The disparities may be greater in the process of news-collection, greatly favouring those (usually the more developed western) countries where agency news is filed directly on to full-speed leased-line circuits. Elsewhere, filing may be via half-speed lines, private telex or national or commercial communications agencies, and sometimes via the communications network of the local national news agency. Choice of mode of communication outwards is determined partly by what is available and the reliability of what is available, and partly by the news priority attributed to any given country by the major agencies and, in turn, by their most influential customers. Where full-speed leased-line circuits are arranged, however, a fixed capacity is assured, and many feel that where there is capacity there is a tendency for news transmission to expand in order to fill it. This in turn may tend to accentuate differences in the volume of news received by the agencies from different countries, although communication technology is probably a mediating rather than a causative factor. On the other hand, increased capacity has enabled the agencies to place their communications facilities at the disposal of other media systems, for a return, and by reducing communication costs for these other systems (also their clients) the agencies may contribute to a media-wide expansion in the volume of news transmissions.

Some of the most important of recent technological developments, such as high-speed news delivery, or AP's 'laserphoto' and 'electronic darkroom', seem unlikely to spread beyond the major industrial countries for some time to come. This kind of unevenness in the rate of adoption and dissemination of new technologies, which reflects differences in the purchasing power of clientele in different countries, is a factor which contributes to the gap between the advanced and developing nations in the quality of agency news services provided.

(iii) Direct and indirect distribution

The full service of each of the world agencies is not everywhere available, either because distribution is via a national news agency which makes severe cuts, or because the time involved in translation imposes its own censorship, or both. Distribution via national news agencies occurs for a variety of reasons. Some governments require their media to take international services in this way; some media prefer this system of distribution because it is less costly for them individually; the agencies may choose to distribute this way where they do not wish to meet the costs of translation and distribution themselves, or simply because the national agency can pay more than the potential market of individual clients. Sometimes it happens that the arrangement with a national agency is not exclusive, and clients have the choice between taking the service in a truncated form through a national agency, subscribing to the world agency direct, or taking the full service of the world agency but through the communications facilities of the national agency.

Where a government requires that distribution be through a national agency, the world agencies cannot do much about it. This has been the case in most black African countries, some Asian countries (spectacularly in the case of India during Indira Gandhi's period of 'emergency rule'), and in communist countries. In South America there had not been a great deal of choice up to the mid-1970s since there were hardly any sizeable 'national agencies' with domestic market monopolies or with sufficiently extensive internal leased communication facilities. As a general rule, AFP has tended to distribute through national agencies wherever there has been a suitable agency, although not always on an exclusive basis. In Germany it distributed independently until, in the early 1970s, it established a deal with the new Germany agency, DDP, but continued to offer a German language service to a relatively small number of individual news media. Reuters' general news service to West Germany was indirectly distributed by DPA until late 1972, when UPI successfully bid for the contract and Reuters turned to direct distribution. Both Reuters and AFP distribute via national agencies in Scandinavia, and in Europe generally Reuters engages in less direct distribution than AP. In Latin America the primary channel for Reuters news is via the continent-wide agency which it helped to establish there, Latin, through which it provides a Spanish-language service. Likewise, in the Caribbean, the main channel for Reuters is the Caribbean News Agency, CANA, which Reuters also helped to establish on the basis of its old regional Caribbean desk. Elsewhere the main factor determining whether distribution has been direct or indirect has been the attitude of the governments of the respective clients' countries. In the Middle East, however, Reuters' scope for direct distribution was greatly enhanced in the early 1970s with the introduction of an Arabic-language news service compiled in Beirut. Figures for world agency sales to 85 non-aligned countries given by Pinch[62] showed that Reuters in the mid-1970s sold to more than twice as many non-aligned country clients than either AP or UPI (cf. Table 2), both in direct and indirect sales (the figures did not unfortunately distinguish between general news and economic news sales). But AP actually had more direct (19) than indirect sales (12) as had UPI (15 direct and 12 government sales). The high number of Reuters' non-aligned sales and especially of indirect, government sales was partly accounted for by Reuters' greater activity in black Africa. This greater tendency for the European agencies to enter into contracts with national news agencies as a proportion of all contracts is well established. UNESCO figures for the early 1950s[63] show that Reuters then had 34 such contracts and AFP had 32, whereas UPA (as UPI then was) had 14 and AP had 9.

The US agencies maintained a preference for direct distribution for much of the post-war period, but UPI in particular reversed policy in the 1970s, and even AP showed signs of retrenchment. Like AP, UPI used to operate translation desks in many West European bureaux for servicing clients direct with a translated UPI service. But in the early 1970s it ceased to compete on these terms with AP in West Germany (where both agencies had, unusually, offered a limited service of West German as well as world news) and replaced Reuters as primary external world news supplier to DPA. UPI's translated services for Scandinavia were phased out in the mid-1970s, and by 1978 the death knell for UPI direct distribution sounded in Europe (outside the UK) with the demise of UPI's French language

Table 2
Sales to non-aligned countries by three news agencies

	No. of Countries	AP Direct	AP Govt.	UPI Direct	UPI Govt.	Reuters Direct	Reuters Govt.
Arabic Region	18	5	4	5	8	7	10
Africa	41	2	3	1	–	5	27
Asia	14	2	4	1	3	3	6
Americas	9	8	–	7	–	5	2
Europe	3	2	1	1	1	2	1
Total	85	19	12	15	12	22	46

Note: The table illustrates, in the case of non-aligned countries, the tendency for AP to resist indirect distribution where possible and the greater degree of direct distribution in the Americas. Note also the greater volume of distribution activity by Reuters in Africa and the Arabic region.

Source: Pinch, Edward T. (1977).[38]

service in France (not replaced by a national agency arrangement, except for the continuation of a new joint venture with AFP for photo-distribution to provincial French newspapers), and its Vienna-based German language service. UPI was clearly unable to sustain the level of service which with the advantages of relatively low rates of pay and available manpower, it had established in Europe after World War Two. It now saw itself, in Europe at least, as a news wholesaler in the sense of supplying mainly to national news agencies and to those individual media prepared to take an English language service. (In Sweden for instance, where the national agency, TT, already took Reuters as a major news supplier, UPI sold direct in English to two leading newspapers). In other major world regions South America was the only continent where direct distribution continued to predominate. However, whereas after World War Two UPI maintained separate translation desks in each South American country, the basic Spanish-language service was now compiled in New York, with a separate Portuguese-language service translated in Brazil for direct distribution to Brazilian media. It is because of its direct South American distribution that UPI was seen to serve more direct than indirect clients in the Pinch study on subscribers among the non-aligned countries.

Of all the 'Big Four' agencies, AP has adopted possibly the strongest line on direct distribution. In the late 1970s, AP's foreign-language services for direct distribution in Europe were still available in France, Italy, Holland, West Germany, Austria, Belgium and Switzerland. Altogether, there was direct distribution in ten West European countries. In Italy, for instance, AP was the only one of the 'Big Four' not to distribute through ANSA. The implication up to the late 1970s therefore was that AP had been prepared to incur very heavy manpower costs (for translation) which other agencies had increasingly abandoned. But this inevitably left a question mark over AP's willingness to sustain costs of this kind, unless it was that as other agencies reduced directly distributed translations, AP was able to pick up more clients. (Reuters picked up ex-UPI clients in Austria and Switzerland in 1978, following UPI's suspension of its French and German language services). Like UPI, AP switched from individual translation operations in South American bureaux in the 1960s in favour of a core Spanish language service prepared in New York for direct distribution, clearly a desirable measure of rationalization. Elsewhere there were many countries, like Kenya, Turkey or Israel for example, where AP was the only one of the 'Big Four' not to distribute via a national news agency. But there were some signs of retrenchment by the late 1970s. In Spain and in Portugal AP distributed via national agencies. (AP did not distribute in Spain until Franco's death, and had no clients in Salazar's Portugal.) In 1976, its Portuguese-language service for Brazil was taken over by the Brazilian agency, Agencia JB (AJB) in partial response to a government prohibition on the distribution of news agency reports dealing with matters related to Brazilian interests. And in Norway in 1978 AP arranged for its Norwegian-language and photo service to be taken over by Norsk Press Service, while in Tunisia it arranged to be distributed by TAP, the Tunisian national news agency. The following year, AP signed a news exchange agreement with the new Nigerian News Agency, also with the Mauritanian news agency, and resumed distribution in Cuba through Prensa Latina, where it hoped to be able to establish a permanent correspondent once more. Hitherto, however, wherever AP has arranged to distribute via local news agencies for whatever reason, and where there has been some choice allowed in the matter, it has often preferred to deal with a privately owned agency. In Norway, Norsk Press Service is private, distinct from the national news agency which distributes news from the European-based world agencies. And in Spain, while the general news service goes to the national agency, EFE, the photo service is distributed via a smaller, private agency. Except for the period of emergency rule in India, AP went through United News, the leading competitor to the principal national agency, PTI, while PTI distributed the services of the other members of the 'Big Four'. In Bangladesh, AP goes via the privately owned ENA, while Reuters, UPI and AFP go to BSS, which is government controlled. In Indonesia, AP has traditionally distributed via KNI, a newspaper-owned private agency, in preference to the government agency, Antara, which takes the other world agencies. Of course, where a government regulates all distribution of news through whatever sources, such a policy of preferring private to government agencies may seem to make little difference in practice. There may be an advantage in being the sole agency (or world agency) to be distributed by a smaller private agency than in being one of four world agencies competing for space on the wires of the larger government agency (but payments to the world agencies would not normally be directly associated with use in this way). And any policy which supports media diversity in any given country may have long-term benefits for the global flow of information. There are partial exceptions to AP's policy: for instance, it distributes via national agencies in the UK (the PA) and in Japan (Kyodo) where there is certainly no compulsion for it to do so: but in both countries it also supplies some of the leading national news media direct, while distribution to provincial media by the national agencies represents a channel of world service influence which otherwise these provincial media might be unwilling to afford.

The most important and visible consequence of indirect distribution is the loss to the client of the full extent of the world agency's news service, since the national distributing agency rarely has sufficient capacity or desire to distribute the full service (particularly if it takes more than one world agency) alongside its own national service. But loss of news volume also happens where, for instance, the world agency does its own translation for a local market. Even where a news agency does its own translation this can reduce volume by as much as 50% or more. If the world agency does its own translation, however, there may be a better chance of a competent translation. Even where the world agency does not translate, the need to render the service easily translatable by others may mean a loss in terms of nuance and complexity. In some instances where world agencies have moved from direct to indirect distribution it is interesting that distributing agencies have hired translators from the world agencies: e.g. Brazil's AJB hired from AP to translate the AP service. Where distribution is indirect and the service also has to be translated the joint impact of editorial selection and pressures of time and cost leads to a further reduction. More important perhaps than decline in volume is the loss of editorial control by the world agency over its own product. Contracts generally include guarantees by the consumer agency against distortion of world-agency news. Constant monitoring of client–agency distribution, however, may be beyond the resources of the world agencies; besides, omission can be as powerful a weapon of distortion as making changes to copy, and clients can debate whether a world agency fulfilled its contractual promise of impartiality. There are some advantages to indirect distribution. For clients of the national news agency it may be convenient to have an edited selection of several world agencies as against the full service of the one agency they might otherwise take. But then the service they get will be exactly the same service as every competing medium also receives. The service may be more suitably packaged to meet national media news requirements, although this should not be beyond the scope of the world agencies either, especially where they distribute via their own national or regional bureaux, staffed by locally recruited nationals. The national news agency selection may permit reception on one or at least fewer teleprinters than would otherwise be needed, thus cutting down on staff time, and may well be cheaper overall, although not all the world agencies are best known for pushing hard bargains which client media can ill afford. For the world agencies, moreover, revenue is sometimes easier to collect from one single source which has an evident need to maintain the contractual relationship. Some clients may prefer a service which, as far as they are concerned, is ideologically safe. Indirect distribution transfers responsibility for any transgression against a government's censorship regulations from the world agencies to the national agency, and may help to make life easier for the world agencies' journalists in those countries where distribution is indirect. Indirect distribution, finally, ensures a wider overall public for at least part of the world agency services, especially among the smaller non-metropolitan media which might otherwise receive no service of world news at all apart from what they can scavenge from broadcasts and metropolitan dailies. But for the world agencies and for client media it would surely be preferable to at least have the choice between direct and indirect distribution and reception.

(iv) Languages

The major languages of world agency transmission are English, Spanish, French, German, Arabic and Portuguese, approximately in that order. (There is also some translation into other languages at point of distribution, particularly in the case of AP, and for bulletin distribution.) These are inevitably the dominant languages of international news flow. TASS and NCNA make their own translations of western world agency reports, as do the Japanese news agencies. The dominant media in many parts of Africa, Asia and Latin America in any case frequently print and speak in English, French or Spanish. But apart from locally-produced local language bulletins, a tiny source of revenue in any case and often dependent on a local bureau manager's estimate of local market demand, there are relatively few concessions to 'minority' languages in world news flow.

Regionalization of news services

The term 'regionalization' as applied to the world agencies is a loose one which broadly refers to the extent to which an agency differentiates between markets, or 'tailors' a service to meet specific client requirements, either individual clients or, more usually, clients of specific countries or geographical regions. There are a number of facets to 'regionalization', and some of these have already been considered under different headings. The main concern in this chapter has been with the general imbalance of world agency resources and services in favour of the world agencies' domestic markets, and this would constitute an example of 'regionalization'. But what is more usually meant by the term 'regionalization' is the extent to which news agency content is tailored for specific foreign markets, and this generally involves additional factors.

Within the domestic markets of the world agencies, with the exception of Reuters which does not operate as a national news agency in the UK, considerable attention is given to domestic regional news requirements. Between a quarter and a third[64] of AP's trunk wire is given to international news; the rest is national or state news. The 'B' wire, which carries less international news than the 'A' wire, is heavily oriented to the different news requirements of individual states. In the 1970s the US agencies invested heavily in computer technology, which greatly facilitated the provision of state, regional and inter-state news. In France, AFP also makes special provision for the inclusion of regional provincial news to clients within each of the major French provinces.

Overseas, the percentage of 'local' news on these three global agency services, or news referring to the country in which the service is distributed, is considerably smaller than the percentage of national and state news on their domestic wires. Generally, it is all but non-existent. Were the world agencies to try and compete everywhere with national agencies or to substitute for national agencies, it is very unlikely that many countries would find this politically acceptable; a few governments do not even find world agency provision of world news politically acceptable. It is also debatable whether world agencies would do as effective a job as national agencies, even if they were allowed to do so, or whether in most countries they would find it profitable. There are a few countries, however, where the world agencies do, in a small way, compete with national news agencies. In the USA, Reuters in 1967 decided not to renew its contract with AP for AP's domestic service when AP demanded a cash payment from Reuters in addition to the UK PA service it received in exchange. Instead, it increased independent coverage of the US and included main national news events in its news service to its relatively small number of media clients, a practice which was eventually of more benefit for its economic and CATV news services. It concentrated mainly on Washington news, and no American newspaper or broadcaster has ever depended solely on Reuters' news. The second country in which world agencies operate to some extent as national agencies, and possibly the second wealthiest national media market in the western world after the USA, is West Germany. Until 1972, both AP and UPI provided services of both national and international news. AP had a considerably larger market share than UPI, and UPI succeeded Reuters as supplier to DPA in 1972. Thus Reuters in consequence also went 'independent' but relying mainly on the broadcast market for revenue with a service which concentrated on the most important Federal news, in addition to news from the international service. In France, AP provides clients with some French news, gathered through its network of stringers but not in competition with AFP, as did UPI to a lesser extent until it ceased its French-language service. Although Reuters operates a French-language service, distribution is partly through a small French agency, ACP, and there is no provision of French news. The only other western or developed country where a world agency operates partially as a 'domestic' agency, other than the base countries of the 'Big Four' themselves, is Canada. UPI operated a domestic news service in Canada for many years, in competition with Canadian Press (CP), the national news agency, which distributes Reuters and AFP international news. UPI maintained bureaux in Ottawa, Toronto, Vancouver and Montreal, while AP did not have even one staff correspondent permanently assigned to Canada, and Reuters did not introduce a permanent general news correspondent (to Montreal) till 1977. In 1979, however, UPI effectively reduced its direct investment on the Canadian market by taking a 20% share in a new formation with the Toronto Star Publishing Group and Sterling

Newspapers Ltd., which was to operate a national service (employing UPI's ex-staffers), taking an international file from UPI.

Outside the western world the only recent recorded cases of world agencies acting as national agencies in foreign markets have been in South America. UPI operated an internal domestic service for Chile even during the presidency of Salvador Allende, although Allende temporarily closed down the distribution of UPI's *international* report in retaliation for a UPI story he claimed was false. And in Argentina, AP operated an internal service from 1969 till Peron's return in 1973. AP's vice-president for world services, Stan Swinton, claimed in a 1976 interview[65] that none of the domestic services in which AP was involved overseas were started on the agency's initiative, but that they were established in response to requests by publishing groups.

Instead of seeking to provide national news of the country in which it distributes to media clients of that country, a global agency has the different option of providing additional international news which is of special relevance to that country. There have been persistent claims from Third World countries that the extent of such regionalization has been slight, or that it has been of the wrong kind. The agencies, on the other hand, have argued that they have always made provision for regionalized services on world markets and that regionalized news constitutes a large proportion of the total. What few academic studies there are are mostly of recent date, so cannot disprove the thesis that regionalization for Third World countries in particular has increased in response to client complaints or to the uncomfortable glare, for example, of UNESCO-sponsored criticism on this issue.

'News of special relevance' is notoriously difficult to define, and much of the debate has focused on the extent to which the news file to any given country includes news of that country's neighbouring countries, its geopolitical region. All the relevant studies up to the late 1970s showed that in general terms the western countries received a very heavy diet of western news. But much less was known about the news files for other parts of the world; studies dating from before 1970 were especially rare. The 1953 UNESCO study examined only one Third World country in detail: India. About two-thirds of foreign news distributed by the agencies in India was 'western' news, the US and the UK predominating,[66] a similar percentage to that carried by the Indian press. A 1956 UNESCO study of Asian news carried by the agencies quoted an AP Tokyo bureau chief who claimed that survey evidence had shown that 19% of AP's file for Asia consisted of Asian news, two-thirds of this coming from Asian points and one-third coming from points outside Asia but dealing with

Asian-related subjects.[67] (The same report quoted research evidence as showing that almost uniformly in all Asian countries, Asian news represented one-fifth of all foreign news carried by the press.) Twenty to thirty years later rather higher figures for 'regionalization' in agency services for the Third World were recorded in *some* studies of *some* services. Continuing prevalence of western news was suggested in Snider's[68] analysis of agency news flow to the Afghan news agency in the 1960s – the US, UK and Russia each got more coverage than any other country. However, a content analysis of Reuters (for one week) and AFP (for two weeks) services to Africa in 1973[69] found that as many as 59% of Reuters and 65% of AFP stories carried mentions of African countries. A remarkable feature of this study is the claim that the 'complete files in both English and French were obtained' although Reuters has five African files (three English, one French, one English and Arabic) and AFP has three (two French and one English) for different regions. Findings indicated that Reuters tended to 'regionalize' more on its English wire, while AFP 'regionalized' more on its French wire. Another 1973-based study,[70] over eleven days from a six-week period, concentrated on Reuters' West African service, but found that it carried only 32% African news, at least partly boosted by relatively heavy coverage of white-dominated southern Africa, and still less than the 43% space given to news of the advanced/industrialized world. This study claimed to find other indications of 'ethnocentric' bias on the part of the world agency: for instance, that coverage of West African news actors was more likely to be given when these acted in an advanced world context, than of advanced world actors in a West African context. Missing from studies of this kind is any analysis of average story lengths across different content categories, any distinction between 'dispatch' and 'story', and any satisfactory definition of what constitutes 'African' relevance. A five-day study of Reuters' South African and AP's African wires in 1974 found much lower percentages of African news (5% of dispatches, 8% of stories in the Reuters' file and 2% of dispatches, 4% of stories in the AP file).[71] But, for Reuters, higher percentages of regionalized news were found in one-day studies of their East African wire (African news: 19%) and the South-East Asian wire, where Asian news dominated over every other source. By the late 1970s, therefore, the evidence for Africa at least suggested that the European agencies gave quite considerable attention to the regional news requirements of African clients, amounting to between one- and two-thirds of the respective news files, but perhaps much less in the case of Reuters' service to white-dominated southern Africa and that of those American agencies whose services had not developed along the same colonial lines. Whether the 'regional' material provided was actually better in any way than alternative western material is open to debate.

Elsewhere there is rather less published evidence. A study of AP's Latin American news flow, based on 1971 data,[72] suggests that AP world distribution of Latin-American stories corresponds with the structure of the material sent by Latin-American bureaux to New York more closely than with AP's US 'A' and 'B' wire selections. This might indicate relatively high 'regionalization' (especially since three out of four items sent to New York were sent in Spanish in order to expedite immediate retransmission back to South America). UPI told UNESCO's ICSCP committee that 45–50% of its service for Latin-American subscribers came from Latin America. A striking 1977 study examined each of the 'Big Four' services for Asia.[73] But the *entire* news content was analysed for only one day, and the week as a whole was absent of 'any dominating story from the Big Powers'. The study estimated that some 39% of all stories were 'Third World news', excluding a mixed category in which non-Third World countries dominated, and that during the full five days, Asian news represented some 58% of all Third World stories (or more than one-fifth of the entire news file). Two of the 'Big Four' wires consistently carried more Third World stories than the other two.

Certainly the world agencies regionalize; but there are differences between them in the extent to which they regionalize and the areas of the world for which each agency concentrates its regionalization effort. For instance, the European agencies are clearly more involved in the African market in this sense than the US agencies, while Reuters is less involved in the South American market. There is 'regionalization' if one means by this the provision of area-relevant news. But is such provision greater than would occur if each agency simply distributed an identically-structured service package across the world? In very many instances, yes, as some of the studies of European agencies clearly suggest, but not inevitably so. A 1974 analysis,[74] for instance, showed that AFP supplied a UK file of which one-fifth was Asian news, and AP supplied an African file of which, again, one-fifth was Asian news, similar therefore to the average provision of Asian news to Asian media in the Schramm study. There are also thorny problems of definition: an emphasis on area-relevant news is not necessarily what the media (or governments) of particular countries really want all of the time, and the needs and wants of various media within a region do not all neatly coincide. A highly 'regionalized' service may in practice be heavily dominated by a few unvarying datelines from within the region and by certain unvarying news categories. A service that is to be highly customer-tailored should strictly begin with an assessment of each individual customer, or at least each individual country. It is difficult to say with much confidence that this degree of tailoring occurs outside the world agency domestic markets, or that if it does it occurs with very great frequencey. But there are grounds for thinking that the conditions for regionalized or tailored news services for world markets have greatly improved.

First, there have been enormous improvements in the volume of news transmitted which have probably benefited all regions and all news categories. For instance the introduction of 24-hour leased circuits for the transmission of news from Latin American bureaux to New York, and of satellite distribution from New York back to South America, possibly increased news flow by as much as five times in the space of a few years in the case of the American agencies.[75] Multiplexing has allowed increases of similar range for high-reliability delivery in many parts of the world. Increases in volume which have affected national as well as world agencies, may have compensated for some of the disadvangates of increased indirect distribution of world services via national agency selections.

Second, agencies have specifically adopted pro-regionalization policies: Reuters, for instance, deliberately designed its West African service in the early 1960s as a regionalized service, having first surveyed the potential demand; similarly, it introduced its Arabic news service a few years later (1972) and established Singapore as a regional Asian base in 1967 (but transferred to Hong Kong in 1980) with particular responsibility for increasing the input of regional Asian news for Asian clients, and Barbados as a regional Caribbean centre 1959–75. In addition to retaining most of its translated services AP increased its South American news files from one to five in 1978; more ambiguously, AP's Keith Fuller, on his accession to the agency's presidency in 1977, announced as his first goal the 'creation of new income opportunities to offset the dwindling revenues from selling services abroad where economic hardship and a shrinking world for honest news distribution are taking their toll'; one such opportunity was to be the fostering of a 'people-to-people oriented foreign coverage'.[76]

Technology and agency reorganization have also facilitated the potential for regionalization but not in every respect, and it is difficult to assess how far potential is actually exploited. UPI's withdrawal of translated services from Europe, for instance, represents a decline of regionalization in one sense, since provision of a translated service is a major convenience for clients. More important, perhaps, is that where a world agency actually translates the service from its bureau located in the receiver country, that bureau in effect has the

C

responsibility for compiling the service. Being closest to the clients, in receipt perhaps of special-interest dispatches (i.e. those likely to be of relevance to only that one country) cabled from bureaux of adjoining countries, the potential for a tailored service might seem to be highest in such conditions. On the other hand, the pressures of deadlines, the laborious work of translation, the inevitable overall volume reduction as a result of translation, the variability of interest of bureaux in adjoining countries in sending specific-interest dispatches, in practice work against full advantage being taken of these conditions. Moreover the insertion of region-specific items can also take place in major regional bureaux, closer to the ground of local client interest than editors in New York, London or Paris. UPI for example established, in the 1970s, Brussels and Hong Kong as 'message-switching' centres for the Europe–MedAf and Asian regions respectively. From 1972 to 1978 Brussels was responsible for intercepting the news from New York and the rest of the world, tailoring it slightly to regional interest, and inserting regional news directed to it by the various bureaux of the region. It also transmitted regional news to New York for the rest of the world. In 1978 the process was extended when regional editing was moved back to London, and the facility there introduced for London to edit news of Asia, a function which before had lain with New York. In other words, there was an extension in the volume and source of the news the regional centre was enabled to edit for its own region. The message-switching centres also permitted individual bureaux to code their own stories, so that stories could move directly from writers to clients within any of the major regions. But the extent to which this latter facility, whereby writers code stories, has in practice increased intra-regional 'regionalization' may not have been as great as the technology itself allows, and by contrast with the impression gained by the author in interviews in the early 1970s, this feature was not greatly emphasized in interviews in the late 1970s. And while direct source-client coding is technically available to the other world agencies, the use to which the facility is put is carefully controlled. Besides, this kind of service differentiation is equally possible from a single centre, with the drawback that centralization can involve a loss of immediacy of contact with local news requirements. AP has preferred a more highly centralized editing system, although some bureaux, London and Tokyo in particular, are responsible for feed-in of regional news, in addition to the differently directed wires from New York, local news interchanges, and nationally relevant news insertions at local level where the service is locally translated and distributed. AFP is possibly even more centralized, editorially, than AP, while Reuters, with its regional news-dissemination from centres such as Beirut, is perhaps less editorially centralized than AP or AFP, but more so than UPI.

It is important not to underestimate the world agencies' regard for the regionalization issue and their need to be seen to meet client needs so far as their market structures allow, a regard which is heightened (though they may be reluctant to admit it) in the wake of criticisms from Third World governments and media. In the short term it may seem that high regionalization adds to costs and is essentially uneconomic. In the long term both political and economic considerations undercut such a view. Politically it is important for the agencies to preserve access to as many countries as possible (though client media are too often slow to apply the necessary pressure from their end as well), and access may be contingent on the provision of services which demonstrate a high regard for local news requirements. Such a response is more comfortable ideologically than to give ground to another potential Third World demand, namely, to be given access in their turn to agency wires. This latter demand can in any case be pre-empted: by depending heavily on the services of government-controlled national agencies where these services are judged reasonably suitable sources (though client media would do well to harbour their suspicions); facilitating a country's diplomatic communications; and through various kinds of consultancy service, measures already employed for example by Reuters. Economically, regionalization should become a great deal less burdensome with the widespread adoption of sophisticated computer aids to editing. But the really important long-term prerequisite for a truly independent regionalized service involves the employment of greater news-gathering manpower, and this expensive item, politically necessary as it may become, constitutes an important short-term obstacle.

Agency–client relations

Much of what has been said already pertains to the character of agency–client relations. Nevertheless this factor is sufficiently important to warrant independent consideration in the analysis of the domestic or local region orientation of the 'Big Four' agencies. It will be considered first in relation to the handling by agencies of non-routine client requirements, since this follows closely the prior discussion on news regionalization. Second, and perhaps more significant, it will be considered in the context of structured channels for client influence on agency policy.

In addition to services provided on a routine basis, the agencies make varying provision for meeting special requests or requirements of individual media. The machinery for such provision, as in the case of the US agencies, is inevitably more sophisticated for the important domestic markets. Much depends on the nature of the request. If it is for news that has already gone out over the wires, the client has merely to be referred to the right number and time of story. If it asks for information which will be covered in any case during the course of the day, or has been covered but not reported, and is therefore easily 'on tap', there is no extra work involved. Problems arise when the request is slightly unusual, raising new angles or issues an agency would not normally bother with. In such cases, a request has more chance when the material which is asked for is also suitable, or can easily be made suitable, for many other clients in the same region or even around the world. But if the material does not have such 'sales prospects', the agency might not be prepared to follow it up, or the client might be charged for the service. Media in the developing world, having fewer alternative sources of foreign news than media in the West, are more likely to have greater need for assistance, but their very geographical situation is likely to heighten the non-routine character of their special needs and they are less likely to be prepared to meet the costs of any extra work involved. Clients inevitably learn to ask only for the kinds of information they have reason to think the agencies can provide. In the case of AP, the important membership connection of the US dailies, who also supply AP with news, works well in their favour so far as available resources for the non-routine servicing of client requests are concerned. But one 1976 account claimed[77] that 'it has been the practice of AP to extend the policy of attempting to satisfactorily answer every request from domestic member newspapers to the agency's foreign clients'.

UPI, in the early 1970s, maintained in Washington a 'regional desk' of seven journalists (established in 1961) to handle an average of fifty special client requests a day from the domestic market (there were smaller regional desks in New York, Philadelphia, Chicago and Cleveland). There was also in Washington an international desk (in addition to one in New York), staffed by nine journalists to serve the interests of overseas clients, mainly covering routine Washington 'beats', but looking for international angles. The international desk had been disbanded by 1978, and instead a similar desk in New York channelled requests to relevant bureaus. Since requests are often more likely to go to high crisis or especially 'newsy' points, the competition can be intense. In Saigon, which the author visited in early 1973, there was such a backlog of requests from US clients that it could take up to several months for an over-stretched staff to clear them.

Client consumption of news stories is monitored by the American agencies around the world, and rather more closely than by the European agencies (which do not compete with each other as directly as do the US agencies). Local bureaux send in to their regional head office or to New York weekly accounts of how the important papers of their area used the material they received from each agency. Scores are compiled to show which of the US agencies 'won' on each important story; the agency which 'loses' may note why it lost: certain angle missed, delay in transmission, failure to back a story with a photograph. In this way each organization builds up a fairly good picture of its relative strength in each client area and in each news area. The feed-back is especially good in the US, however, since agency sources are normally clearly identified and used verbatim, and because AP and UPI are virtually the only competitors for the media market: and it is this US data which carries the most weight, since it is US media which pay the most money. The agency reports, AP *Log* and UPI *Reporter*, are sent to every bureau for perusal.

The US agencies also make structural provision for the collective expression of member or client concerns; again, it is the domestic market which gains most. Such provision is in addition to any influence exerted by virtue of any media ownership control. In the case of AP it takes the form of the Associated Press Managing Editors Association (APME), which comprises all the domestic member daily newspapers and which each year establishes a number of committees which sit to discuss and organize research into aspects of AP functioning and of their own newspaper problems. More than 500 editors sat on APME committees in 1971, for instance; 19 committees reported to the convention in 1977 (see Table 3), including the well-established Foreign News Committee. Many of these committees attempt surveys of member clients to assess strengths and weaknesses of relevant AP coverage – in sports news, for instance, or business news – and while there is a natural sympathy for AP in such reports as they make, the pictures they present are by no means automatically flattering. A survey conducted by one member of the Business News Committee in 1971, for instance, reported that businessmen generally agreed that AP was 'shallow' in its coverage of business news,[78] while the Foreign News Committee in 1977 complained that in its coverage of the Quebec election 'AP appears not to have given the election the priority and consideration it deserved'.[79]

In addition to the nation-wide APME Association, there are state-wide AP groups. Georgia and South Carolina, for instance, have active AP news councils, organizing APME-style committees and seminars and awards for journalistic performance. In Illinois, the

Table 3
APME Committees, 1977*

General News Committee
Writing/Editing Committee
Washington News Committee
Business and Economics Committee
Professional Standards Committee
Sports Committee
Foreign News Committee
Journalism Education Committee
Membership Citations Committee
Publications/Information Committee
Freedom of Information Committee
State News Committee
Newsroom Management Committee
Modern Living Committee
Changing Newspaper Committee
New Technology Committee
Photo/Graphics Committee
Membership and Performance Committee
Surveys and Research Committee

*Order in which reports appear in APME *Red Book*, 1977 (Associated Press).

local AP group is one of several in the US, which has fostered the practice of 'team reporting' since 1971, and the 1977 APME State News Committee reported that 'the AP bureau likes the solidarity that has emerged among the membership working towards a common purpose'.[80]

Although APME's research may sometimes not meet academic standards, there can be little doubt that the AP relationship with its members through APME helps create a unity of identity amongst members, a reliable and powerful means of feedback, an impetus to excellence in professional practice and a forum for new ideas that is not matched by any of the other agencies, certainly not by the European agencies. It is not a criticism of AP members to say that they look after their own interests first, and APME membership, like AP's full membership, is mainly of US media, but it is important for an understanding of world news flow to identify this concentration of organizational vitality on home ground.

UPI, in emulation to some extent of the APME Association, established something similar in 1973. UPI had traditionally held a conference of editors and publishers every year (EDICON), and had organized a network of regional client associations in the US, but these did not have the continuous backing features of APME. The EDICON meeting held in Mexico City in 1973 voted overwhelmingly in favour of the establishment of a national newspaper advisory board. The main function of the board would be to 'assist and advise UPI executives on ways the agency may carry out its goals and purposes for the benefit of the profession'.[81] The fifteen-member Newspaper Advisory Board, whose original membership came together in response by certain publishers to invitations from UPI itself, held its first meeting in Chicago in the spring of 1974. Board members were chosen to represent UPI's three major US divisions, five per region, and to represent at the same time the different circulation levels. It is the Board which appoints new members in a process of annual partial replacement. An early intention to include non-US media representatives did not materialize but was said to be still under discussion by vice-president Frank Tremaine in an interview with the author in 1978. There is not the same range of committees serving the NAB as is to be found in the APME structure. There is concentration instead on three general areas: the Services Committee studies and makes recommendations concerning the various UPI services, including news and news pictures; the Management Committee consults with senior UPI executives on operational matters; and the Technology Committee monitors and evaluates relevant technological developments. A later development of the UPI Advisory Board in 1974 was the introduction of a committee of New England editors whose stated function was to assist UPI in meeting the news requirements of newspapers in a six-state region. And in parallel with AP's decision in 1976 to give broadcast members representation on AP's board of directors, UPI established a Broadcast Advisory Board that same year, with a similar brief to that of its newspaper counterpart.

No organization similar to the APME Association or UPI's NAB exists among the European agencies. These organizations do not maybe monitor client consumption of their material quite as rigorously as their American competitors, who in any case compete with one another much more fiercely than the European agencies need to do. Naturally, there is a great deal of interaction of an informal day-to-day kind between the European agencies and their clients, but this interaction seems rarely to be systematized for wider audiences. Nor would there seem to be quite the same incentive as with the Americans, since neither European agency depends on the media market for the bulk of its revenue, although the media services might well benefit by some form of more systematic scrutiny. Another reason in the case of Reuters, and possibly to a lesser extent in the case of AFP, is that they do not have leading markets which are both so large in numerical terms and so homogeneous. If they were to gather together sufficient numbers of editors and publishers every year on a scale similar to the American agency annual conferences, they would have to cope with problems of language and of great differences of interest and situation between media of different countries. They would have to organize truly international conferences, whereas American agency conferences are almost entirely domestic affairs, even if UPI does vary their location from country to country. There are organizations which try to do for the international market some of the things that the American agencies (and other US media organizations such as the publishers' body, ANPA) seek to do for their domestic markets. There is the International Press Institute, for instance, which amongst other things produces an annual report on censorship and freedom of the press around the world, and seeks to intervene in cases of harassment of journalists. And both American and European world agencies sometimes come together with national agencies (an important client category) and other media in international forums, such as the International Press Telecommunications Council, to help fight for causes they share in common.

2
Structure and process

Media studies have considered two central issues for much of their relatively short history: the question of the effects of media outputs on audience beliefs and behaviour, and the question of the processes whereby media outputs come to be selected and packaged in the first place. Treatment of both issues has undergone considerable sophistication. From dependence on stimulus-response models, effects studies have progressed to consideration of the uses and gratifications to which individuals put different kinds of media material, and the influence of social and group identity on that process.[1]

Some early studies of news selection considered this in terms of an identifiable filtering process, where certain individuals were responsible for eliminating or channelling forward the information they received. This 'gatekeeper' approach was based on a psychological model devised by Kurt Lewin for a study of how the housewife channelled various foodstuffs into her home.[2]

This kind of approach, exemplified in David Manning White's study of a telegraph editor whose job it was to select news from the wire services for inclusion in his newspaper,[3] was not without merit. White's 'Mr Gatekeeper' did manifest some prejudices which directly influenced his choice, and it is significant that usually very few people are involved in this formal kind of filtering process, and that these few may well share certain similarities of social background and belief.

More recent studies of news selection, however, see this aspect of the process as but one segment of an enormously more complicated reality. The issue of selection is seen to involve consideration of the structure, ownership and management of media organizations; the social backgrounds, career patterns, and attitudes of professional communicators; patterns of interaction between communicators and other related occupational groups; and the influence of prevailing cultural values.[4] Increasingly the media are seen in relation to the characteristic mode of production in society, as functional sustainments of the 'corporate economy'.[5] And in the field of news, attention now focuses on the active participation of professional public relations and non-professional informants outside the media industry, for whom the media have strategic importance in their pursuit of private goals.[6]

A study of news agencies is itself a contribution to the study of the general news-source environment on which 'retail' media feed, while also demonstrating how the processes of selection in the agencies are likewise subject to a complex interplay of external and internal factors. This chapter considers some of the internal arrangements for news selection and processing. But in respect of both internal and external factors, an essential key to the continuing viability of these organizations is their combination of respect for what their important markets require, their refusal to be 'sidetracked' by alternative ideological theories as to what their 'proper' function should be, and the extraordinary economy of their news-processing machinery, an economy which owes as much to unspoken traditions of editorial fluency as to technological developments.

Editorial controls

A preliminary consideration is whether the nature of agency work exhibits sufficient regularities to allow for any kind of general statement about the extent to which news flow is an *intended* and *controlled* activity. Many personal biographies of journalists after all emphasize the absence of routine in news-gathering and see there a constant anticipation and celebration of the unpredictable. In situations of extreme crisis and in areas of very poor communication, agency news-gathering is as inspirational and unpredictable as any journalism can be.[7] But for the most part agency work is characterized by a tight *scheduling* of activity. This by no means precludes 'organic' or 'non-routine' organizational features: considerable initiative may be displayed, for instance, in the logistical planning of news coverage, and much news itself tends to be unpredictable, though less so than many people imagine, even if organizational responses to news occurrences are routine. (This is not meant to imply that the concept 'news' is anything other than a social construction.) Nor does scheduling necessarily imply a great degree of bureaucratization: in fact the number of levels of authority in the structure of the agencies is relatively small, and at the news-gathering end authority is a diffuse, ambiguous and perhaps irrelevant concern.

The essence of agency schedule is a *continuous* deadline. In a way this *is* a figure of speech, but it does denote one major difference between agencies and other media: newspaper journalists may have a day to pursue and develop and think about a story; weekly newsmagazine journalists of course have much longer, and this is evident in the breadth, depth, and quality of their writing; television and broadcast journalists may have one- or two-hourly intervals between broadcasts – their schedule begins to approach the schedule of agency journalists, except that broadcast journalists can often update their material simply by reference to incoming agency reports.

A 'continuous' deadline is in a sense an absurdity. Events have to happen, have to be recognized as relatively complete news-items or news-developments before they can be transmitted. The definition of when a news-event has sufficient meaning, either on its own accord, or by reference to some broader set of events, is a social construction on the part of the agency journalist. And that construction must take into account the necessity for some degree of personal and organizational order.

But in terms of the shortness of interval between stories or dispatches, the agency journalist, as a general rule, is working to a much tighter schedule than any other media journalist. For one thing, an agency journalist is working for the deadlines of clients in many different countries, in different time-zones, whereas other media journalists are working simply to the deadline of their own employing organization. Freelance journalists usually have the good sense to work for newspapers within the same time zone.

The character of agency schedule has some important consequences. One of the most evident is the emphasis on speed, which is especially acute in agency journalism. Enormously expensive technological innovations are introduced to save only a few minutes in transmission or processing time. The 'scoop' which some believe has gone out of fashion in daily newspaper journalism is still a very important objective for an agency bureau chief, one that is nourished by various forms of feedback from head office: e.g. weekly and monthly records of the agency's success relative to competing agencies; messages warning of news delvelopments on rival wires; queries from client media.

Speed affects the logistics and style of coverage. It binds the agency journalist to his office. Even in the battlefield he stays close to a phone, or to a plane, and does not usually plan to be away from the office for longer than a day. He must try and ensure immediate transmission of the news story. And his office may need him to work on some other, perhaps totally different development somewhere else. There are never too many staff.

The 'story' for an agency is usually what other media would consider a development within a larger story. Agency journalists do not wait to integrate, explain and package. They send *now*. Head office may do any fundamental integration and packaging that has not been done and is considered necessary for client consumption,

'Background' or feature pieces can normally wait for quieter periods – the Sunday wires for instance.

The pressure of agency schedule, finally, has consequences for the internal communications of agency organizations. Not simply for the sophistication of communications technology, but for the absolute volume of such communication. Bureau chiefs are in frequent contact with their head offices. Stories transmitted from any given bureau arrive at the desks of head office or regional head office almost instantaneously, and elicit, if they are going to elicit anything, almost instantaneous feedback. The output of the agency is received on one or more teleprinters in each bureau, so that the organizational image, the selection criteria it employs, its constantly developing definition of news vis-à-vis any given set of world circumstances, is constantly present, regardless of distance between bureau and head office. Communication networks in agency life, perhaps more clearly than any other single variable, account for the apparent uniformity of agency product, and the degree of control and integration so evident in the news-processing cycle.

Studies of other kinds of multi-national corporation have shown that distance is no necessary obstacle to control by head office over far-flung divisions and branches. Nor is the extent of bureaucratization a necessary indication of the extent of actual organizational control of its members. One comparative[8] study of organizational structure found that centralization of decision-making upwards is an *alternative* mode of control to the high structuring of employee activity by setting prescribed tasks, rules and procedures to regulate behaviour. But in the case of agency organization it is not so much 'prescribed tasks, rules and procedures' that are sources of control, but rather the continual statement and restatement of values and norms through the process of communication on specific issues. It is a constant process of predicting the reaction of organizational colleagues and adjusting strategy in the light of that prediction. This is the basic process that underlies the closely integrated professional and organizational solidarity that is characteristic of full-time agency journalists. It eliminates the need for highly centralized decision-making. Although exceptional dilemmas are passed up the hierarchy (from editorial to executive levels), no time-consuming decision-making machinery is suitable for agency work, for otherwise by the time a decision is taken the story will be dead.

The very organization of the task, therefore, its combination of world-wide scope and complex differentiation of service, imposes its own form of editorial control. But this in itself cannot be sufficient to ensure an acceptable consistency of standard through wildly varying sets of circumstances: the communication process is not so

Structure and process

efficient that all news-gatherers are in possession of all the relevant information, all the necessary expertise, all of the time, in order to know what to do, and when and in what form to do it, given specific situations, without some more explicit or direct intervention between the stages of production and 'consumption'. There is a need for a built-in machinery for quality control and what machinery there is exhibits certain basic characteristics:

(1) Editorial control is above all a process of *elimination* in relation to copy. It is a negative control. Some stories are delivered on one or more wires; some stories are not used.
(2) Positive editorial control in relation to copy is relatively low-key. It concerns such things as the deletion of certain parts of a story in the interests of precision, accuracy and length, or the addition of some very basic explanatory groundwork (the title of the person quoted, for example, or a sentence of backgrounding to cover the development of the story prior to the latest report). Stories developing in more than one country at a time may be compiled by a central desk from individual items sent by different bureaux. There may be spelling mistakes, stylistic 'errors' (that do not accord with the style guidelines generally printed for editorial use by each agency), or expressions which do not suit the colloquial usage of the market for which the story is being considered. But most editing has a straightforward technical as well as marketing character, which does not query the basic substance of a story, does not seek alterations in its basic structure and choice of information.
(3) Editorial control which involves person supervision rather than copy alteration is similarly low-key. There may be instances where major revisions are required, and the editorial desk will ring back to the bureau of origin, maybe to demand further information, or to check the character and quality of sources of information. The bureau of origin will typically be informed of alternative or parallel accounts appearing in competitive media, and asked to investigate these. This kind of person control is also often forward-looking: a regional head bureau or head office may ask a bureau chief about predicted stories for the next week or month, and then recommend certain angles he should cover (and which if he is experienced he would probably cover on his own 'socialized' initiative anyway). Control is often in the nature of feedback: what the rival agencies are saying; reports in the London, Paris, and New York press that need to be checked out and developed. The most

extensive and protracted form of person supervision occurs, as it would for any organization, in relation to the new members or the 'incomplete' members: entrants still on probation, locally recruited journalists, or locally recruited bureau chiefs reporting to larger regional bureaux. Many newcomers have already worked on newspaper or broadsheet media (one survey of American journalists found that 'radio and the wire services . . . show a relatively strong propensity to recruit experienced journalists')[9] and are therefore deemed to have already internalized many of the desired norms. One very important induction procedure is to place new recruits on the central editing desks so that in this way they may learn, through constant exposure to on-going story developments and editing decisions, what qualifies as 'acceptable' copy.

(4) At each editorial stage only very few people are involved in the task of surveillance of copy. The general pattern is that there is only one or perhaps two copy-tasters per editorial desk at any given time, and these will be the only people likely to see the entire file of incoming copy directed to that desk. Any sub-editor assistants they have will correct and revise copy given them by the copy-taster(s), and may often be instructed as to what is needed. The number of assistants does not extend much beyond three or four on even the most important desks dealing with a very sizeable proportion of the entire volume of world news. The flow of copy for so few people is such that they work at a rapid pace in any given shift: the essential feature is that there is really no *time* for much more than the elimination process, the simple kinds of change mentioned in (2) above, and, when the occasion calls for it, a more extensive and detailed check-up on 'problem' stories.

(5) The elimination process is maintained at such a feverish rate that it is inevitable that selection occurs on the basis of a few simple variables, about which there is consensus between copy-tasters and agency executives. These have to do with (a) the cultural/economic/political *relevance* of a given story to one or more major world regions; (b) the *dimension* of the story: the more countries involved the better; the bigger it is, whatever it is, the better – whether it be an earthquake or political demonstration – but in certain fields, such as education or scientific development, it has to be very big indeed; hence the third variable (c) is *content appropriateness*: certain categories of news get high coverage by agencies, others do not. Politics, economics and sport rank high; education and

science do not. For the agencies, therefore, 'news' tends to occur towards the top levels of national, decision-making institutions, especially those whose decisions have fairly direct international implications; (d) its *technical adequacy:* in other words, provided the story passes on competence, in terms of language, sources approached, and 'impartiality' of presentation, it is a candidate for selection on the basis of the other criteria. If it does not pass those other criteria it will not be selected; if it passes those criteria but does not pass on technical adequacy, a check back to bureau of origin or an on-the-spot rewrite may be attempted.

The dominance of the elimination function reflects both the need to cut down on incoming copy, as well as the basic purpose of the outgoing wire, which is to provide huge choice of usuable material for clients in any given area. So while selection has to be made between some material and other material, the selection does not have to be so rigorous that it becomes a bureaucratic obstacle, since it is important to provide much more copy than any single client will want to use. The aim is both precision *and* bulk.

Centralization of editorial control

Editorial control is something that need not be centralized: indeed the perennial conflict of media organizations between professional autonomy and bureaucratic convenience generally requires some measure of decentralization or devolution away from the top echelon of executive authority. One of the strengths of the news agencies has been their ability to resolve this conflict more to the favour of 'bureaucratic' requirements (if by this is included the dictates of both organizational economy – its schedule for example – and external market pressures) than might be expected of such extraordinary diffuse operations.

One important indicator of the extent of centralization is the size and importance of each agency's headquarters, located respectively in New York, London and Paris, and the location in these headquarters of the major executive functions, performed mainly by nationals of each agency's respective 'home country'. It could hardly be otherwise. The top executives who manage these organizations from headquarters not only invariably have had journalistic backgrounds themselves, but also include many who continue to head important news divisions. UPI and AP's major news divisions are headed by vice-presidents, for example, most but not all of whom work from New York. Reuters, in a surprise 1977 reorganization, however, removed from its executive committee the two representatives of the editorial departments, Reuters World Services and Reuters Economic Services. Instead, Reuters appointed a London-based Editor-in-Chief responsible for both departments, and reporting directly to the Managing Director. Editorially, the agencies' respective headquarters also exhibit a significant concentration of editorial functions for the distribution of world services. AFP's Paris HQ in the late 1970s housed some 1,000 staff of whom 400 were journalists. Almost all news filed by AFP correspondents and bureaux was channelled via Paris. Dispatches received by the central desk in Paris were channelled by it to any one or more of six other desks, distributing services mainly in French, English, Spanish and German, to different world regions, as well as desks catering for French clients and dealing in specialist areas of news such as economics or sport. This heavy concentration was justified by AFP on the grounds that it gave it greater control and permitted economies of scale: for instance manpower, even 'specialist' manpower, could be rotated from desk to desk as the need arose. Minor regional news services were distributed from centres such as Singapore or Cairo (where MENA translated AFP copy for an AFP Arabic service), but did not amount to much in wordage: daily wordage of regional news distributed from Hong Kong for Asia, for instance, was in the 7,000 to 9,000 range.

In its international services, AFP is possibly the most centralized of all the 'Big Four' agencies. AP too is fairly heavily centralized. Its World Desk in New York is primarily responsible for putting together the basic news items that make up its services for Europe and Africa (with some input in London), and Asia (with some input in Tokyo), in addition to any localized insertions at the point of local distribution. The Latin-American services are likewise based in New York. The continued high level of *in situ* translation and direct distribution represents an important measure of decentralization. However, the bulk of news transmitted to any individual bureau for translation passes through New York.

The dynamics of editorial control in relation to centralization, technology, economy, professional autonomy and client need were well illustrated by Reuters and UPI in the 1960s and 1970s. For much of the post-war period, Reuters exhibited a heavily centralized pattern. Until 1966 there was a large Central Desk in London, with a total editorial staff of about 30, which transmitted copy to regional desks located in close proximity within the same building.

Each of the regional desks worked for a different schedule or deadline, depending on the common press deadline times in their respective regions. The Central Desk might give help, advice or recommendations. For instance, it might initiate a round-up of stories of similar substance but involving more than one region. Most of the translation work was done at the receiving end, by national news agencies. A long-established French-language desk did exist in Paris for France and French Africa. Translation into Spanish for South America was done on location in Buenos Aires. In the mid-sixties, the role of the Central Desk was further accentuated when it was renamed the World Desk and its role vis-à-vis the regional desks became more powerful, to the chagrin of many of the regional specialists. Before 1966, each regional desk had sifted for itself through the incoming Reuters material to compile a regional service. After 1966 the World Desk did the basic sifting for all the regional desks, whereas before it had performed this function only for areas with no special regional representation, and handed out to the regional desks the copy which it considered suitable for each desk. The regional desks could still monitor the incoming regional copy directly on their own teleprinters, but the only copy they now changed was regional copy.

Increasing the centrality of the World Desk was part of a programme of production rationalization which culminated in 1968 with the introduction of computerized operations: Automatic Data Exchange, or ADX. This was a multi-addressing system whereby dispatches could be sent, simultaneously, to appropriately coded addresses through the world. It eliminated the need for repunching of the same material for different destinations, and made possible the direct flow of news from source to client without intervention in London. In practice, London still did exercise intervention, except on stories of very great importance, like an American election, when the New York bureau would be given the go-ahead for direct coding of stories for immediate world-wide distribution.

The computer transmitted copy to the same broad destinations that were once covered by the regional desks. But these desks now seemed technologically redundant. Regionalization of news distribution was largely in the hands of the World Desk copy-taster and sometimes, at the discretion of the World Desk, of the bureau originating a story. The role of the 'regional' desks was now shifted largely from centralized news-distribution to augmentation of regionally located news-gathering and local news distribution teams. They moved out of London to Singapore for South-East Asia, New York for North America and to Beirut for the Middle East. The establishment of the New York regional desk followed the break with AP's domestic service and the Dow Jones economic service, although of course there had always been a news-gathering bureau there. Largely because of the importance of the economic news services, North America later became a separate 'revenue' centre for Reuters, ploughing back North American revenues into the further development of Reuters' establishment in that region. The French-language desk was brought back to London from Paris, possibly to help rationalize the selection and translation of French wire copy for France, Francophone Africa and Canada. Translation centres were now established in Bonn for German (when DPA switched to UPI for provision of international news) and in Beirut for Arabic. In effect the general climate of rationalization, symbolized by the introduction of computer, led to greater editorial centralization in the compilation and distribution of a basic Reuters world news service, but at the same time (possibly to better deploy existing resources) increased the extent of decentralization in regional editorial control of news-gathering and sometimes allowed very considerable discretion in regional handling of regional copy, further enhanced in the late 1970s by the extension of computer technology – for instance the establishment of an ADX system in Hong Kong.

UPI introduced a similar computer operation to Reuters' ADX in 1971, but it was exploited in a different way. Installed in London, this MSC (message switching centre) system covered Europe, the Middle East and Africa. (It was later moved to Brussels.) Its main purpose was economy, the elimination of manual copy repunching, but the opportunity it gave for a more regionalized and flexible news service was also extolled as a major virtue. The burden of coding dispatches was increasingly transferred to bureau level. An individual bureau could therefore become responsible for determining to which major world regions (or even countries within its region) it considered a story should be sent. This was a radical change in traditional agency editorial practice. The change was preceded by a nine-month training or simulation programme. Correspondents had to be taught to write copy in a way that would be immediately acceptable to clients. The training period, in other words, was designed to help correspondents internalize the practice of sub-editors. They were being asked to make the same decisions that previously sub-editors at Head Office would have made: for instance, they now had to decide what priority they should give a story – whether it should be urgent or ordinary. To write too much, or to send a story to too many places, might threaten to overload the system. In fact, one mode of control available to the regional centres was to let bureaux know when the system was near to full capacity. The correspondent still generally wrote one story for different client areas. But he could code the opening paragraphs for a wider market area than the closing paragraphs. One consequence may have been

Structure and process

to introduce a greater division of authority at bureau level, since it now became more important that the transmitting journalist not only had a good knowledge of codes but that he was also fully competent in English usage and an excellent news writer. There was now less editorial control from outside the bureau, particularly within each major region. So certain people were debarred from transmitting stories on their own authority. Those authorized to file tended to be the American bureau chiefs or chief reporters. In some instances reporters with poor linguistic qualifications (in English) were made redundant. To counteract this trend, the reduction of editorial work in the London bureau meant that some senior journalists were freed for location news-gathering.

UPI established a similar message-switching centre a little later in Hong Kong. Brussels would code Europe/MedAf news to both New York and Hong Kong; Hong Kong would file Asian news to New York for the Americas and for Europe. From 1978 it was possible for London to receive Asian and American news without any prior intervention at all in New York, thus accentuating the UPI tendency towards greater decentralization of news distribution. UPI's South American desk remained in New York.

UPI's experience of the 1960s and 1970s has also clearly demonstrated the extraordinary flexibility that modern communications systems permit. For instance, UPI transferred its London operations for Europe and the Med/Af area to Brussels in the early 1970s. It was argued that Brussels had become the political centre of Europe and, in American eyes, the news centre; that Brussels was at least as good a communications centre as London; that the Belgian government was prepared to make certain tax concessions in order to encourage new investments; and that labour problems were not nearly so acute in Brussels. On some of these points the agency was to be disappointed. Expected tax concessions did not materialize, and the communications, though good, were not notably better. Labour problems did begin to catch up on the British rate after a few years and, for UPI at least, the London labour situation improved (so that UPI journalists were allowed to use video-display editing terminals in London before the print unions were prepared to make the same concession for Reuters' far larger London operation). Nor did Brussels become quite the news centre that UPI had hoped for. In 1978, therefore, the London bureau once again became the headquarters for Europe, Middle East and Africa, although the message-switching computer remained physically in Brussels while London was linked into UPI's New York information storage and retrieval computer network. And, to quote another example of bureau mobility, UPI's Asian centre switched from Tokyo to Manila to

Hong Kong in the space of a few years spanning the late 1960s and early 1970s.

Within domestic markets of the global agencies the extent of decentralization is rather greater than on international markets, suggesting both that client needs are perceived as more complex here, and that local bureaux can be given greater discretion. Strangely, Reuters' domestic counterpart, the UK national agency and its part owner the PA, is more centralized in its domestic distribution than AFP or the American agencies on their respective domestic services. For instance AFP's Paris headquarters suspends its incoming and outgoing domestic communications with the regional bureaux for a few periods each day to allow provincial bureaux to transmit to one another, and to newspaper clients, stories of primarily local or regional significance unlikely to appeal on a nationwide scale, and which do not therefore require handling in Paris. More so than AFP, the US agencies both produce high volumes of local state and interstate news, and state or regional bureaux have considerable responsibility for the compilation of continuous state wires, coding stories for transmission on national trunk and broadcast wires, and for inter-bureau communication and combined state-trunk wires.

The structure of news-gathering operations in all the agencies is considerably more decentralized than that of news distribution. The basic component of the news-gathering machinery is the individual bureau. But there is a hierarchy of bureaux. Each of the agencies has some important regional centres, as we have seen. In the event of a news-crisis, the appropriate regional centre may well take responsibility for the logistics of coverage, ordering the transfer of correspondents from one point to another, arranging new patterns of communication if necessary, advising correspondents of related developments in other parts of the world and helping them establish some form to what at the front line may still seem hopelessly fragmented. Bureaux may also be differentiated by their place in the lines of communication. Many bureaux, for instance, do not code their stories directly to their respective head offices, or on to major distribution circuits, but either to a major regional bureau, or simply to the bureau in a neighbouring country. For instance in 1973 the Malaysian bureau in UPI's South-East Asian structure reported to Singapore. It tends to happen that the bureaux which *receive* the communications of others in this way are more important, have more authority, than the ones which do the transmitting. This is not so true of developed areas of the world, which are extensively covered by agencies' leased cable networks. Stories from Moscow, for instance, pass through Scandinavia, Germany or Belgium on their way to London or Paris, but the Moscow bureau is no less 'important' than the bureaux through which communications pass. Nor is any attempt made to edit the material which passes through. In other cases, however, it is more than simply a matter of passage. Stories are stopped or at least monitored at the point of passage, and the bureau chief at this point may have the right to query the bureau of origin on certain facts or suggest new modes of approach. This happens very often where the smaller bureau is headed by a locally recruited journalist, or a junior staffer. It happens particularly when there is no full-time representation at all, but a trusted stringer or stringers.

In some cases, however, and especially in Africa, inter-country communication is very poor, and it is easier for a stringer or local correspondent to file his stories direct to head office (London or Paris in the case of Africa, no matter whether the agency is European or American); but there will be some supervision of news-gathering by the bureau chief of the nearest sizeable bureau. The bureau chiefs of Nairobi, for example, have responsibility of this kind for several countries of East Africa; a similar situation is found in South America, where the smaller countries liaise with bureaux in the larger ones; and in the Middle East, where Beirut and Cairo bureaux sometimes lead for others in the same region. In Europe some of the East European bureaux are really subordinate to Vienna; and in Scandinavia, Stockholm tends to be the senior bureau. The politics of inter-bureau superordination–subordination is a flexible and mobile phenomenon in people terms. But since some countries consistently rank low both as centres of news and in terms of communication facilities, these same countries are especially vulnerable to being considered subordinate to bureaux in neighbouring countries which are considered of greater newsworthiness.

The bureau system

The bureau system is the essence of news-agency operation. Despite the speed of modern communications, and the preparedness of individual newspapers or broadcast media to resort to the 'roving correspondent' or the 'firefighter' instead of maintaining residential correspondents, the agencies have by and large retained a pattern of local representation, and indeed have expanded it to most parts of the world.

Their insistence on local representation is a reflection of the nature of the task: relatively *continuous* surveillance of the nation (from primarily a metropolitan vantage point), on behalf of a heterogeneous *international* clientele; and *distribution* of news to each nation, with some filtering in of news which is of specifically local interest. The agencies have business relations with most of the countries they cover: they need a representative in each country not simply to gather news, but also to sell news; they need continuous presence, or the nearest to this they can afford, because unlike the firefighter of a newspaper they cannot rely on some other source to tell them when a crisis has occurred; an agency has to tell other people when a crisis is about to occur; and it is as well that it should have representation inside a country at a point of crisis, since sudden closure of customs-posts and airports might otherwise restrict coverage by firefighters altogether.

Table 4
Twenty-eight countries in which agency bureaux were visited or which supplied questionnaire evidence: 1972–4

Argentina	Malaysia
Austria	Mexico
Belgium	Morocco
Brazil	Kenya
Cambodia	Philippines
Colombia	Singapore
Cyprus	Sweden
Egypt	Taiwan
France	Thailand
Hong Kong	Turkey
India	United Kingdom
Israel	United States
Japan	Vietnam
Lebanon	West Germany

There is, nevertheless, a considerable measure of compromise. A great many countries are covered only by stringers for the agencies, with a more general surveillance from a regional centre. Stringers are especially vulnerable at times of crisis, more so if they are local nationals; but the stringer is commonly relied on for non-crisis, routine coverage in many smaller Third World countries. As soon as events inside a country look like becoming what to the global agency's staff appears a matter of international concern, or a national matter of such magnitude that it must automatically be of international concern, a full-time agency staffer is generally sent in to take main responsibility, if entry is permitted or possible.

There are some agency 'rovers' and 'firefighters'. Like their newspaper counterparts they sometimes enjoy a relatively high prestige, but without quite the same degree of autonomy. A 'firefighter' is a correspondent who travels to the country where the latest crisis is happening, to take immediate responsibility for coverage; a 'rover' on the other hand is one who has some broad region to cover, but may wander from country to country to a greater or lesser extent at his own discretion, within the region, without any obvious or significant base. Two kinds of coverage are implied: the 'firefighter' for spot news in a time of crisis; the 'rover', although he may cover crises as well, for 'informed' coverage of a background or featurish character.

Anyone in an agency, virtually, can be a firefighter. Once a crisis flares in any particular country, reinforcements from other bureaux are normally directed to the spot, often with a great deal of ingenuity on the part of the regional bureau chief or news editor who is organizing the logistics of the operation. There is no identification in the agencies of one or two people who should spend most of their time 'fire-fighting'. In a newspaper this is more probable because there are so many countries in which a newspaper has no local representation: therefore it is convenient to develop certain individuals for this role. But agencies have men in most areas: the problem is the *number* of men they need at a given time.

There is nothing especially prestigious about being a firefighter. There are however certain individuals who are recognized as 'roving correspondents' although their numbers are small – perhaps about a dozen for all the agencies combined. They are generally senior journalists. The role implies less autonomy than might be thought. Roving correspondents report to the local bureau chief of the country they are in, or the nearest bureau chief. They do not generally spend long periods away from the office, or out of reach of the office. But they are often employed to write features and commentary pieces. There is no trend towards increasing the number of such correspondents. Precisely because a degree of extra prestige is attached to this role, there is the danger of upsetting local bureau chiefs; and by allowing certain individuals to develop an expertise and freedom which is not typical in agency work there is the danger of undermining the organizational authority on which the system rests. There is also a financial disincentive: by creating 'stars' the agencies would be developing correspondents they could not hope to afford; other media would step in with offers of higher salaries, and a great deal of training and expense would have been wasted.

The bureau, then, is the core organizational form of agency operation, the point at which local coverage is organized and managed, and at which the agency's services can be promoted. The bureau chief is a crucial status link between the organizational executive and local correspondents. He takes legal responsibility in any given country for what goes out over the wires about that country, and for general employment and business matters, although occasionally a 'bureau manager' is especially appointed to take care of these and so free the bureau chief for more news-gathering work. The bureau chief finds local journalist staff and stringers; he does much of the coverage of important news stories, liaises with local clients and is responsible for collecting revenues from them. His role is absolutely indispensable, and although he may work on a team basis with his colleagues in the matter of news-gathering, he is first among equals, and represents a useful vantage point for the analysis of actual agency operations at bureau level.

Bureau scope, size and composition

A study by this author in the early 1970s involved obtaining interview data from bureau chiefs and other correspondents in twenty-three countries; together with standardized information obtained in response to a questionnaire from representatives in fifteen bureaux of nine countries (four world regions),[10] and some further data from a previous study concerning groups of UK specialist correspondents. The information yielded a certain number of basic observations about bureau responsibilities, structure, news-gathering and news-processing operations. Because of its standardized nature and because it closely reflected the evidence obtained in interview from a much larger number of bureaux, the questionnaire responses usefully illustrate some features of bureau organization and news-processing.

The geographical area covered by any one bureau can vary enormously. The range amongst the questionnaire respondents, for instance, varied between one country or territory and sixteen (the last being a regional bureau with general oversight over several other bureaux in the region), and only three of the questionnaire respondents had responsibility for coverage of only one country. Table 5 provides some instances of multi-national responsibility for direct coverage. (Single country responsibility, however, is the norm for most of Western Europe, North and South America, and the more developed countries elsewhere.) As has been seen, there are other bureaux with multi-nation responsibility but in the sense of maintaining a general surveillance over other bureaux in a large world region. In 1974 this was true for instance of the UPI bureau in Buenos Aires, which had a general supervisory responsibility for the whole of South America, and of the Reuters Singapore bureau which had a similar role vis-à-vis South-East Asia.

There was also great variation in the size of agency bureaux, in terms of full-time staff. Among the bureaux covered by the questionnaire, the range was between 1 and 148, but the higher figure again

Table 5
*Selected instances of bureaux with multi-nation responsibilities in the early 1970s**

Bureau location	Range of coverage
Cairo, Egypt	Egypt Libya Sudan
Beirut, Lebanon	Lebanon Jordan Syria South Arabia Iraq Yemen
Nairobi, Kenya	Kenya Tanzania Seychelles Madagascar Uganda Somaliland Burundi
Bangkok, Thailand	Thailand Burma Cambodia
New Delhi, India	India Bangladesh Ceylon
Mexico City, Mexico	Mexico Central American Republics

*With variations these instances applied fairly closely to all four agencies; stringers were usually maintained in the 'subordinate' countries, and in one or two cases there were full-time but locally recruited correspondents, reporting to the major bureaux.

belonged to the regional bureau claiming on behalf of all bureaux within its region. Eight of the questionnaire respondents said their bureaux employed between six and fifteen full-time staff.

Not all full-time staff are journalists, however. Journalists were defined as 'staff who spend all, or nearly all, of their time directly engaged in news-gathering or news-processing'. Among the questionnaire bureaux there were between one and ninety-eight such journalists; in ten cases the number of journalists ranged between three and fifteen.

The fifteen bureaux covered by the questionnaire accounted for 194 full-time journalists between them, out of a total of 364 full-time staff. In other words, 53% of these agency staff were directly engaged in the news process; the others were ancillary staff, including messengers and technicians. Most of the agency journalists were generalists, with no specific function other than the gathering or processing of news. Of the 194 full-time journalists, only 39 or 20% were 'specialists', that is, journalists who spent at least half of their working time covering only certain kinds of news. Of the 39 specialists 24 were accounted for by the one regional bureau in the sample, answering for all the bureaux within its area of responsibility. The others were accounted for by six bureaux. 34 of the 39 specialists in fact were photographers, their speciality lying in a technique rather than a news-field, therefore, all of them employed by the two American agencies (the European agencies having no comparable photo services). The remaining five specialists included two whose speciality was sport, and three who covered mainly political affairs.

In addition to their full-time reporting staff, the fifteen bureaux recruited the help of at least 187 stringers (because one bureau did not give a precise number, but a range, the total figure is a minimum estimate). The number of stringers per bureau ranged from 2 to 35. This did not include cases where special arrangements had been made for journalists of local news agencies to report for a global agency bureau. A minority of the 187 stringers (35%) were not paid a retainer, but were paid only in terms of linage used.

Most of the full-time staff were resident in the country in which the bureau offices were based, and not in the surrounding countries or territories for which the bureaux were responsible. There was a tendency to compensate for the lack of full-time correspondents by the recruitment of stringers in these 'peripheral' areas. A higher percentage (30%) of all stringers was reported as resident outside the country of the bureau's location than the percentage (8%) of all full-time staff or journalists.

The larger bureaux, as we have seen, are those situated in the major capitals of the developed world or which are well situated to serve as regional centres. The most highly staffed of one American agency's bureaux were London (40), Paris (26), Rio de Janeiro, Brasilia and São Paulo combined (21), Tokyo (16), Beirut (15), Saigon (14), and Rome (13). This same agency's Latin-American reportorial staff (writing and editing) in the early 1970s was reported by Hester as shown[11] in Table 6. These Latin-American bureaux varied from 1 (e.g. in Asuncion, Paraguay) to 14 (Buenos Aires). But many were 'basically writing for internal consumption within their country'.

Table 6
AP *employees engaged in international news handling in* **Latin American** *bureaux, 1971.*

Asuncion, Paraguay	1
Bogotá, Colombia	2
Brasilia, Brazil	1
Buenos Aires, Argentina	14
Caracas, Venezuela	3
La Paz, Bolivia	1
Lima, Peru	5
Mexico City, Mexico	8
Montevideo, Uruguay	2
Panama, Panama	1
Quito, Ecuador	1
Rio de Janeiro, Brazil	5
San Juan, Puerto Rico	9
Santiago, Chile	8
São Paulo, Brazil	11
St Thomas, Virgin Islands	1

There was also one roving correspondent for Latin America. Total: **74**. The author comments 'Many of these, however, basically are writing for internal consumption within their country'.

Source: Hester, 1974, p. 87.

The nationalities of agency employees was discussed in Chapter 1, and the questionnaire evidence illustrated the general trend quite clearly. Among the journalists there were many more locally recruited staff than 'foreign' staff. The 'foreign' staff were mainly nationals of the agency home countries. There were three and a half times as many locals as there were non-local journalists. However, despite the high number of local journalists employed it is clear that the agencies prefer control to rest mainly in the hands of nationals of their home countries, or less frequently in the hands of nationals of other western countries. Of the fourteen respondents who gave details of nationality and birth-place on the questionnaire, thirteen were American, British or French and the other was a West European.

Locally recruited bureau chiefs, the interview evidence suggested, very often were to be found in charge of the smaller bureaux, possibly filing all copy to a larger neighbouring bureau under the control of one of the agency's own nationals. In the UPI network at that time, for instance, locally recruited bureau chiefs included a mainlander Chinese on Taiwan, filing to Hong Kong; an Indian in Kuala Lumpur also filing to a more senior journalist (in Singapore); while the local representative on Cyprus was a stringer, editor of a pro-Greek English-language newspaper.

Of the five locally recruited bureau chiefs in the UPI network for which information was available, four had been long-time employees of the agency. The Egyptian bureau chief had worked for the agency since 1945; the Cypriot and Dutch bureau chiefs had worked for the agency at least ten years, and the Taiwanese bureau chief for eighteen years. This might suggest that local recruits who are appointed to the position of bureau chief tend to be extremely 'trusted' men who, once appointed, are left in their bureau rather than regularly transferred – as happens in the case of the western bureau chiefs, few of whom have been in one place for more than ten years and usually for much less. However, considerations of expense may have made it more likely that the proportion of local bureau chiefs will have risen subsequently. Photographers were also found frequently to be local recruits: in Italy, for example, all four of UPI's photographers were locals.

Stringers are more likely to be locals than full-time agency journalists. Of all the stringers reported in the questionnaire evidence from 15 bureaux, only 8 were American, British, or French, while the remaining 157 were reported as locals. The percentage of stringers who were locals (95%) was higher than the percentage of full-time journalists (78%). Non-journalist 'support' staff were mostly locals: of the 108 support staff reported, 106 were locals.

Strength of local representation in the bureaux of global agency offices is perceived as a significant factor and many respondents in the interviews commented on this. Although most agency journalists are locally recruited, most bureau chiefs are not; and not many locally recruited journalists, proportionate to their numbers, filter into the international circulation process whereby journalists are transferred from one bureau to another. Several reasons were advanced for the relatively low number of locally recruited bureaux chiefs. It was said that they would occupy posts which the agencies needed to hold open for their own nationals as a line of promotion for good work in domestic offices (provided the candidates had the right linguistic abilities, etc.). But more usually the reasons given had to do with coverage rather than promotion. Most important for the American agencies, it was felt there was a need to have local news coverage in any given country at least guided by an American presence, since only an American was likely to have an authentic feel for the important requirements of the American market. There was also the technical problem that the locally recruited nationals were often not up to the linguistic standard required to feed news into a system which depended on an English-speaking market for much, if not most, of its revenue. This was the reason why locally recruited journalists in non-English-speaking countries were sometimes not allowed to file directly into UPI's computer controlled distribution network. A locally recruited journalist was also seen as more susceptible to formal or informal pressures imposed by his government or by other local interests, since family and property were immediately to hand, while too much pressure on a foreign journalist, especially a journalist from a major power, could create something akin to a diplomatic incident (although such reticence seemed to be on the decline during the 1970s). There was the possibility that the local journalist, despite screening, might be markedly biased in his attitude towards his own government (such bias being considered more likely in the case of a local than in the case of a foreigner). The possibility of bias therefore makes it all the more surprising that in three out of the four bureaux on Taiwan in the early 1970s the local bureau chief was a mainlander Chinese – although it could well be argued that only a mainlander on Taiwan could have had easy access to Taiwan government sources. The use of Greeks in Cyprus raised similar doubts about access to the Turkish community; or the employment of Indians in Malaysia rather than Chinese or Malays. In each of these three cases, of course, the bureaux did not operate with the same autonomy as bureaux headed by nationals of the agency countries.

For many reasons it is to the advantage of the world agencies to depend on locally recruited manpower for much of their journalistic labour. Local journalists of course are often cheaper to employ by contrast with the cost of maintaining expatriate staff overseas at salary plus living allowances, education expenditures etc. For another reason, they have close grass-roots experience of the country of coverage, which it may be difficult for any foreigner to acquire in less than a few years. They will be more fluent in the local languages, and are of great value for the translation of news services, where this occurs, and for the translation of local media content. In many countries, moreover, it is impossible for the world agencies not to depend largely on local labour, because of local restrictions on the employment of non-local labour.

Data on the personal background of bureau chiefs was not consistently collected in the course of interviewing in categories other than those described, but fourteen of the questionnaire respondents replied to questions in this area. These respondents had worked for their agencies for time spans of between one and twenty-nine years. In nine cases the bureau chief had been with his agency for longer than ten years. Ten of the fourteen had worked in journalism prior to joining the agency that now employed them, and of these six had worked for newspapers and four for other agencies. Of those who had worked on newspapers before, their newspapers were either provincial or regional papers of their own country or foreign-language newspapers in other countries – this experience obviously being a relevant qualification for agency work.

Respondents had joined their agency between the ages of 18 and 37, but in thirteen of the fourteen cases the range of recruitment was between 18 and 26. They were all American or West European in nationality; nine came from provincial towns or cities of their home countries. In three cases there had been a father who was also a journalist, and six others came from a middle-class background, only two coming from a working-class background in addition to two whose fathers had been members of the armed services

Ages ranged between 26 and 54. It is clear that it is possible for an agency correspondent to be appointed bureau chief of a medium-sized foreign bureau in his early thirties. Ten were graduates. Nine were married, three divorced and two single. They had worked at their present posts for between one and twenty years; but ten had been at their present bureau for four years or less – in six cases for eighteen months or less. Twelve had been bureau chiefs from the moment of their arrival, indicating therefore that as a rule bureau chiefs are not recruited from the bureaux of which they become chiefs. Of the other two, one was not a bureau chief, and the other had been recruited locally.

In 1974, Reuters respondents earned between £4,000 and £8,000 per annum; French respondents between Fr.100,000 and Fr.140,000 while the Americans grossed $12,000 to $24,000. Only two respondents said they took on work in addition to their agency commitments, but one of these was essentially a stringer or part-time bureau chief in any case, and the other was not a bureau chief.

Data was also available from an earlier, 1968 survey.[12] This concerned ten Reuters correspondents in four western capitals.

These were mainly reporters, not bureau chiefs. They tended to have worked on newspapers before joining their agency. Half were graduates, and most were of middle-class background. There was no outstanding feature in terms of their political sympathies, as measured by voting intentions. Salaries ranged in that year from £2,000 to £6,000 and only two admitted to earnings from other sources, substantial in only one case. Ages ranged from 22 to 53.

These findings suggest that bureau chiefs and agency journalists as a group tend to be young to middle-aged (by the mid-fifties most will either have been promoted to executive posts in head office bureaux or central editorial jobs, or will have left for other forms of journalism), and that their salaries are not outstandingly high. They have usually had some prior experience of journalism before moving to their agency. Bureau chiefs who are not local nationals are moved around from post to post at quite frequent intervals; they are rarely recruited from the bureau for which they have responsibility.

At work: in the office

Agency journalism, perhaps surprisingly, can be very much of an office job, especially in the case of bureau chiefs who, in addition to their work as journalists, must usually concern themselves with internal management and client and government relations. All but one of the questionnaire respondents spent 60% or more of their time in the office, and eight of them spent between 75% and 90% of their time there. In the 1968 survey, eight out of the ten respondents spent more than 50% of their time in the office, and in four cases it was 75% or more.

The single most time-consuming activity for these respondents concerned news-gathering and news-processing. In eleven cases this accounted for between 50% and 85% of all working time (1974 survey). The next major time-consuming activity for this sample was bureau administration, which ranked highest in eight cases followed in importance by the handling of communications and sales problems. In sum, news-gathering or processing, and bureau administration accounted for between 60% and 100% of the respondents' working time.

Within the general work category, 'news-gathering and news-processing', the single imost mportant component was the writing up of news stories; ten respondents claimed to spend eleven hours or more a week in writing news stories. The next most time-consuming component was reading the local press in the search for new stories and in the process of keeping well informed generally. Eight of the fourteen respondents who answered this question spent more time on this than anything else under this work category. Third most important activity tended to be editing or filing of copy. Other activities were fairly equivalent in importance, except for 'planning future coverage', which got the lowest overall score.

Respondents were given a rather different set of activities to rank in the 1968 study, but here 'writing and sending stories' consumed the most time – nine of the ten spent ten hours or more a week on this activity. Next most important activity for this sample was telephoning sources, which consumed between 5–9 hours a week in nine cases and more than 10 hours in the tenth. Taken altogether, it is clear that the writing-up process was a dominant activity for all respondents.

Travel

Respondents were asked about the extent of their travel, both within the country in which their bureau was located, and outside it, in the space of a six-month period in the second half of 1973. Most of them had spent some time outside the city, inside the country in which they were based. Altogether the fifteen had marked up 203 days of travel inside their country of coverage in the six months. A similar period, 213 days, was spent on travel outside the country in which the bureau was based, but within the region for which the bureau was responsible. Only three correspondents had travelled outside their area of responsibility, and in one case this was for home leave in the US. 1968 respondents also reported a fair amount of travel a year, from between twelve days to three months. Overall, these findings might suggest a certain metropolitan bias in coverage. If there were areas anywhere near as important in agency terms as the capital city of the country in which the bureau was located, this would presumably be reflected in a higher degree of travel outside the city in the provinces.

News sources

The single most important news source for agency correspondents appears to be the press media of the country or countries covered by their respective bureaux. In other words, 'news' is determined to a large extent by what other journalists have already defined as being 'news', and the global agencies are partly, at least, in the business of relaying national journalistic definitions of news on an international level (although these definitions in turn will have been influenced through constant exposure to the news definitions employed by the agencies).

Respondents were asked to identify by rank order the most important initial source of news. The highest overall score went to press media of the country or countries covered; ten out of the fifteen respondents, or two-thirds, recognized the local press media as source of at least 31 % and usually more of all stories. The second most important news source was information which the agency had solicited from individuals or organizations, followed by local radio or television media, stringers, unsolicited information and competing news agencies. Taken altogether, therefore, it seems that the local press and broadcast sources are extremely important. It is significant however, that these respondents believe solicited information is more productive than unsolicited information, and this, if true, contradicts to some extent the impression of passivity given by the high dependence on local media. This impression is confirmed by the 1968 data. Nine of the respondents then claimed they made more telephone calls to sources in a day than they typically received; but half felt that sources helped journalists more than journalists helped sources; the others thought it was about equal.

Wordage

Each of the fifteen bureaux put out between 500 and 8,000 words a day, in the week prior to their completing the questionnaire. In eleven cases the output varied between 1,000 and 8,000 words a day, a very wide range. The percentage of the daily wordage which was 'spot' news as opposed to 'soft' news of a featurish or background nature was estimated as high as 75 % or more in all but two cases. The percentage of news which was international, that is, pertaining to two or more countries, varied: in seven cases it was estimated at 60 % or more of news output, and in seven cases less than 40 %. But content analysis suggests that international stories do indeed predominate in the final dissemination, suggesting a possible weeding-out of the 'national' stories in the process of editing. Respondents were asked to rank varying kinds of news within both national and international news categories. There was a clear tendency to regard non-violent political news as the most prominent category, in terms of the amount of wire space it consumed, in both national and international news categories, a finding largely supported by content analysis data.

Markets

Who did these respondents consider they were writing for? Nine considered that their bureaux were primarily in the business of

D

reporting news of world-wide interest, whereas six thought their news was of interest mainly to a specific geographical region (e.g. the Middle East). Local clients within the country of coverage were in most cases considered of little or no importance, in this respect.

Competition

It is clear from the interview evidence that the agencies perceive their business environment as a competitive one, and that in many ways this inter-agency competition influences the news-flow, often but not necessarily always in the direction of greater uniformity. The questionnaire respondents were asked to say which other agencies they considered to be their most important competition for clients in their area of coverage and for clients around the world generally. In six cases AP was mentioned as the most important competition for clients in the local area of coverage, twice as often as Reuters was mentioned and three times more often than AFP or DPA. (DPA was mentioned only once.) AFP was mentioned as second most important competition in seven cases, probably reflecting its relatively good position on the South American market. This was better than second-place mentions of AP (five), UPI (three), and Reuters (three). Reuters was mentioned as the least important in five cases, UPI in four, AFP once. Reuters' poor ranking here may reflect the over-representation of South American bureaux in this very small sample.*

Mentioned as the most important competition for clients around the world generally, AP again received most mentions (ten), many more than Reuters (three), UPI (two) and AFP (two). Reuters got the most mentions as second most important (six), AFP (five), and UPI (three), and also as the least important (five), followed by AFP (four) and UPI (three). AP's lead in both kinds of competitive position is better than it at first seems since there were more AP respondents than any other agency and they were not able to mention themselves. On the other hand, the over-representation of South American bureaux would have worked to the advantage of AP (most likely to be identified by UPI and AFP as main competition) and against Reuters, whose South American operation is its least extensive on world markets.

---

* By contrast, Golding and Elliott (1979) report that in their study of broadcast media in Sweden, Ireland and Nigeria, Reuters was 'widely regarded as the best of the agencies' by the journalists they questioned.

Forward planning

Respondents experienced agency news-work as relatively unpredictable, and it has been seen that little time is given to planning future coverage (although this could be part cause as well as part result of the unpredictability attributed to news events). They were asked what percentage of stories in the previous week had required prior preparation, either a day in advance of their occurrence or more than a day. Participant observations in other news media, including TV news-studios and newspapers, had shown that quite a high percentage of stories were predicted and in some way prepared for in advance. In the case of the agencies it was clear that most stories seemed to require no advance preparation. Eight respondents said that 50% or more of the stories of the previous week had required no advance preparation (in two cases, between 80 and 100%). In no case did stories which required preparation within a day of the occurrence of the news event account for more than 50% and very little preparation of more than a day's duration was reported. This question did not cover the *anticipation* of stories before they happen, as opposed to the more active concept of planning. If almost 40% of all stories require some kind of advance preparation, the stories which are simply anticipated and internally prepared for, so to speak, without the necessity for overt planning activity might well increase the percentage.

Selection criteria

An attempt was made to identify some of the criteria of initial news selection, by means of asking questionnaire respondents to score up to twelve stories which had been constructed in pairs to test hypotheses generated from interview evidence. The scores given suggested that stories were more likely to be selected for transmission, other things being equal, if they were concerned with a capital city or major metropolis, if they had clear international repercussions, if they had a clearly established general market interest (e.g. sport as opposed to medical research), if they were violent and if the news sources were prestigious. Many stories were rated more highly if they were ready for transmission at non-peak activity periods. Some story scores fluctuated widely between respondents, indicating lower levels of consensus in certain news areas. Respondents were also asked if they would report certain types of story known to represent special difficulties of diplomacy, journalist-source relationship etc. (e.g. 'monarch/prime minister arrives drunk at annual celebration function and is incapable of delivering speech'). Most reporters claimed they would report such incidents, but many insisted on the need for impeccable sourcing. One major problem in news-gathering of course is that it is often difficult to find an impeccable source for a story that few people want to admit to, and especially difficult if an 'impeccable' source needs to be someone of high official status. There is also the question of when a respondent chooses to quote his own observations as an impeccable source.

Freedom to report

Comparatively few questionnaire respondents had been at the receiving end of serious source sanctions – retaliations, that is, for activity which sources disapproved of. Four correspondents had never experienced any of a list of sanctions presented to them during their experience in their present bureau. Two had been expelled and six had been threatened with expulsion at least once. Three had had experience of being refused all access to official sources, and more than once. Only one had been imprisoned. Three had been forbidden to file any stories out of the country and four had experienced selective restrictions on filing, even when other media were free to file as they chose. Eight had experienced informal 'warnings' a few times or often, and three had actually been subject to physical intimidation by sources. Altogether, therefore, the fifteen respondents put up thirty allegations of sanctions, experienced, at least once and sometimes quite often. However, the respondents were asked about their experience in their present bureaux, and in some cases this experience was of only a few years' duration. The findings would have been more remarkable, possibly, had they been asked about the sum total of their sanction experiences. Sanctions experienced by respondents in the 1968 study were rare, usually mild, amounting to insistence that a correction appear in print or a letter of protest or correction be sent to a journalist's senior. This low profile on sanctions reflected the relatively open and secure journalist-source relations of the western countries covered in that survey.

In comparison with journalists of local media in the country or countries they covered the agency respondents mostly felt they were freer to report whatever they considered newsworthy (nine out of fourteen), while five felt they had the same degree of freedom. However, in comparison with other (non-agency) foreign correspondents, only four out of fourteen felt they had more freedom, while seven thought they had the same amount of freedom and two thought they had less. Interview data supported very strongly the impression that agency journalists as a rule felt freer in reporting whatever they wanted to report than local journalists, especially where there existed a strong degree of government control over domestic media. But of course there are several countries where the agencies are not even permitted access and the question does not arise. There are a number of possible explanations for the perception of greater freedom to report:

(i) A government's concern for internal security may lead it to exercise more caution in relation to the flow of information to its own public than the flow of information to overseas countries.
(ii) Harassment of foreign journalists is more likely to create an unfavourable impression abroad than harassment of domestic journalists. Foreign journalists will tend to report their own experiences of harassment, especially if there is nothing else to report. Harassment of foreign journalists can take on the character of a 'diplomatic incident'.
(iii) The kind of information which the government may wish to control need not necessarily be of great interest anyway to the foreign press: the foreign press may be interested in the general character of restrictions on, say, internal political opposition, without being concerned with the instrumental details of how this restriction is achieved in practice, the kind of details which the government might find embarrassing or dangerous to itself.
(iv) The agencies are themselves careful to avoid what they consider to be needless provocation of the authorities.
(v) The sanctions which a government feels it can apply against foreign nationals are sometimes less severe than those which can be applied against its own domestic journalists.
(vi) Governments need the agencies to present the government point of view internationally, and need the services of the agencies to keep informed of international affairs.
(vii) In some countries the revenue to the local PTT from communication costs incurred by the agencies and other foreign correspondents may be sufficiently great to discourage excessive harassment of foreign correspondents.
(viii) Governments are often interested to know how their policies and performances are viewed by the foreign press – if they are repressive governments, the foreign press may be one of the few forms of non-dependent feed-back available (though the foreign press may be seen as reflecting interests inimical to those governments).

This finding of relatively high correspondent autonomy may have been a finite cultural phenomenon, reflecting the tolerance for western media which many Third World countries showed for the first decade or so of independence. But by the mid-1970s there was some feeling that western media credit was close to zero. Martin Woollacott, the *Guardian*'s Far Eastern correspondent, argued this case in response to developments in India, Bangladesh and Vietnam in 1975 (though restrictions were lifted in India in September 1976):

> The great era of the Anglo-American foreign correspondent, a person as privileged in some ways as a diplomat, travelling around combining the roles of adventurer, entertainer, reporter, and moralist, is coming to an end. But it is to be hoped that the rising tide of censorship and other restrictions will in time recede for, in spite of all the excesses and stupidities of the Western press in Asia and Africa, there is nothing else to take its place.[13]

And this trend was further exemplified by the so far unsuccessful attempts of some nations to seek UNESCO endorsement of government control over international news communication in or out of national boundaries. By the late 1970s the crisis of access was clearly an established feature of Third World coverage. AP, for instance, complained in 1978 that it had been unable 'for some time' to send correspondents into Angola, Uganda, and Mozambique; its resident correspondents in Ethiopia and Nigeria had been obliged to leave, and visas were difficult to obtain. In South America, severe pressures existed in Argentina, Chile and Uruguay. Access was generally impossible in Vietnam, Cambodia or Laos. Between 1975–7 AP correspondents were expelled from six countries: the Philippines, Peru, the Soviet Union, India, Zaire, and the Central African Empire.

To say that a foreign correspondent experiences greater freedom than local correspondents in a good many cases where foreign correspondents are permitted access at all may not be saying a great deal in any case, given the vast array of means whereby important news sources can frustrate foreign and local journalists alike in so many countries. While formal and informal means of censorship, reprisal, intimidation etc. are an extremely important issue in the general analysis of international news flow, there is little more that needs to be said about them in a study that is concerned specifically with news agencies rather than with foreign correspondence in general.

News content

Agency news content is comparatively difficult to obtain. Newspaper content can easily be preserved, and access to it is generally possible through central libraries. Radio and television material can be recorded from private sets. It is not always easy to determine what is agency material and what is not in a newspaper, and it is even less easy in broadcasts. If the agencies are credited with some stories there may be others, uncredited, which are also agency material. What can be said about agency material collected from a newspaper which is truly about the agency and not about the selection criteria of the newspaper? What can be said about the public impact of the agencies, the effect of their reporting, if agency coverage reaches the public only via the newspapers served by the agencies?

A study of wire-service coverage must arrange to obtain agency content direct, unmediated by any newspaper or similar agency. It can do this by subscribing to agency services, which is not only expensive but can only provide it with a limited range of the total services put out by each agency (because not all services are everywhere available). Or it can go to a newspaper or an agency bureau and ask to pick up a complete wire or wires for the purposes of study. This is often inconvenient for the newspaper office or the agency, and they may refuse the request. But if they do agree, neither a newspaper nor an agency bureau is likely to be able or willing to provide more than one or two services, and even then there may be no record of materials inserted at the point of distribution in certain countries. And the study will need several days' worth of material for each single wire examined. Its conclusions will necessarily be limited, because different parts of a single country, different countries or regions, often receive different versions of the same basic service, or different sets of services, from a single agency. It has to assume that the services provided for the study are the actual services as they were initially distributed, not ones which have been doctored in any way, or which for one reason or another are incomplete. Any conclusion drawn from the basis of one or two agency wires must be qualified by an awareness that the material distributed to clients is not necessarily the material that was transmitted by correspondents initially (material that is generally difficult to obtain); that the material received by some clients is not always the same as that received by others; and that clients sometimes have supplementary services or alternative sources of their own. Apart from the number of qualifications that must be made for each finding, a further deterrent to research is the sheer volume of agency output, and the tedious work of content analysis required to master it.

Despite these difficulties, most studies of the agencies have been primarily studies of agency content. Such studies have tended to fall into one of two broad categories.* The first category of *structural* studies is the more reliable of the two in as much as it involves the statistical analysis of all agency output on one or more given wires over a given period of time. Studies within this category have typically asked such questions as: which countries or world regions are given the most prominence or what are the most important kinds of news coverage on these wires – political, economic, sports etc.? The second category of *evaluative* studies generally attempt to draw conclusions about the quality of coverage with respect to specific news stories, or specific places and people. The reliability of the data is usually more questionable, more subjective, in this second case, although the conclusions may sometimes seem more insightful. However, there are some studies which are primarily structural but which, through the use of particularly sensitive statistical categories, are also able to move more towards the kind of in-depth, qualitative and content-specific conclusions usually more typical of the evaluative category.

Given the enormous volume of output, and the great diversity of wire services, it is truly remarkable that there is broad continuity over time in the principal structural characteristics of wire-service content. Above all, the wire services are conveyors of news about government affairs, international relations, and economics. The 1953 content analysis survey sponsored by the International Press Institute found that two-thirds of the copy provided by AP, UPI, INS and Reuters to US subscribers concerned war, politics, foreign relations, defence and economics; as did two-thirds to three-quarters of the content of five agencies transmitting news into Europe, and of four agencies transmitting news into India at that time. Although academics frequently use different systems of classification, studies by Cutlip (1954), Adams (1964) and Hester (1971) of AP's trunk wire in the US suggested somewhat smaller overall percentages for these kinds of news (approximately 50% in all total), but noted that the percentages were higher for foreign dateline stories than for domestic, and higher for news of developing rather than for developed countries. Weibull (1971), in a study of Reuters and AFP news supply to the Scandinavian news agencies, found that some three-quarters of agency content concerned politics, war, international relations, defence and economics. Somewhat exceptionally, Hester (1974), in a study of Latin-American news transmitted by AP's Latin-American bureaux and retransmitted from New York, found that the general categories of political, economic, military news

*For full details of studies quoted in this sub-section, see Bibliography, p. 263.

etc. accounted for less than half the items transmitted and less than a quarter of those retransmitted. But Bishop's (1975) study of Reuters and AFP services to Africa shows that the categories of economics, domestic and international politics and war accounted for 72–77% of their respective files; while Harris (1975) showed that in Reuters services to West Africa, politics, economics and military affairs accounted for 64% of the total. Harris (1977), in a study of Reuters, AFP and UPI services to their respective domestic subscribers, found that politics, economics and military affairs accounted for between half and two-thirds in each case. The author's own survey (1976) found rather lower percentages, ranging from 44% to 49% in the case of Reuters' South European and South African wires, and AP's European and African wires, but accounting for the more usual 50–60% range in the case of UPI and AFP services for UK subscribers. Schramm's (1978) study of 'Big Four' Third World news coverage for Asian media showed that between two-thirds and almost three-quarters of each agency's Third World news coverage was committed to the categories of military/violence, foreign relations, and domestic government, confirming the suggestion of Hester (1971) and implicit in Bishop (1975) that news of developing countries is more likely to be in one of these categories than news of developed countries.

Two other categories that tend to rank highly after these others are crime/legal and sport. In Hester's (1974) study of AP Latin-American news, 'crime/criminal violence' accounted for 14% of all stories transmitted from Latin-American bureaux to New York and an astonishing 48% of Latin American stories on the US 'A' wire at that time. A category of 'crime, violence, disaster' accounted for only 6% of Reuters and AFP stories for Africa in Bishop's (1975) study and in Schramm's (1978) study of Third World news in the 'Big Four' wires for Asia, 'crime/judicial' was only 4%. Sport gets a similar range of percentages: 8–11% of Reuters' and AP's European and African wires (and UPI's European) in Boyd-Barrett (1976), 8–18% in Schramm (1978), as high as 28% of Latin American stories retransmitted for AP's Pacific–Tangier wire in Hester (1974), but only 6% in AFP's English-language UK wire in Boyd-Barrett (1976).

Inevitably, there is little scope for large percentage scores in other categories of news; but it is important to remember that while percentages may remain fairly static over time, there have been enormous improvements in absolute volume. Categories that typically rank poorly include: 'technology', 'education', 'culture', 'religion', 'race'. Some typical instances: 'cultural' scored between 0.4% and 1% in Harris (1977); 'education' scored an average of

0.3% in Schramm (1978), while 'labour relations' scored an overall 1–2% in Boyd-Barrett (1976). However, a more composite category compiled by Boyd-Barrett, headed 'social' and including science and technology, social and welfare, education, religion, and culture, yielded scores of between 8–10% for all the major agencies, comparing more realistically with the similarly composite nature of categories such as 'domestic politics' or 'economics'.

Boyd-Barrett's content analysis of all four major agencies found that between half and two-thirds of all foreign service stories were 'international' in the sense of pertaining to two or more countries, possibly because, other things being equal, international stories have a wider market appeal than national domestic stories.

While there is evidence of a substantial diet of regional news in many of the agency services for the Third World (see Chapter 1), there is abundant news of the US and Western Europe on all wires. On US agency wires for US subscribers, for instance, Adams' (1964) study of AP's trunk wire showed that 45% of foreign news stories came from Western Europe; similarly Western Europe accounted for over 38% of foreign stories on AP's trunk wire in Hester's (1974) study (but 42% of the 'B' wire), and approximately one third of UPI's 'A' wire foreign coverage in Harris (1977). For non-US destinations, naturally, the US becomes a major foreign story. Together, the US and Western Europe accounted for more than 42% of incoming agency news to the Scandinavian agencies in Weibull (1971); between 55% and 63% of stories on Reuters' South European and South African wires, AP's European and African wires and UPI's European service and 38% of AFP's English-language European wire in Boyd-Barrett (1976); 55% of Reuters' European wire and 50% of AFP's English-language wire in Harris (1977). News of the advanced/industrial world accounted for 42% of Reuters' West African service in Harris (1975).

For US clients, studies by Adams (1964), Hester (1974) and Harris (1977) identify Asia and the Far East as the second most important region of foreign coverage after Western Europe, accounting for between 15–26% of foreign news stories, followed by Latin America, which in all these studies accounts for a remarkably constant 9–11%, with the Middle East scoring a similar percentage, and with news of regions like Africa and Eastern Europe trailing far behind: e.g. Africa accounted for 6–7% of AP and UPI 'A' wire coverage in Hester (1974) and Harris (1977), while the USSR and Eastern Europe accounted for 5–6%. For non-US clients in the developed world there was less similarity between the agencies in their ranking of non-western regions, but Africa and Eastern Europe still tended to trail behind, with the exception of AFP's coverage of Africa in its

English-language European wire (Boyd-Barrett 1976). These general findings have also been reflected in dateline analysis. Top five datelines in Weibull's study (1971) were New York, Paris, Washington, London and Moscow; and in Harris (1977), the UK, France and the USA accounted for a third of all datelines for Reuters and AFP wires.

Despite these broad similarities in content balance, however, there are also important differences. This is evident in such features as length and typical number of stories carried per day. For instance, examining eight different daily wires, Boyd-Barrett (1976) found differences in length from 24,000 to 62,000 words, the low figure of 24,000 referring to an American agency wire in French translation. There were also great variations in numbers of stories: e.g. in a three-day period in 1974, UPI carried 256 stories on its European wire, while AFP carried 418, but AFP's stories were shorter; in a five-day period that year, AP's European wire carried 602 stories, Reuters carried 528, but Reuters had more individual dispatches (stories were counted on a daily basis, with a fresh count for each day). On one of the days studied in the comparison of AFP with UPI, only 27 stories were carried by both wires, accounting for only 22% of AFP's total and 42% of UPI's. In the comparison between Reuters' South African and AP's African wires, only one-third to one-half of the stories carried by Reuters were also carried by AP, accounting for between one-fifth and one-quarter of the AP wire.

The same observation of dissimilarity in specific content within a framework of consensus on content *balance* is made by Schramm (1978): 'The apparent similarity of wires and papers in categories of content does not extend to individual stories. The wires are quite different, not only in total size and length of stories, but also in the particular stories they choose to cover and the kind of coverage they give events within a country'.[14] Some of these differences emerge in the analysis of the more detailed sub-headings of major categories of story location and content type: e.g. in Boyd-Barrett (1976) AFP was shown to have a far wider spread of datelines within many world regions than UPI; in his comparison between Reuters and AFP in Africa, Bishop (1975) notes that AFP put more stress on stories of regional cooperation, foreign cooperation and industry, labour, and mining; whereas UPI's major region for European clients was Western Europe in Boyd-Barrett (1976), AP's was the USA. Whether such features are temporary or permanent is more difficult to establish. But it seems probable that major structural characteristics of these agencies should be reflected in their respective services: some fruitful hypotheses for example might be that AP and UPI are consistently more generous in their provision of Latin-

American news than the European agencies: that Reuters, precisely because of its revenue dependence on RES, is less inclined to go in for economic detail within its general news services than, say, AFP.

The category of 'evaluative' analysis covers a wider range of studies in terms of questions typically asked and methods of investigation. Some are highly systematic, dependent on a data base of content analysis of a structural kind, but looking in detail at, say, a specific category of news, region or country, or a particular news event or development. What they have in common is a concern for specific substantive content as opposed to the structure or form of agency services. But they share important limitations. The short time-span of most of these studies is a more serious limitation in studies of specific content than studies of general structure: it is less easy to conclude that a two-week period of coverage of one particular country is as valid as a general description of content balance across an entire agency wire, especially since single-country studies are so rarely replicated – this author cannot in fact recall any agency and non-US replication of a study of the coverage of one particular country. This question is very relevant for instance in relation to the Bishop (1975) study of Reuters and AFP coverage of Kenya and the Ivory Coast, in which he concludes that the image provided of Kenya was 'totally inaccurate and inadequate' in the balance of news stories presented, and lacking any 'really critical coverage'. Above all, there is a problem in the rationale of choice. Harris (1977) chooses too exceptional a case in looking at the coverage of the 1976 UNESCO conference in Nairobi, an event in which the agencies had an organizational interest, but which they might very well have concluded from previous experience was unlikely to get good play in client media unless it focused on the conflict between super-power interests.* Bernstein and Gordon's (1967) analysis of

---

* Salinas (1977) describes interesting patterns of selectivity in AP's coverage of the 1976 Costa Rica Intergovernmental Conference. It is a useful study but problematic in that (i) the agency had an organizational interest in some of the issues discussed; (ii) this kind of event is relatively low-ranking among general priorities the major agencies attach to news; (iii) most western news organizations, agencies included, perceive a need to go beyond conference rhetoric and to contextualize conference events in the light of alternative information concerning underlying power strategies. In regard to this last point there is considerable controversy in the 'free flow' debate. Many people, in developed and developing countries, might agree that much discussion at conferences such as these is rhetorical, but it can also be said that it is precisely from proposals at intergovernmental conferences that changes in the world balance of power may eventually emerge; moreover, while scepticism is often considered a healthy attitude to politics, the perspective which the sceptic adopts is often culturally determined. (cf. Salinas, Raquel: News Agencies and the New Information Order: in Varis et al., 1977.)

events leading up to the 'Bay of Pigs' invasion, an excellent study, is nevertheless too exceptional to tell very much of everyday practice: if the US agencies were too respectful of Pentagon sources then, this had changed by the early days of American involvement in Vietnam. The choice of stories is especially problematic in studies such as Aronson's (1970) analysis of US media coverage of the 'cold war', where the author's choice of critical issues and of the evidence to support his views is arguably not backed by a sufficiently comprehensive description of the total package of output from which they are drawn. Like Braestrup's (1977) analysis of Vietnam war coverage, the central concern is with the general performance of US media, and not enough attention is given specifically to the agencies and to the task of supplying international markets. Furthermore, there is the problem of the standards to be applied. The implicit standards with which the agencies are compared sometimes seem too much to do with scholarly comprehensiveness and depth and not enough to do with coping in the heat of daily battle (often literally). Greater explicitness about the standards being applied would probably generate more constructive debate in many instances. Some judgements of agency content appear to be based not so much on direct studies of content as on agency stories which appear in the local press. But agencies are also sometimes accused of relying too heavily on the local press. Speaking in the context of Bolivian coverage, Knudson (1977) complains of the 'propensity of wire service reporters to cull much of their material from the national newspapers where they are stationed – thereby rehashing an essentially conservative version of contemporary history written to please the oligarchical owners of much of the hemisphere's press'.

It is this author's opinion that 'evaluative' studies can be at their most useful and insightful when they pay close attention to the descriptive circumstances in which coverage occurs, when due account is taken, therefore, of situational constraints on perspective and interpretation, and when the implicit standards, if any, share a certain respect for those same professional standards which agency journalists might recognize as relevant.* Braestrup's study is one such example: his finely-sifted evidence does successfully illustrate some of the negative consequences of intense inter-agency competition (e.g. haste, duplication); the difficulty agency reporters face in establishing the general significance of specific news developments

---

* But it can be useful to compare 'Big Four' agency content with the coverage of a different kind of agency. For example, Robinson (1977) establishes a useful line of enquiry in her analysis of AP coverage in comparison with Tanjug coverage for one day of 1966: she concludes, for instance, that Tanjug gave less emphasis to élite nation interests.

in a situation of rapid change; problems arising from high staff turnover and consequent loss of organizational 'memory'. Similarly, Aronson's (1970) critique of 'cold war' coverage is at its most telling in relation to specific instances of failures of professional cynicism: as in relation to the 'discovery' of a 'Vietcong camp' in Cambodia, 1967. Braestrup (1967) gives several examples of UPI stories which, 'faithful to the New York rewrite tradition', tended to exaggerate accounts in highly coloured prose; the same phenomenon was discussed in Barnes' (1964) analysis of UPI Latin-American news, in which he criticized the use of value-laden 'nutshell epithets' to describe political leaders on the 'wrong' side of the cold war fence. One further feature of the 'evaluative' tradition, therefore, has been a tendency for researchers to stick to familiar lines of enquiry: the reporting of 'cold war' politics has been a particular favourite. Moreover, it is particularly difficult to engage in studies of specific instances long after the event, when other retrospective material is available, because the total volume of agency output is not generally available, least of all the copy sent by individual bureaux to agency head offices before editing and retransmission. It is impossible to rely on the use to which client media put agency reports as a valid record. But the enormous power and responsibility of client media in selecting, adding to, and detracting from agency stories should not be overlooked in evaluative studies which sometimes seem to place an unrealistic burden of responsibility on agency shoulders for client news reports. Matta (1979), for instance, discusses the failure of some of the larger Latin-American media to provide independent coverage of some important regional stories. (Where some independent coverage is provided, 'Big Four' agencies may have a better indication of what is required locally.) He also gives an instance of an important Third World story which was provided by the agencies but ignored by many Latin-American media. A further consideration is the extent to which various 'gatekeepers' reduce the volume of news, as was first and well established by Cutlip (1954), who found that as much as 98 % of all the news copy received by AP's national office in New York could be eliminated by the time it had been filtered through the bureau manager responsible for the trunk wire; the state wire manager, the newspaper editor and, finally, the reader's own process of selective exposure. The process of elimination was accompanied by a narrowing of content range. At each stage of the downward flow, from trunk to state newspaper levels, certain categories of news increased as a percentage of the total and others decreased in importance.

Conclusion

As organizations the world agencies are simultaneously both highly dispersed and highly controlled. News-gathering, inevitably a very dispersed activity, is held together by the bureau system, with its relative absence of freewheeling 'stars', and exhibiting important routine features of operation such as the heavy reliance on local media as news sources. Any disruptive consequences of a dispersed news-gathering structure are in any case held in check by relatively centralized systems of editorial control and news-distribution, together with a concentration of major executive tasks in the head offices and in the hands of groups of fellow nationals. The high degree of editorial control achieved is reflected in the startling consistencies in content-balance of agency coverage over time, although differences of substance in coverage of particular events and places between the agencies are sufficient indications of real competition and differences of market orientation, and exemplify the principle that the dominance of the 'Big Four' system hitherto has been founded on a fine blend of similarities *and* differences.

3
Wholesale news and market control: Domestic

The home or domestic markets of three of the world agencies have, throughout their history, been by far their most important sources of revenue. The importance of the domestic market for Reuters has declined considerably in the post-World-War-Two period and in 1977 yielded only a sixth of the total. This might still be considered a large fraction for any single country and the domestic market has significance for Reuters in many other ways. Certainly, the future development and viability of the world agencies has much to do with their struggle for supremacy in the world's affluent markets (especially the domestic markets in the cases of AP, UPI and AFP) which in turn helps determine the potential scope of their activity in other markets. There are parts of the Third World (particularly Latin America in relation to the US agencies) which do yield appreciable revenue and for which regionalized services are made possible on that basis. But overall the sophistication of Third World services provided by the 'Big Four' must be greatly influenced by 'Big Four' viability in major markets, and it is with these that any analysis of the existing pattern of world news provision must begin.

The European agencies faced two major problems with respect to their domestic markets, which were, first, how to secure the best possible market position, and second, having attained that position, how best to contain actual or potential competition in the domestic market from either external or internal sources. A third problem was what to do when, having secured the best possible market position, that market proved not to represent a sufficiently sound financial foundation.[1]

Reuters

Four salient features characterize the strategies which these problems generated for Reuters. The key to Reuters' dominant market position in the sale of international news to the British newspaper press was its relationship with the Press Association, the national news agency established by the provincial daily newspapers and formally constituted in 1868. This helped protect Reuters from potential sources of internal competition, while the international news agency cartel of which Reuters was a leading member helped further secure the domestic market from external competition until after World War One. A sympathetic but not necessarily an intimate relationship with the Establishment, especially in the inter-war years, was also of some importance, but not so useful a security as the shift from private ownership to an ownership structure in which the provincial press and later the national press were major powers. This provided a framework for the post-1945 period of initial financial security, independence from the threat of state intervention, legitimacy and prestige which enabled Reuters to expand its services within and beyond media markets, and in particular those services for the financial and commodity markets on which the agency eventually came to depend for the bulk of its total revenue.

The Reuters–PA alliance

In the United States and in France, domestic news agencies set up machinery for international news gathering and distribution after they had first established themselves at home. In the case of Reuters the first important home market was the finance, not the newspaper market. Unlike the other international agencies, therefore, Reuters did not start as a domestic agency for newspapers. But the domestic market quickly became important to it nonetheless. Baron de Reuter had signed up most of the London dailies as clients for his service of foreign news before 1860 and very soon supplied some of the leading provincial newspapers. But the provincial press mainly relied on the telegraph companies for services of national and foreign news. Such services had been developed by the companies to exploit night-time surplus wire capacity. The newspaper clients found them very unsatisfactory: they were not exclusive services for newspapers only, and were considered both to be inferior in quality and exorbitantly expensive. Such dissatisfaction was the main impetus behind the formation of the Press Association, a cooperative enterprise owned by the morning and afternoon provincial newspapers of Britain. The Press Association adopted the task of disseminating national news to its member-clients, and also lent its support to the campaign for the nationalization of the telegraph, which came about in 1870.

Recognizing the significance and the strength of the Press Association, Reuters was happy to enter into a cooperative relationship with it whereby the PA received its service for exclusive distribution to many (and eventually all) its provincial newspaper members, beyond a 15-mile radius of Charing Cross, and the PA in return supplied Reuters with its domestic news service for incorporation into Reuters' service to overseas clients. The exchange was not an equal one, since the PA made an additional and substantial payment to Reuters. But the cost to individual PA members was greatly reduced from the previous cost of individual subscriptions. Reuters had established for itself a secure domestic market by virtue of this arrangement, without needing to involve itself greatly in the activities of domestic news-gathering. At the same time, it maintained a direct relationship with the most lucrative end of the market: the national newspapers of Fleet Street. Since the PA initially undertook to rely solely on Reuters for its foreign news, the competition was to that extent curtailed by the simple strategy of removing the possibility of a broad, national revenue-base for any competing news organization.

Domestic and external competition

It could not eliminate competition entirely, however. A second major domestic agency, Central News, was established in 1863, primarily as a parliamentary news agency, which from 1871 also gathered foreign news. Although it had nothing to compare with Reuters' overseas facilities, and did not enjoy the same reputation for accuracy, it did compete seriously on liveliness of coverage. Sufficiently so, indeed, to prompt the PA to observe in 1887 that some of its members were beginning 'to think that Reuters was a channel for official messages rather than a news agency'. If Central News could compete in this way the solidarity of the PA would itself be threatened. At home and abroad the Central News could afford to be more selective in the areas and kinds of news it wanted to cover because it did not have the responsibility of producing anything that claimed to be a reasonably exhaustive service. In other words it could concentrate expenditure on the maximum revenue-producing areas.

Reuters' relationship with the PA was remarkable in the sense that it contributed to the strength of the provincial press relative to Fleet Street, yet only exceptionally did it alienate Fleet Street from the services of either Reuters or of the PA. The London newspapers did sometimes resent their growing dependence on Reuters' news. No paper could afford to provide for itself in as extensive a fashion; and in times of war and similar catastrophe, important news sources had already discovered the advantage of speaking to the press as a whole through a single news agency reporter rather than a clutch of nervous competitors. The wealthier a newspaper the more likely was it to resent the role of Reuters, since the agency functioned to minimize the advantages of substantial independent overseas reportorial strength. *The Times* especially recognized this, in a period when it was also concerned by the growing success of its daily competitors in the adoption of techniques of popularization borrowed from the United States. Hoping perhaps to kill two birds with a single stone, *The Times* began to support possible alternative sources of news to Reuters. The most likely of these turned out to be Dalziel's agency, established in 1890. The agency was an exponent of the American 'new journalism' and, although owned by the publisher of the London *Morning Standard*, was largely financed by American capital and concentrated its coverage on relatively sensational fare from America. By 1892 Dalziel had persuaded a number of provincial newspapers to switch over from Reuters by offering to accept half the normal subscription to its service in the form, not of cash, but of advertising space – the method which Havas agency had employed to such advantage in France.

Dalziel's day was short. Because much of the agency's news was American it was popular, but it wasn't altogether necessary in the England of that time, since the rise of the popular press to this point had been mainly confined to the news weekly (and by the time the *Daily Mail* was established in 1896 Dalziel's agency in England had disappeared). Reuters offered a global, and in particular an imperial news service which Dalziel hardly began to match. Dalziel's reputation for accuracy was poor and it scored only on sensationalism (sometimes based on rewrites of Reuter stories). For most provincial papers the importance of a cheap domestic and foreign news supply was far too great for them to risk losing it for what was in effect an agency of a fairly specialized character.

Neither the competition of Central News nor of Dalziel succeeded in changing the nature of client demand so radically that the Reuters–PA alliance was seriously undermined. But it did succeed in provoking the established agencies into improving their own performance. In reply, for instance, to the threat posed by Dalziel, Reuters launched a 'special service' to which the PA contributed half the cost and which offered papers material that was more interpretative, more 'sensational' (in the sense, mainly, of giving more attention to the kinds of news now labelled 'human interest' as opposed to hard political and economic reports) than they received in the regular service. A third competitor, Extel, established in 1872, also maintained foreign correspondents in important news-centres and these were increased in times of major crisis. The Extel service circulated mostly to the metropolitan press, usually as a supplementary agency, taken in addition to the other agencies. As a competitor it was of more concern to the PA and to the Central News, especially in the fields of financial and sports reporting, than to Reuters. From 1906, the acrimony of its relationship with the PA was alleviated through the establishment of a joint Extel–PA service in the reporting of sports reults.

The development of a different mode of internal competition appeared in the form of foreign news services established by certain national newspapers towards the turn of the century, and of exchange arrangements between British and overseas newspapers. None of these, however, supplanted Reuters. Their prime beneficiaries, moreover, were the newspapers or newspaper groups involved: there was no question, for example, of extensive sales to the provincial press or to competing newspapers (Dalziel was the major exception). Nor did they achieve the degree of comprehensiveness of coverage accomplished by the news agency cartel, although they did help compensate for foreign government manipulation in the supply of news from Reuters' allies in the cartel.

At the very time that Reuters was consolidating its position on the domestic market through its exclusivity agreement with the PA, it was also securing itself from external competition in a series of cartel agreements with the other two leading agencies of the time, Havas in France and Wolff's Continental agency in Germany.[2] The cartel was inspired by the concern of each agency to protect its domestic market, and by the need to find a way round the very high expense of cable costs in the gathering of international news. The market for news was not so lucrative that the agencies felt free to establish local news-gathering networks wherever they wished. Instead, they relied very much on each other. Under the cartel's agreements the agencies agreed not to poach on one another's territories for clients, and to exchange their respective news services. They could not recoup news-gathering costs through local sales in areas which were not 'theirs', so they tended to concentrate their news-gathering resources inside their own client areas.* For Reuters, these were, initially, Britain and all parts of the British Empire, Holland and its dependencies, Australia, the East Indies and most of the Far East.

* Not entirely, however: 'As information from these (other agency) sources was apt to be coloured by the views of the governments of those countries, Reuter appointed special correspondents in the principal European capitals, as well as in great centres outside Europe, to give their own versions of events. It was, however, understood that these correspondents should not duplicate news which the semi-official agencies in their respective countries might send automatically, and should keep their independent accounts as close as possible to the bare facts without personal gloss or interpretation'. (Steel, W., 1938, p. 202)

There were modifications as time went on, but the basic character of the cartel remained constant until the 1930s when the leadership of the European agencies was effectively challenged from America. AP had begun to establish its own independent reporting system in Europe well before World War One, but it did not sell overseas. AP was a junior member of the cartel, which owed its initial survival to the exclusive contract it had signed with Reuters for the supply of news from the cartel in exchange (plus a cash payment) for its own news of the United States. It was permitted to expand to a few territories considered 'natural' AP property, like Puerto Rico and the Philippines, but in most respects AP's dependency on the cartel continued well into the twentieth century. It was from UP (later UPI) that the European agencies first felt the American threat. UP had no link with the cartel and, in order to secure new sources abroad, often established relations with other agencies outside the cartel system. But by the time of its emergence as an international competitor, Reuters had already begun to develop new strategies for the retention of a special relationship with the British market.

Relations with the Establishment

The commercial convenience of the alliance between Reuters and the PA was greatly augmented by the social and political legitimacy accorded both organizations by clients and sources alike. For Reuters this was reflected in the elevation of its founder to the status of Baron by 1871, not much more than a decade after the agency first began to supply newspapers, and he was later to receive from the Queen a Royal Warrant which granted him and his heirs the privileges of the foreign nobility in England. Reuters' services, meanwhile, were supplied free of charge to the Queen and her ministers. But while he no doubt won many informal concessions from Establishment sources in the receipt of early intelligence (Reuters' correspondents overseas often had close ties with the ruling political and business élites), there was little in the way of a formal relationship. This suited both the agency's need to be seen as the 'honest broker' in international news, and also suited the government for whom some aspects of the agency's business activities, exemplified in its struggle for the Iranian railway concession,[3] might otherwise have been diplomatically embarrassing.

A number of factors conspired to jeopardize this balance between government and agency. The declining profitability of the agency in the period leading up to World War One, first of all, exercised government concern. The initially secret purchase of Reuters by Roderick Jones, its new managing director, was a partial solution to the agency's financial difficulties, especially after the failure of its ventures into banking and financial advertising.* The move occurred with possible government encouragement as a means of avoiding a takeover by American interests, or even by Marconi who was also thought to be interested. Financial difficulty may also help explain why Reuters was unable or unwilling to maintain complete independence of the government during the war. The agency agreed, for example, to disseminate official allied communiqués and news to neutral countries, the British Empire, and the allied troops. This service was barely distinguished from the regular service by a change of prefix from 'Reuter' to 'Agency' or 'Agency Reuter'. The government financed the new service by paying the transmission costs of the telegrams, which amounted to £120,000 per annum, and contributed to the material expansion of communication facilities. Roderick Jones accepted a post in the Department of Information, supervising its cable and wireless services, while maintaining his ties with Reuters. One of the agency's board of directors, the novelist John Buchan, left it in 1918 to become Director of Intelligence in the new ministry formed out of the Department of Information under Lord Beaverbrook. Roderick Jones, who by this time had been given a knighthood, was asked to become full-time Director of Propaganda. He accepted the post without remuneration, but did not consent to handing in his formal resignation as Reuters' Managing Director. Questions were raised in the House of Commons alluding to this dual responsibility, and in the same year Roderick Jones resigned from the Ministry due to ill health.[4]

The war demonstrated both the importance of Reuters to the government at a time of crisis, and the willingness of its board to share reponsibility for government objectives at such a time. The relationships and outlook nurtured in those days seemed to continue into the post-war years. Government ministers, and even royalty, were to express hopeful concern in these inter-war years about the role of Reuters in disseminating British news in competition against propaganda agencies of other countries.[5] Roderick Jones encouraged this fusion of interest between state and agency. Discussion between Reuters' executives and the British General Post Office in this period, for example, concerning the wireless broadcast of news throughout the world, often alluded to the agency's responsibility for the 'national interest', a responsibility which Reuters was willing to affirm if only in order to obtain material concessions in communication rates and the goodwill that would follow a coincidence of values.[6]

---

* Jones turned the company into a private trust which bought up all its share capital; he was appointed chairman with full control.

New ownership structure

In practice, any subtle agency-government 'understanding' was insufficient to solve the agency's growing financial insecurity during the inter-war period, given the absence of direct and substantial subsidies of the kind which in France persuaded Havas to maintain its international network of bureaux. A different mode of solution was adopted to consolidate the agency's market position at home and to improve, or at least bring about, its profitability. Jones's tendency to look to the government for support in solving the agency's problems may have proved unwise, but perhaps helped to precipitate a successful eventual outcome. Continued financial deterioration during the thirties (arising from the depression, non-payments, and competition on international markets both from the American agencies and from the new agency services of Germany and Italy which now sought to establish themselves as equal to the dominant agencies) probably encouraged Jones to enter into secret negotiations with the government on the eve of World War Two which might have given the government some control over senior appointments.[7] Press concern over this development was a contributory factor in the eventual decision of the Newspaper Proprietors' Association (NPA) to become joint owners of Reuters along with the PA and later the Commonwealth Press Associations.

Roderick Jones had gone half way towards this solution in the inter-war period by bringing in the PA. His purpose in doing this was to establish a firm capital base for the agency, which the previous strategy of maintaining good relations with the government did not succeed in doing of itself. At the same time he also offered 50% control to the national papers, represented by the NPA. The NPA did not agree to come in on that occasion (1926), partly because Jones was unsympathetic to suggestions from some NPA members that the news operations of the agency should be separated from its commercial news services. World War Two, preceded by the scandal of Jones' approach to the government, created the right climate for the NPA's participation, and the present ownership structure was established in 1946 (although the Press Trust of India later withdrew, leaving majority control in the hands of the NPA and PA and the remainder divided between the press associations of Australia and New Zealand). This arrangement merely tightened the alliance between Reuters and the PA which had always existed. But whereas Reuters before the war had continued under the effective control of Roderick Jones, despite the participation of PA-appointed directors, the post-war solution promised more democratic control.

Bringing in the national papers to part-ownership tightened up that end of the market in Reuters' favour.

Post-1945 market competition

Competition to the Reuters–PA alliance which had existed before the war had a less favourable outlook after it. Central News went under during the thirties. It was supported for some years by Extel, which had feared that the property might otherwise fall into the hands of a foreign agency (the principal stockholder of Central News had been American) against the interests of domestic agencies. After the war, however, Central News was finally parcelled off between Extel and the PA. Extel itself later virtually disappeared from the field of general news. It informed the Royal Commission on the Press in 1948 that although most of its revenue came from non-media interests, its primary purpose was the general news service. In 1965 it divested itself of most of its news-gathering activities with the claim that there was no way in which these could be made to pay, even though it was then making a handsome profit from its racing services to bookies following the legitimation of off-course betting in 1961. Today, Extel's interest in news is mainly confined to sport (racing in particular, in which field its joint partnership with the PA continues), and finance.

The other major source of competition has been the rival global news agencies. Well before World War Two the foreign news service of UP had reached the British market through its English agent, British United Press. BUP was actually financed from Canada, where UP, as in Britain, eventually took it over altogether. BUP's first English client was secured in 1927 and before World War Two it claimed a total clientele of 70. Most of its staff were English, and some of them later rose to senior positions in Reuters. Its attraction was faintly similar to the earlier Dalziel agency: it was North American, popular in tone, heavy on human interest, rather brash. UP's significance in the post-1945 era is probably less now than it was. It is no longer so unusual in its approach to news, while Reuters has left behind its 'official' image of the thirties and has secured greater domestic support through its new pattern of ownership. The PA, by arranging with the other American agency, AP, to distribute an edited version of AP's services to PA clients (PA takes the AP service in return for supplying AP with its own), helped succeed in siphoning off any major threat of competition posed by both American agencies. The proportion of AP to Reuters news that was appearing on the PA wires in the mid-1970s was only about 10%, but this was sufficient to provide clients with a reasonable semblance of variety. The arrangement also means that AP does not distribute directly to provincial newspapers, and that there is not a great provincial market for UPI – which does however sell to the London offices of some of the larger provincial chains. The other attraction of this arrangement is that through the PA–AP exchange the provincial press is given relatively cheap access to foreign news-photos, which Reuters does not provide, without upsetting the provincial newspapers' major allegiance to the Reuters–PA alliance.

The situation by the mid-1970s was that Reuters was by far the most significant supplier of international news to the provincial newspaper market, largely via the PA news network (although a few larger provincial newspapers subscribed directly). Every national news media orgnization also subscribed to Reuters, despite the fact that its service was considerably more expensive than the services of the American agencies, and several also subscribed to some of its economic news services. Most but not all national news media also took both the American agencies, for both general news and news-photos, while a few subscribed to AP–Dow Jones, the economic news service. Only two organizations subscribed directly to the fourth global agency, AFP. For domestic news all organizations subscribed to the PA.

Development of the finance market

In the post-1945 era, therefore, Reuters accomplished a long-term consolidation of its domestic market dominance through a change of ownership structure. But it could not rely on that market to finance the cost of sustaining and expanding its international news operations: the newspaper industry was neither large enough nor wealthy enough to perform a function similar to that played by the North American markets for their respective agencies. The idea of a government-subsidized news agency was also clearly anathema to British newspaper tradition (barring minor and indirect subsidies, as through communications). The development of an alternative source of revenue, one which also contributed to the growing internationalization of the agency's revenue base, took the form of diversification of services beyond the media market altogether and into the finance and commodity market. For Reuters it has meant a far greater degree of liberation from economic dependence on the domestic market, and even on the world media market, than is possessed by the other agencies. But by structure and tradition it is still closely tied to its domestic media base in other ways. This raises questions about the long-term potential for conflicts of interest between its ownership base and the agency's economic internationalization, and between its involvement in general news and its involvement in economic news, which will be pursued further in later chapters.

Havas/AFP

Havas operated as both national and international news agency. Its techniques of market consolidation, and the strategies subsequently employed by AFP, depart from the Reuters experience in a number of important respects. And while domestic market revenue has remained more important to AFP than to Reuters, its hold on that source of revenue is also considerably more problematic. Up to the time of its disappearance as a news agency in World War Two, Havas' relationship with the domestic market exhibited three salient features. These were, first, its developing ability not just to control the news services in France, but to influence the infrastructure of media economics through its involvement in advertising. It was far less cautious than Reuters, second, in its relationship with the government and benefited much more financially from this relationship. Third, as with Reuters, the international news cartel helped protect its internal market position from external competition. The first of these strategies was made impossible for AFP by the nature of its constitution, which because it also restrains the possibility of diversification has obliged that agency to depend increasingly on the second strategy of dependence on state revenue. This in turn has had problematic consequences for its internal and external stability.

Master of clients

Founded in 1832, L'Agence Havas had the distinction of being considered first of the modern agencies. It quickly became both a domestic and an international news agency. But in its relationship with domestic clients, Havas was very different from the British Press Association. It was not a cooperative spawned by common media interests; it was no servant of the press, and, when it seemed profitable to do so, it ignored the interests of its newspaper clients, for example, by providing certain financial services to non-media rather than media clients.[8] One factor common to the emergence of cooperatives in both the UK and the USA, namely, press dissatisfaction with the news services organized by competing electric telegraph companies in an effort to exploit night-time surplus wire capacity, did not apply to France. L'Agence Havas was established before the coming of the electric telegraph, and when the telegraph came to France it quickly became a state monopoly, with Havas as one of its most important users. Perhaps in time the financial difficulty of depending solely on a news service as a source of revenue might have brought about a cooperative structure, but Havas quickly established alternative but related sources. Given the prior existence of an agency, the French daily newspapers were deprived of one important issue on which they might have cooperated, and in the absence of a cooperative machinery Havas was able to play clients off against one another.

In the 1840s, Havas sought to counter the competition threatened by the business of Mathieu Lafitte, who leased newspaper pages and then sold this space to advertisers, while supplying the newspapers with a free news bulletin. Havas successfully proposed a scheme whereby it would provide its superior news service to its provincial subscribers, on condition that they would make Lafitte their advertising representative, and on condition that Lafitte would cease his news bulletin. Havas would also enjoy a percentage of the advertising income.[9] In effect the two businesses pooled their interests and were later to merge completely.

What Havas had achieved was an extraordinary four-way relationship between itself, its clients the newspapers, the financial and business community for whom this represented a low-cost system of advertising, and the government, which in addition to subsidies which it already provided, was itself an important advertiser. Precisely because it was so rational a system it was not readily apparent to any of the four groups why they should dissasociate from it until very much later when the 'hidden' costs – e.g. the concentration of power in the hands of Havas – became meat for left-wing politicians.

In all, Havas engaged in three major kinds of advertising activity: advertising as normally understood; dissemination of government propaganda, of the kind often leaked to prepare the public for future decisions; and *'publicité financière'*, which consisted of creating a favourable atmosphere for the floating of security issues or loans. There was therefore no clear-cut distinction between editorial and advertising. One notorious instance of indirect propaganda dissemination was the payment of bribes to Havas (and other French media) by an agent of the Russian Czar in the period 1904–16 with the intention of bolstering the confidence of French financiers in the Russian economy.[10]

Even as early as 1845 Havas is credited by Desmond as having had a 'near-monopoly on the distribution of foreign news in Paris and most of France'.[11] By 1857, in addition to supplying most of the Parisian newspapers with national and international news services, Havas had some two hundred provincial newspaper clients. Its influence in Paris grew considerably in the early 1900s when the major Paris dailies grouped their commercial and financial advertising into one conglomerate under the management of Léon Renier, a co-managing director of Havas. Havas now had the right to sell their advertising space anywhere in the world. But Havas did not identify too closely with the Paris dailies which, after World War One, were in fierce competition with the growing power of the provincial press. Provincial newspapers had lower distribution, labour, and production costs, and operated in what were often monopoly conditions. For Havas, they were also crucial to its dual news-advertising network. So, with Hachette, Havas resisted attempts like that of *Le Petit Parisien* to set up regional editions in competition with provincial dailies; just as it helped bankrupt the attempt of François Coty in 1927 to undercut other Paris dailies with his *L'Ami du Peuple*, by refusing to deal with its publicity. No wonder that the New York correspondent of *Le Petit Parisien* was later quoted as saying that 'to alienate Havas may mean for a newspaper the loss of practically all its advertising revenue',[12] or that it was said that Havas news 'was often, if not always, bent to fit its enormous volume of advertising'.[13] Editor of *Le Petit Parisien*, Pierre Lazareff, described Havas as one of the most dangerous of all the poisons which undermined French public opinion.[14] By 1939 it was estimated that Havas controlled 80–90% of all advertising that appeared in French newspapers.[15] The agency's historian, Pierre Frédèrix,[16] tends to downplay the importance of advertising to Havas. Between 1879 and 1918, he claims, the advertising branch made a loss on five occasions, while for the period as a whole the news branch made two and a half times as much money as the advertisement branch, accounting for 70% of the organization's receipts. But this ignores the essential interconnectedness of the two operations, while veiling the government's dual role of news client and advertiser. Moreover, advertising revenues soared in the 1920s; and although they slumped in the Depression, the poor economic climate merely served to weaken still further any media potential for independence from Havas. It is possible, as Frédèrix claims, that the agency's critics exaggerated the actual number of newspapers it controlled. But their criticisms had a profound political reality which first seems to have surfaced during the left-wing government of Léon Blum which considered either stripping Havas of its advertising business or nationalizing the agency. While Havas in fact remained intact until the German occupation, the practices with which it had been associated ensured a radical restructuring after World War Two.

Government ally

Possibly on the strength of political connections originally acquired by Charles Havas during this period as supplier to the Napoleonic army in Portugal, the French agency established close ties with the government very early in its history. Desmond says that the agency was actually in receipt of a subsidy by the late 1830s, although at least part of such a 'subsidy' was simply a payment, generous perhaps, for a special government news bulletin which Havas began in 1840. Whether subsidy or payment or both, it went up when Havas, by his merger with Lafitte, added to the agency's influence and hence its usefulness to the government. In its foreign news service the influence of the government came to be felt most strongly in the following century, between the two world wars. This was a period of great intensity in propaganda warfare between the great powers. In the 1920s Havas, even while its advertising revenues soared, accepted undertakings from the Quai d'Orsay to underwrite Havas 'losses' in unprofitable markets, notably in South America. In the agency business of course it is a moot point whether news coverage of a country which does not yield much revenue should be considered a 'loss' or a cost contribution to revenues obtained in other markets. In 1931 Havas was persuaded by Briand, with none too great a reluctance it seems, to have the Department of Foreign Affairs reimburse the agency up to as much as 800,000 francs a month for expenses incurred in the reinforcement of its bureaux and foreign services in Europe, America and Asia. Total government payments to Havas that year for all services totalled 36,000,000 francs.[17] The Foreign Office budget for 1932 stated that the effort of the department had concentrated on the reorganization of the foreign services of the news agencies, principally the Agence Havas.

Domestic competition

The special relationship with which Havas cemented media clients, the government and finance institutions left little room for competition. Its key position as a member of the European cartel helped protect it against possible invasion by the other giant agencies: there was one such short-lived invasion attempt by Wolff and Reuters, later compensated for by the cooperation extended to Havas by Reuters in the aftermath of the Franco–Prussian war. Further and largely unsuccessful attempts were made between the two world wars, by UPI and INS amongst others.

There were few serious threats from internal sources. Perhaps helped by its special government relationship, Havas' strategy was to incorporate competition where possible, as it did to great advantage in the case of Lafitte's advertising and news service. Clients who wanted a more elaborate service than basic 'spot' news were catered for by a special service of political commentary from Paris, not altogether dissimilar in purpose to the Reuters Special Service. Like Reuters, Havas also had to contend with Dalziel's agency, but Dalziel's success was as short-lived in France as in Britain.

Much of the competition appears to have been concentrated in the provision of stock-exchange prices. In Britain, Extel secured an early exclusive contract for this information in the 1870s and Reuters, which had initially taken it direct from source, thence took it for many years from Extel. In Paris no one organization won an exclusive right to distribution, which meant that the market here was open. Henri Houssaye, then in charge of the Havas telegraphic service, wrote to a colleague in 1871 concerning a competitor:

> L'Agence Continentale is nothing. You know that anyone can find out and telegraph the stock exchange quotation list, and set himself up as an 'agency' with no one to say him nay; this is the case with L'Agence Continentale . . . which just like us has the means to telegraph the exchange quotation list.[18]

This was also largely true of a later entrant into the field, L'Agence Fournier, established in 1919 to compete with Havas, which took a foreign news service from UP in partial exchange for its service of French news. Eventually taken over by Havas, it specialized in finance, dealt mostly with Praisian clients and did not distribute by teleprinter. Much the same applied to L'Agence Economique et Financière. There were also instances of generally ill-fated local or provincial competition. One such was L'Agence Ewig which, like Havas, sought to combine advertising and general news interests but could not compete with Havas' superior credit, communications and expertise.

Agence France Presse: the reaction

It may be that had there not been a war, the advertising and news businesses would in any case have been split asunder eventually under pressures of a more enlightened public opinion. In fact it was the Germans who effected the split by taking over the advertising branch until after the war, when it was acquired by the French government. Undesirable as the old system may have been from an ethical point of view, it did at least represent a relatively stable economic achievement. The post-war situation for Agence France Presse has been very different. Characterized by considerable political instability for the first decade of its history, and a far less docile clientele, under great pressure from those very interests least certain of the desirability of AFP's continued expansion, and far too dependent on revenue from government clients for comfort, the new agency has had to pay far too high a price for the benefit of a moral virtue in which not everyone has been prepared to believe anyhow.

During the war Havas the news agency ceded to the official Office Français d'Information, dependent on the government for 90% of its revenue. In London, meanwhile, ex-Havas journalists established L'Agence Française Indépendente in cooperation with British official information services and with Reuters. Ex-Havas correspondents abroad were divided as to whether they would work with OFI or with AFI. A non-Gaullist branch of AFI emerged in Algiers (AFA). When AFP emerged after the war, therefore, it contained the seeds of numerous factional possibilities, interacting with a situation of general political instability. There was a rapid turnover of director-generals until the appointment in 1954 of Jean Marin, who was consistently returned to office until 1975.

Until 1957 the agency had only provisional status; its formal constitution passed by the Assembly that year gave it a cooperative-style management structure under public ownership. This comprised both media and government clients, who, since they suffered the consequences of rate increases, had a vested interest in moderating the agency's growth. This, as was seen in Chapter 1, brought about a crisis in the mid-1970s leading to the departure of Jean Marin.

The original intention of the National Assembly in 1944 had been to give the new agency the sole right of circulation of foreign news. This caused a storm of protest from the American agencies and from Reuters, who had hoped to establish solid markets in France. UP's John Degandt, for example, had worked his way up from Cherbourg to Paris via the underground even before the Liberation, to set up office, start a news service, and work out tentative contracts with newspapers which had not yet been licensed by the Provisional Government. In response to the 1944 decree, Reuters and AP severed their connections with the new agency, withdrawing their services of foreign news before it had time to establish its own. A further potential for leverage may have been the supply of agency equipment from the US. In any case the decree was soon lifted. While AFP fairly quickly regained and increased its newspaper clients at home and abroad, helped by privileged access to government information and preferential treatment in the allocation of cable networks, it had to contend with a scale of competition from other global agencies greater than that experienced by either the American agencies or Reuters on their home grounds. All three of these agencies soon had French-language services distributing in France. But whereas Reuters and UP confined themselves to providing only foreign news, and subscribing to AFP's domestic news service for their overseas coverage of France, AP also sold French news in France. By 1946 every daily paper in France received one or other of the US services. AFP tried to rid itself of the AP competition with an unsuccessful proposal for an exchange arrangement with AP, on the condition that AFP would have had the sole right to distribute AP news to French newspapers.

The period of political instability at home, together with AFP's clear dependence on government revenue, helped convince many domestic proprietors of the need for secondary news sources. Overseas the potential market may have been negatively influenced by the, albeit necessary, government subsidy: foreign media were encouraged in this negative view by the propaganda of rival agencies, although even the latter would concede that on matters not affecting French interests the AFP service was as objective as any. This did not prevent it from greatly expanding its overseas news-gathering machinery by comparison even with pre-war Havas. And in South America, where Reuters had nobly looked after and then returned AFP bureaux at the close of the war, AFP continued as strongest of the European agencies, helped by its Catholic image and a reputation for good football coverage. But the overseas operations would not have been as extensive had it not been for government subscribers at home. The alternative of seeking out some lucrative non-media and non-government market may in any case have been foreclosed by the agency's constitution, which laid down the agency's obligations specifically in relation to the provision of news. Although an economic news service was established in 1968, the non-media market for economic news may already have been cornered by Reuters, and AFP's operation did not seem destined for similar growth. The growth of Reuters' involvement in non-media markets, like that of some national news agencies, may have inclined some French observers to wistful recall of the old Havas news-advertising empire (a pattern still practised by some national news agencies, such as Argentina's official Telam). For even within its domestic market, and despite a continued growth of sophistication of its domestic services, AFP faced competition from moves by some newspaper groups to establish their own independent news sources in cooperative attempts to cut news-gathering costs and to increase editorial independence. One such competitor was Agence Centrale

Wholesale news and market control: Domestic

Parisienne de Presse (ACP), established in 1951 by Gaston Deferre, Mayor of Marseille, which was mainly controlled by a group of regional daily newspapers and subscribed to AFP until as late as the early 1970s. By 1976, ACP's clientele included 26 daily provincial newspapers, some of whom had abandoned AFP altogether, thus increasing the pressure on ACP, with a staff of 35 journalists, to duplicate some of the services hitherto the sole preserve of AFP (e.g. racing results). Although it had no intention, wisely, of attempting to become a global agency, its own foreign coverage extended to North Africa, while in the early 1970s it began a subscription and exchange arrangement with Reuters, providing Reuters with a provincial outlet and a source of news of provincial France. Reuters had ceased subscribing to AFP in the early 1970s, and AFP now ceased to supply ACP with any of its services. This prevented indirect Reuters access to AFP's service via ACP and hurt ACP, while also requiring ACP to expand in order to survive. ACP, given its regional daily newspaper base, could also claim to provide a service more closely tailored to its smaller client group than AFP; and by 1976 it no longer stressed its socialist origins – its new editor, Michel Bassi, had come from the conservative *Le Figaro*. A similar cooperative, Aigles (L'Agence d'Informations Générales, Locales, Economique et Sportives), was established in 1967 by two leading daily newspapers (*Le Dauphiné* and *Le Progrès*) in the Rhône–Alps region. It was designed to cater for the specific news requirements of seven dailies in Lyon, Grenoble and Saint Etienne. Aigles had a photo service, and planned to develop its news-coverage to all France. In an attempt to reduce AFP's market advantage its constituent newspapers imposed a ban on all stringer cooperation with AFP, thus establishing an effective monopoly on regional news sources, leading AFP to temporarily (1967–73) reduce the size of its Lyon bureau and to increase its dependence on the Aigles services to which it, like AP and UPI, also subscribed. At one point, UPI had considered an exchange relationship with Aigles.

AFP has therefore had to operate to a far tighter brief than Havas ever did, and has faced many difficulties which Havas, a free entrepreneurial organization, had long ago overcome. Nevertheless, despite these difficulties, there was no sign in 1979 that the government or the public had reached a point where they could envisage the disappearance of AFP as a global agency. Indeed, for all the tightfistedness of client-patrons on the AFP board or in the Assembly, it is remarkable that AFP has managed to bring itself into the computer era, greatly modernized its accommodation and been something of a leader in the development of satellite communication for agency news. Moreover the continuance of an assertive French role in world affairs has very likely worked to the benefit of the agency. But of the 'Big Four' in the 1970s AFP seemed the junior partner in some respects, albeit within a context of a rapid increase in numbers of clientele. While it had a better image than some of its senior partners so far as supply of news to the Third World was concerned, it was precisely in this particular and unremunerative sphere of agency operations that competition had suddenly become the most intense by the late 1970s, mainly from agencies such as Tanjug, the Non-Aligned News Agencies Pool, and regional agencies in South America and Africa, whose moral credentials for Third World operations were possibly more convincing even than AFP's if not more effective.

AP and UPI

In the US the situation was very different. Even by the turn of the century the US newspaper market was the wealthiest in the world, large enough to support two, even three, major agencies. Government patronage and non-media diversification in the history of agency development have never been so evident in the US as in Europe. But while monopoly may not have seemed an economic necessity here, it may well have been an aim. The history of agency competition in the US is partly one of relentless invasion of one another's 'exclusive' or preferential markets, creating ever broader market strategies that have in turn minimized or tended to eclipse the old divisions of interest between metropolitan and non-metropolitan, East and West, A.M. and P.M. papers, press and broadcasting, that once seemed so important. That there has been an overall winner in this protracted battle may seem to some observers increasingly clear, and should the dust ever rise from the battlefield the question of future development may seem as much political as economic. But meanwhile the rich diversity of supplementary agencies which coexist alongside the giants preserves an element of volatility which should not be underestimated.

Early conflicts: the metropolitan interest

The broad drift of agency development in the US as, to some extent on world markets also, has been a move away from sectoral market orientation towards the colder waters of the open general market. In particular this trend involved first of all a reaction against the New York, and to a lesser extent, big city interest; the decline of 'exclusive' distribution practices; equal treatment of both A.M.

and P.M. papers; and development of equal concern for print and broadcast markets.

The 'metropolitan interest' was originally New York, and New York media struggled unsuccessfully to retain a dominant control over the news agency network in the US. Associated Press was the creation in 1848 of six New York dailies, and the New York influence was an early cause of resentment for many non-New-York clients. Editors of the Memphis *Commercial Appeal*, for instance, included among their many complaints about the AP service in the 1860s that it was too much dominated by news from New York, and trivial news at that, while other cities of more proximate interest and distance to Memphis, like New Orleans, Galveston, or Charleston, received hardly any attention at all.[19]

The formation of a Western AP by mid-Western papers in 1862, designed to counteract this bias, was inspired by local reaction to the New York City emphasis of the agency's coverage of the Civil War. Western papers also objected to AP's policy of confining itself to routine news so that smaller papers would not compete too much with the metropolitan press. When the Western papers were eventually admitted to a role in AP's management, they 'demanded more enterprise and a report of a more varied character. The policy of limiting the field to "routine news" was abandoned, and the institution began to show evidence of real journalistic life and ability'.[20]

That there should have been resistance to New York was inevitable. Three other major regional press cooperatives were established, exchanging news with New York and with each other. But on this drift away from New York dominance there operated several remarkable catalysts. There was, first, the interaction between the rivalries of the press associations and the rivalries of the telegraph companies. In the conflict between AP of New York (NYAP) and Western AP (WAP) over a proposed secret deal between NYAP and the non-cooperative UP (the old UP, not directly connected with UPA, founded in 1907), for instance, Western Union changed its allegiance from NYAP to WAP, hoping that UP's demise would also kill MacKay's Postal Telegraph Company, with which UP did business and which was a threat to Western Union interests. There was also the excessively entrepreneurial character of the old UP, in whose subsidiary Cable News both NYAP and some WAP members were discovered to have interests. It used NYAP and WAP news reports for a service which it sold at a lower rate. The scandal this represented, well exploited by WAP which was to supersede NYAP and become the nucleus of *the* Associated Press in the 1890s, provided an extraordinary and permanent boost to the idea of a news-cooperative catering equally for all its members. Finally, there was the key role of the other global agencies, the European cartel. The dominance of the NYAP initially rested on its control of the transatlantic cable head in the US, giving it a lead in the provision of foreign news which it then secured by an agreement with Reuters in 1872, followed by similar agreements with other members of the cartel. When WAP first struggled with NYAP for a stronger role in the sharing of costs and facilities, it temporarily subscribed to a service from Wolff, then in disagreement with its cartel partners. This prompted NYAP to send a man to London to select NAYP news material from the Reuters file at point of origin, so as to maintain a lead in terms of speed. Then NYAP and WAP resumed relations, and shared the cost of a Reuters subscription.

In the 1890s, largely because Reuters chose to sign an exclusive agreement with AP of Illinois (as it was known temporarily after the battle between NYAP and WAP over relations with UP), AP survived but UP did not, although UP had struggled along with minor agency services such as that of the London Central News.

By 1900 the 'new' AP was itself incorporated in New York. Had it remained in Illinois, state law could have claimed a right to surveillance of AP as a public utility, and might have obliged it to sell the service to anybody who could afford to subscribe. But AP wanted to protect the market interests of its existing members, and to exclude many of the Scripps newspapers which had been clients of the old UP. By excluding them (and it may have suited Scripps to be so excluded) it inadvertently ensured the emergence of at least one rival news agency.

The New York influence persists today in that for both AP and UPI New York is the location for head offices and for many top executives. But the 'metropolitan interest' is now more diffuse. Schwarzlose,[21] for instance, considered that AP's board tended to over-represent large-city newspaper properties in the period 1893–1964. But constitutional safeguards restricted the total number of votes available to any member, and required that at least three of the eighteen directors each represented a newspaper published in a city of less than 50,000 population, and not controlled by any other newspaper published in a city of more than 50,000 population. Another possible source of imbalance has been reflected in complaints by West Coast editors that the agencies devote too much space to East Coast news. A 1974 conference of Californian publishers[22] identified possible East Coast bias in terms of the pegging of stories to Eastern Daylight Times, a slowdown of news flow from New York after close of business in the East but before close-down in the West; direct omission of Western points in round-up stories;

and ignoring West Coast stories of equal significance to East Coast stories. In reply, AP representatives pointed out that the Los Angeles bureau alone accounted for 17% of all non-Washington and foreign stories on the 'A' wire and that the four states in the Los Angeles regional news area produced 30% of non-Washington national copy.

It so happened that at that time, as AP's president informed an APME conference later the same year, Washington news had reached 50% or more of trunk wire copy 'on many days' in Watergate coverage, but that it was AP's intention to return to pre-Watergate proportions.[23] Possibly the problem of 'East–West' imbalance has been more psychological, a reaction to the role of New York as head office, and the promotions that have taken good newsmen step by step to the giant New York and Washington bureaux from all over the US. But Chicago is also a major centre of agency activity, and AP has several important regional or 'hub' bureaux. UPI in particular has been less tarred by the 'East–West' conflict image, with its traditionally strong market position in California and its association with the Scripps empire which was largely mid-Western and Western. A more important source of structural imbalance might have been identified between media-saturated states and others, with its implications for news-gathering investments and news service provision: in the mid 1970s, for instance, only a one-man bureau reported Alaska for AP, and a 'state'-wide wire service was not established for Puerto Rico until 1966, while many East and West Coast bureaux ran into double figures and state news services were in general well established.

Exclusivity

Just as the European agencies sought to protect domestic and imperial markets from external competition by means of the cartel system, US agencies sought to establish protected enclaves within the general domestic market. Each regional Associated Press agreed not to poach on the other's territories and forbade its clients to subscribe to alternative news services. Likewise the old UP operated on a franchise basis. Franchise-holders could waive their right of protest against the sale of UP to other papers in their territory in return for rate reductions. Scripps claimed he had so many reductions that UP was actually subsidizing his own Scripps League Service for Scripps papers.[24] AP continued its franchise system even after its victory over the old UP in order to reward its established clients and protect them from the competition of papers like those of Scripps. Together with its rule forbidding members to subscribe to alternative news agencies, this clearly limited the possibility for expansion of membership. The new UP, founded in 1907, and with nothing to lose, had abolished the principle of exclusivity. In order, therefore, to attract clients who subscribed to UP but did not necessarily want to do without AP, the rule on alternative news agencies was lifted in 1915. But the franchise system was more difficult to drop, since it so clearly benefited the existing membership. This membership restriction was not struck down until in 1944 the US District Court ruled that AP could not exclude any newspaper from membership by reason of its competition with a member newspaper. The Association's by-laws consequently forbade members or directors, when voting upon an application for membership, to take into consideration the effect such an application, if successful, might have on competing members in the same city or field. Assuming that the by-laws in fact eliminated this possibility, it seemed there might still be ways in which both agencies could if necessary make life awkward for new entrants, in order to cushion the competitive impact on more established customers. During the hearings of the Subcommittee on Antitrust and Monopoly of the Senate Judiciary Committee in 1967,[25] publisher Evan Mecham claimed that UPI charged very heavily and demanded advance payment when his paper in Tucson wanted UPI, because a rival paper in the area already subscribed to the service. He had to deposit $53,000 to get the wire 'in the door'. Other instances were given by different publishers of requirements to pay one or more years in advance, although these were not necessarily in towns with more than one newspaper anyway, and there are other reasons why an agency might prefer long contracts. Despite borderline cases, however, it is clear that neither agency any longer depends on local monopoly territories for protection, although exclusivity contracts are common among the smaller 'supplementary' news services and the position of some secondary services of the major agencies is unclear. The ending of exclusivity may in fact have worked to the disadvantage of agencies such as UP and INS which had emerged initially in response to the needs of newspapers excluded from the cooperative network.

A.M. and P.M.

The morning (A.M.) press was AP's special constituency in its early days and concentration in this sector (overnight telegrams were cheapest), helped create its own competition. In 1869, the American Press Association (APA) was established, mainly to represent the evening papers which felt that AP's service was too much geared to morning press needs – little news was provided, for example, after morning press deadlines. It was APA that later became the UP so badly routed by Western AP in 1892. The evening press (P.M.) complained of discrimination not just from AP but from the telegraph company whose favourable (night-time) rates supported AP's early growth: Western Union. Western Union charged APA heavily (daytime rates) and forced it to turn to other weaker telegraph companies. UP did not secure the kind of relationship with a telegraph company that AP had then established with Western Union. The AP alliance with Western Union was nevertheless costly: about three-quarters of all AP's revenue went to the telegraph company, until under Kent Cooper attempts were made to seek less expensive routes and to employ competitive bidding. UP, failing to get cheap standard rates, started leasing wire circuits. AP's larger members (mainly A.M.) were reluctant to see the agency expand too quickly. A strong agency would help smaller papers, which would include many P.M. papers, compete with them. They wanted to restrict AP to coverage that would suit their interests:

> The Associated Press had been founded mainly by morning newspapers. The most powerful members of the organization were still in that field. They were jealous of their rights; they had insisted that the 'evening wire' should close at four o'clock – that any news which 'broke' after that time of day should belong to the morning newspapers. This precluded those 'sporting extras' which have become of late years such a prominent feature of journalism, for almost all sporting events, notably baseball games, are finished after four o'clock in the afternoon.[26]

Such limitations could hardly be maintained for long in face of the sure expansion of these smaller papers anyway, and of the competition against AP which such policies helped generate. But the A.M. dominance was in fact accentuated in 1900 when the reconstitution of AP gave extra voting privileges to existing members (mainly A.M.) by issuing low-denomination bonds that carried voting rights. The result was that the larger and older morning papers kept control of the Board of Directors despite the growth of evening papers, which by 1908 already accounted for half of the AP membership (but much less than half of its revenue).

Into this situation came the new United Press. UP was in effect a merger of three other press associations, representing West Coast, mid-West and Eastern papers respectively, set up by E. W. Scripps (whose papers were mainly P.M.) after the collapse of the old UP in 1897. UPA, later simply called UP, concentrated on the afternoon market and on that other neglected market, Sunday morning newspapers. Another major publisher whose interests had been affected by the exclusivity of many AP contracts, and who also owned evening papers whose interests were not adequately served by AP, was William Randolph Hearst. He established two agencies in 1909–10, one for morning papers (International News Service), one for evenings (National News Association) and these were combined into one, International News Service, in 1911. UP set out to do for afternoon papers that which AP had disdained to do. It abolished the principle of exclusivity, and adopted a brash, colourful style. It installed a sporting service that ran between four to seven o'clock in the afternoon, and included in the sporting service any important news which 'broke' later in the afternoon so that UP clients, unlike AP evening clients, could publish 'late night extras'. To help smaller papers in outlying areas, it organized a telephone news service much cheaper than the telegraph.

Despite UP's concentration of energy in the evening field, AP could still boast more evening papers amongst its members than UP could claim P.M. clients. P.M. papers represented the major growth area of the industry, and were soon to greatly outnumber A.M. papers (by four to one in 1974).* Women were believed to prefer the more popular P.M. style of journalism, and department store advertising wanted the women. In 1908 only 362 of AP's 774 newspaper members were P.M. By 1930, P.M. papers accounted for 897 of AP's total of 1,286. UP started solely in the P.M. field with 300 in 1907, and 515 in 1914 (its A.M. clientele, started in 1919, climbed slowly to reach only 118 in 1928 and 150 in 1935). There were still several advantages of AP membership and disadvantages in subscribing to UP which overrode AP's initial lack of consideration for its evening membership: AP was a cooperative, and was more established amongst important institutional news sources, while the Scripps ownership of UP possibly alienated many non-Scripps evenings worried by the Scripps brand of popular radicalism, which might also have worried news sources. An AP franchise was a valuable property in itself.

Numerical growth of the P.M. press and the appearance of UP spurred AP to a more pro-P.M. stance. It established a sporting wire in imitation of UP, and then in 1915 extended its full service to afternoon subscribers, from 9.00 a.m. to 9.00 p.m. In response, UP in 1919 started its service for morning papers, after a suggestion to this effect from the newly-founded *New York Daily News* which had been unable to obtain an AP franchise. Despite UP's endeavour to

* By the late 1970s there was a trend for some P.M. papers to print morning editions or simply to convert to A.M. papers. Ease of production schedule, and reading habits of the young, were among the cited reasons given by editors.

establish a sectoral market 'enclave' in the P.M. area, therefore, it was in fact AP which enjoyed the stronger position in both A.M. and P.M. fields (cf. Table 7). Its total penetration of the P.M. market rose from 50% to 65% in the 1934–74 period, but still less than its total penetration of the A.M. market which peaked at 83% in the early 1960s and fell to 77% by 1974.

Table 7
Morning and evening strength of major US agencies

	AP				UP/UPI			
	% papers subscribing exclusively to AP		% papers taking AP		% papers subscribing exclusively to UP		% papers taking UP	
	M(1)	E(2)	M(3)	E(4)	M(5)	E(6)	M(7)	E(8)
1934	45·4	38·8	68·2	50·3	13·0	26·9	35·8	37·4
1948	33·3	40·1	58·3	53·3	9·6	26·1	34·6	39·3
1962	34·3	43·1	83·0	62·9	14·4	31·8	63·1	51·6
1966	36·9	44·7	82·0	64·5	15·4	30·8	60·5	50·6
1974	37·6	48·6	77·2	65·0	17·4	29·4	57·0	45·8

Sources: 1934–66 figures computed from Schwarzlose (1966).
1974 figures computed by the author from the *Editor and Publisher Yearbook* (1974).

Print and broadcasting[27]

The growth of broadcast news was problematic for the agencies. Newspaper members or clients feared radio newscasts would undermine circulation, although their ranks were split between those which had radio interests and those which did not. But for a surprisingly long period the view prevailed that only newspapers were the rightful vehicles for news. During the 1920s AP expelled members who allowed AP news to be broadcast on stations which they owned or who engaged in independent news-gathering for radio news, and radio chains were excluded from AP's customer list. A 1933 AP referendum established that the AP board would permit only AP members to use AP bulletins. Sponsorship of AP-based newscasts was considered out of the question. In South Dakota AP obtained an injunction which forbade radio stations to read fresh newspaper reports. A later decision by a Seattle court held that AP had no property rights in news after publication. But of course the agencies could refuse to supply (especially effective in foreign news). UP and

INS initially picked up many of the stations which AP refused to supply, but had to withdraw in face of the same newspaper pressures. At this point CBS organized its own news-gathering operation under the direction of an ex-UP journalist for sale to radio stations, taking foreign news from Reuters and Central News of London. This prompted concerted action from the print media (ANPA, AP, UPI, INS, Universal Service, Scripps–Howard Newspapers) to establish, in conjunction with CBS and NBC, a special news service for radio, the Press–Radio Bureau. Its main function was to select a limited volume of daily bulletins of state, national and international news from the wire services for use by broadcasters. Each bulletin was restricted to thirty words (this clause was later dropped as impractical), and the broadcast periods were restricted to two a day, not exceeding five minutes each. CBS agreed to terminate its own agency, and NBC agreed not to enter the news-collection field: they could hardly afford at that point to be blacklisted by the major news organizations.

But the Press–Radio Bureau agreement applied only to network-affiliated stations: while the networks owned 20 stations, and were affiliated with 150, there was already a total of 600. Inevitably, this other market attracted new suppliers. An ex-editor of the CBS service, Herbert Moore, set up a cooperative venture for the independent stations. This fell apart when, unusually, Eastern stations complained the service was too much dominated by West Coast and mid-West stations. Moore then established the Transradio Press Service, with a subsidiary, Radio News Association, for remote and less affluent stations. By 1936 Transradio claimed 260 clients by comparison with Press–Radio's 160 or less, and by 1938 Press–Radio sank without trace. Like the CBS service before it, Transradio took foreign news from Reuters and Central News of London. Reuters was retaliating, perhaps, for AP's withdrawal from the European cartel. At home in Britain it also combined with publishers to control use of news by radio. In Britain the government, via the Post Office, had established a radio monopoly (albeit 'autonomous') in the form of the BBC. Newspaper and agency interests negotiated to ensure that the BBC depended entirely on a carefully limited supply of credited agency news, a control which remained effective up to World War Two.

The collapse of the Press–Radio agreement, the growing acceprance of radio power and the profitability of print-radio joint ownerships, the realization that radio did not in fact damage circulations to the extent feared or, more important reduce the advertising revenue available to newspapers, all these factors combined to give both AP and UP an eventual free hand on the broadcast market.

Operating freely, they eliminated much of the competition. Transradio, which incidentally also provided a translated version of AFP news after World War Two, disappeared in 1951. But for a long time broadcast clients were given 'second citizen' status. UP had sold to sponsored news programmes in 1936; AP did not lift its ban on the use of its reports on sponsored programmes till late in 1939. In 1940, the AP board gave its general manager the authority to contract with individual radio stations and broadcasting networks, and quickly hauled in almost 50% of the market available. Both agencies were given to imposing tough contracts: for instance, requiring five years' subscription in advance. In 1967, however, the FCC adopted a rule prohibiting broadcasters from signing news service contracts which extended longer than three years. AP extended only associate membership to radio clients, and then not until 1946; not until 1976 was board representation made available to radio client-members. But in the meantime there had been very important advances by both agencies in the broadcast field, from the provision of special broadcast wires to audio services to (in the case of UPI) televisual news.

Market trends, 1970s

Official figures released by the two major agencies each year seem to suggest that in terms of daily newspaper sales on the domestic market, UPI lags only a little behind AP. Other sources suggest that the discrepancy is actually greater. One such source is the *Editor and Publisher Yearbook*, which for each daily newspaper lists the news agencies to which it subscribes. Analyses of *Yearbook* data by Schwarzlose[28] and Boyd-Barrett,[29] for instance, provide information ranging the period 1934–74 (cf. Table 8). The accuracy of *Yearbook* data is unknown but there is no reason to believe that any failures to keep the material up to date should favour one agency against another. Perhaps not surprisingly, the *Yearbook* analysis is in line with figures independently compiled by AP (1977–8).

These figures show that AP had a clear lead in overall market penetration and amongst single wire service subscribers; this lead appeared to be increasing, partly as more subscribers switched from having two to only one wire service (in line with the great decline of intra-city newspaper competition), partly because there appears either to have been a decline in 'no service' papers, in AP's favour, or because the reliability of the data on 'no service' papers has been inconsistent. (The general findings are supported also by Trayes (1972) and Singletary (1975). These show, for instance, that while AP's market reach declined slightly from 1,186 papers to 1,171 in

Table 8
Market penetration by US news agencies to US daily newspapers, 1966–78[a]

% of dailies subscribing to:	1966[b]	1974[c]	1977[d]	1978[e]
AP only	43	47	53	55
UPI only	28	27	29	27
Both AP and UPI	24	21	19	17
None	4	6	NA[d]	1
Total market penetration of				
AP	67	68	72	72
UPI	52	48	48	44
No. of dailies	1,748	1,754	1,736[d]	1,743

Notes
a. Percentages are rounded.
b. *Source:* Schwarzlose (1967), based on *Editor and Publisher Yearbook* data.
c. *Source:* Boyd-Barrett (1976), based on *Editor and Publisher Yearbook* data.
d. *Source:* Associated Press. This compilation did *not* include papers receiving no service, so that the percentages in this column may be slight underestimates.
e. *Source:* Associated Press, but this time including 'no service' papers.

1960–73, UPI's dropped more sharply from 917 to 799 in the same period. Fewer publishers subscribed to both the major wire services in this time – a drop of 4.3% – mainly at UPI's expense.)

The 1974 data suggested that in terms of individual states AP had an even greater lead, having more subscribers than UPI in 36 states (70%) while UPI led in 11 (22%) and elsewhere the agencies tied. In 16 states AP's lead was by 10 or more clients (in Iowa it led by 27), whereas UPI's lead was of this dimension in only one state: California, where it had 26 more clients than AP (eroded by 1978 to an AP lead of 3, according to AP figures). It led in 4 more states than in 1963, but the AP figures for 1978 showed that UPI now led in only 8 states by comparison with AP's 41.

The agencies' official figures on domestic broadcast clients – and there are no alternative sources to this author's knowledge – suggest that in this sphere UPI was in the lead in the 1970s. Unlike AP it had involvement in television newsfilm via UPITN, although the extent of its holding declined from 50% to 25%. In 1977 UPI claimed 275 CATV clients as against AP's 247; 900 clients for audio services as against AP's 537; and a total of radio/television clients of 3,650 as against AP's 3,487. These figures are substantially higher than those for daily newspapers, helping to explain why such broadcasters seem less and less the 'second class citizens' of agency clientele/ membership, though as sources of revenue they are said to account for only a fifth of AP's revenue, but approaching half of UPI's.

UPI's secondary position on the daily newspaper market was underlined by an announcement in 1978 of a five-year plan to recover its financial position. Its situation had deteriorated under pressure of high computer investment costs, dollar devaluation and a 1978 21% increase in distribution costs following increased ATT rates. UPI spokesmen had strongly favoured the possibility of a joint ANPA–wire-service transfer to distribution of domestic services via satellite, involving small receiving stations either in individual client offices or in most of the major cities. Such a scheme however could make the news system more vulnerable to enemy guided missiles, and would probably still require a landline back-up provision. For AP it could even be a disadvantage if UPI's market position was thereby strengthened. AP did initiate an experiment with satellite distribution for its broadcast audio services in 1978/9, followed by UPI, possibly in a bid to capture some of UPI's lead in this market.

UPI's market predicament was dramatized at the UPI annual luncheon in April 1979 when the president of E. W. Scripps, Edward W. Estlow, claimed that the corporation was tired of losing money on UPI. The agency had lost 5 million dollars in 1978, and had not made money for several years. Estlow warned that the current control of the company rested with a family trust 'which will some day terminate'.[30] But methods and means were being explored for the purpose of strengthening UPI and to further its perpetuity. UPI's management and the UPI Newspaper Advisory Board were participating in this study: the Advisory Board, represented by its chairman Richard Capen of Copley Newspapers, continued to urge the further introduction of technological improvements to improve efficiency and reduce the costs of news collection and delivery.

In July of the same year, a story in the *Wall Street Journal* argued that the decline of dual subscriptions from 25% to 18% of the daily market had worked against UPI, that only 35 of the top 100 US newspapers subscribed to UPI, and that UPI had recently initiated spending cut-backs of between 10–15%. UPI's President later denied that UPI was losing out to AP. The agency's investment of more than $21m., in the course of the preceding ten years, in computers, video-terminals, newspicture receivers and transmitters and other technical improvements, and the $10m. communications and computer centre opened in Dallas in 1979, the President argued, were not characteristic of the seige mentality suggested by the story in the *Wall Street Journal*. Only a month later, E. W. Scripps Co. and Hearst Corp. sent out a prospectus to a select number of US newspapers and broadcast organizations, offering 45 limited partnerships units. Under the new proposed organization, E. W. Scripps Co. and Hearst Corp. would be general partners with a 10% share of UPI's domestic business, but continuing to own and operate UPI's international operations. No organization was to acquire more than five partnerships, i.e. a 10% share. Of the $6m. working capital required annually for domestic operations, $1·5m. would be contributed by the general partners and the other 45 units would each provide $100,000. The general partners would be responsible for day-to-day operations with the limited partners having veto rights over budgets, capital expenditures and senior management changes (cf. Postscript).

The future of UPI, whether it can overcome its financial difficulties, improve or at least sustain its domestic market situation for the forseeable future, is a key issue in the survival of the present 'Big Four' configuration. The evidence seems to suggest that even in a market as media-wealthy as the US the underlying 'natural' trend is in favour of monopoly. Until 1958 there were three major agencies although the Hearst-controlled International News Service could more accurately have been described as a half-way house between 'major' and 'supplemental' agency status, with a specialist interest in overseas news. In 1948 its total US market penetration was 19%; the precariousness of its position as a major agency was illustrated by the fact that well over half its clients also subscribed to AP and UPI. The general trend since then has been a decline in multiple subscriptions to major agency services. An important UPI strength, by contrast, is that since the 1930s it has been able to hold on to a substantial clientele who subscribe only to UPI: since 1934 this clientele has fluctuated only a few points between 23 and 29% of the total market.[31] A future deteriorating hold on the Californian market might indicate the possibility of slippage. UP seems not to have gained considerably from the merger with INS, although its number of sole subscribers did rise after that. It may have gained more on the overseas market, where INS claimed a total of 2,000 clients in 1957 (out of a global total claim of 3,000); which suggests that INS, perhaps like UPI at certain points of its history, sought to overcome domestic obstacles to expansion through foreign expansion. The INS news-gathering resources were not as extensive as those of rival agencies, and it used Reuters for news of the Middle East and Africa (and had the sole right of distribution at that time of DPA's overseas service in the western hemisphere). It was said that INS had gone into the red by as much as $30,000,000, most of it covered by Hearst newspapers at a rate, in its last three years, of $1,500,000 a year, despite the alleged acquisition of 247 clients in 1957.

As for UP, an *Editor and Publisher* report at the time of the merger[32] commented that 'the foreign service kept in the black but the domestic operation was in-and-out of red ink by small margins'. In the wake of the merger UPI made a bid for a stronger hold on the domestic market, and announced that, unlike AP, it would not require clients to provide it with routine 'non-exclusive' news – an impossibility anyhow, given its non-cooperative structure. But it did not catch up with AP, and it is unlikely to have been independent of support from its parent company in subsequent years. UPI spokesmen have claimed that AP's cooperative structure makes it easier for AP to secure rate increases, but AP figures show that the average UPI increase in 1956–78 was 7% as against AP's 5% (or 9% against 7% for 1967–78). While there seemed little doubt that the parent company would be able to maintain its involvement for the immediate future, the agency's recent history of financial difficulty at least posed the question of its continued survival as a major agency, and whether it might, for example, revert to being a supplemental agency. This might seem an attractive proposition to AP, for whom such a trend would generate more members and more revenue, and therefore more scope for news-gathering improvements. In overseas news, it might be possible to use the new possibilities for expenditure in such a way as to produce a more even spread of news-gathering resources across the different continents and regions, and to move away from the kind of media resource duplication and concentration on a few major news centres, which is one of the costs of competition. On overseas markets Reuters and AFP would still offer considerable competition.* But in the US it is unlikely that the media industry would for long tolerate an effective monopoly situation, and loyalty to the competitive tradition might in the end prove a constant and unwelcome embarrassment to AP, leading to the growth of one or more of the supplemental agencies into something approaching a second major news agency once again, but perhaps this time an agency of a more specialist kind, one that rather than being a spot news agency with features, might be a features agency with some

---

* Reuters' media market in the US might of course grow. In a recent study of Middle East news coverage in leading US media (Mishra, 1979), it was found that while AP was the major source of agency items (14% of all items), Reuters and UPI were neck and neck (7·7% as against 7·1%). But Reuters would need to invest much more heavily in general US news-gathering to compete with AP in the US, and its prospects might be very uncertain.

spot news. Of course this could happen, to a limited extent is already happening, even in the current duopoly situation. In the meantime it seems unlikely that UPI would wish supplemental status upon itself. The indications now are that the setting up of the National Advisory Board was the first step in a long-term policy whose aim has been to transfer control from a private basis to something that may turn out to be a new kind of media cooperative, its losses therefore sustained by its membership, and the agency being more directly accountable to its clients. An alternative route might be through mergers with some of the existing leading supplemental agencies. If the market could sustain the continued existence of a second major news agency, any such development would doubtless be regarded as a healthy one by the US media industry generally. But the evidence that it can in fact sustain a second agency at this point is not altogether favourable.

The 'supplementaries'

The competitive relationship between AP and UPI is further complicated by the existing pattern of 'supplementary' agencies. In the US there are a large number of smaller agencies, ranging from syndicated feature distributors to relatively large-scale teleprinter networks for general news services. Subscriptions to the smaller news services, the supplementaries, are registered in the annual *Yearbooks* of *Editor and Publisher*. Over 60 are recorded there for 1974, but only 12 of these were recorded as having more than 10 daily newspaper clients. Most important of these were the fast-growing *New York Times* News Service which distributed to 141 daily newspapers in the US, and the *Los Angeles Times–Washington Post* News Service, recorded as having 108 daily US clients.[33] (By 1978 the *New York Times* News Service claimed over 400 subscribers in 49 states. The proportion of these which were daily newspapers is not recorded.) Both these services used material intially written for the newspapers that controlled them, and both had extensive sales as well (the NYTNS went to 119 overseas newspapers in 42 countries in 1972, and the LAT–WP service went to 100 papers in 346 countries). Table 9 shows the leading smaller news agencies at that time.

The pattern of subscriptions to supplemental agencies suggests several important features: (1) such subscriptions were an increasingly common feature of the media scene in the 1960s and 1970s; (2) it is the papers who seem least to 'need' the supplemental agencies, those already supplied with many services and with generous facilities, that most use them; (3) to a limited extent the agency services may be taken as alternative sources to one (but never both) the

Table 9
Leading supplementary agencies in order of their percentages of total daily newspaper subscriptions to supplementaries

	1966 News Service	%	1974 News Service	%
1	New York Times (NYT)	14·5	New York Times (NYT)	20·0
2	Chicago Daily News (CDN)	12·7	Los Angeles Times–Washington Post (LAT–WPN)	15·3
3	New York Herald Tribune (NYHT)	10·2	Chicago Daily News (CDN)	9·8
4	North American Newspaper Alliance (NANA)	9·5	Newspaper Enterprises Association (NEA)	9·3
5	Newspaper Enterprises Association (NEA)	8·6	North American Newspaper Alliance (NANA)	6·1
6	Chicago Tribune–New York News (CT–NYN)	8·3	Copley News Service (CNS)	5·8
7	Reuters News Service (RN)	7·3	Gannett News Service (GNS)	4·8
8	Dow Jones News Service (DJ)	6·1	Dow Jones News Service (DJ)	4·7
9	Copley News Service (CNS)	5·4	Reuters News Service (RN)	4·0
10	Los Angeles Times–Washington Post (LAT–WPN)	4·7	Christian Science Monitor (CSM)	2·0
11	Gannett News Service (GNS)	2·9	Chicago Tribune–New York News (CT–NYN)	1·8
12	Scripps-Howard Newspaper Alliance (SHNA)	2·3	Scripps-Howard Newspaper Alliance (SHNA)	1·7
13	Hearst Headline Service (HHS)	0·5	New York Herald Tribune (NYHT)	1·3
14	Other	7·0	Other	13·2

Sources: Schwarzlose (1966) and figures computed from the *Editor and Publisher Yearbook* (1974).

major agencies; (4) the supplementary industry has become increasingly concentrated in the 1970s; and (5) many of the supplemental agencies themselves have significant links with the major agencies which might further reduce their potential as competitors with major agencies.

Singletary[35] records an increase in supplemental subscriptions from 382 in 1960 to 655 in 1973 (among daily newspapers). The proportion of all daily newspapers subscribing to supplementals also increased. In 1974, Boyd-Barrett[36] records that 390 or 22% of all daily newspapers subscribed to one or more supplementals, an increase of 7% on the previous year; while in 1966 the percentage was only 16%.[37] In the period 1966–74 there was a slight decline in the proportion of papers taking AP, UPI and a supplemental agency, and a slight increase in the proportion of smaller papers taking supplementaries. Only 191 dailies, or 11% of the total in 1974, appeared to take a supplementary as substitute for an alternative major news service. These papers subscribed either to AP or UPI, but not both, and had one supplementary (at least) in addition. 72% of these papers took AP for their major news service.

There was an increasing trend towards concentration among supplementaries in the 1970s. The three most important services in 1966 accounted for 37% of all daily newspaper subscriptions to supplementaries, and for 45% in 1974, while in 1973 the NYTNS and the LAT–WP together reached 62% of all newspapers subscribing to supplementaries. There were also several mergers. In 1974, for instance, two of the smaller news services, Knight Newspapers and the *Chicago Tribune–New York Daily News* Service, joined forces. A joint sales operation between the *New York Times* News Service and the *Chicago Daily News/Chicago Sun-Times* was discontinued that year, but the two services continued to share a transmission wire. Two small agencies of a newer generation merged in 1978: these were States News Service and Capitol Hill News Service, both specializing in Washington news and serving 77 newspapers on the basis of a fifteen-man staff.

Three leading supplemental wire services and some of the smaller ones have indirect links with UPI by way of Scripps-Howard Newspapers. One of these is the Scripps-Howard Newspapers Alliance (SHNA), founded in 1917, with 12 daily newspaper clients recorded in 1974, and distributing to Scripps-Howard newspapers. Another is Newspaper Enterprises Association (NEA) founded by Ellen Scripps in the 1920s, which in 1974 served 66 daily clients, in addition to overseas sales. In 1976, NEA became a subsidiary of another Scripps-Howard service, United Features Syndicate, and in 1978 was amalgamated with it to form United Media Enterprises Inc.

UME also incorporated North American Newspaper Alliance (NANA). Whereas SHNA in 1974 distributed to papers which also took either UPI alone or UPI and AP (but not AP alone), NEA was taken by more papers whose major agency was AP or who took both AP and UPI. Another leading supplemental service, that of Gannett News Service, had a long-standing relationship with AP in that Gannett's chairman, Paul Miller, was president (later called chairman) of AP from 1963–76 (he had previously worked for AP). Perhaps a more significant link between AP and many of the leading supplementaries is the expanding role of AP as a communications agency for such services. In 1974, for example, AP agreed to provide a leased wire to LAT–WP, and in 1977 it was reported that DataFeature, the AP high-speed transmission system for feature material, was carrying material and syndicate copy of some fifteen supplementary agencies, including some of the Scripps-Howard supplemental agencies such as United Feature Syndicate. This material, however, went only to AP clients, while UPI carried similar material on its wires to UPI clients. Both agencies carried NYTNS copy for instance. (The NYTNS electronic editing system established in 1976 was programmed by AP and is maintained at AP's New York headquarters.) UPI's National Advisory Board in 1977 recommended UPI's management to explore all possibilities of sharing with 'others in the industry' the cost of support facilities, such as communications, computers, maintenance and/or data-processing. A UPI source told this author in 1978 that such activity in the communications piggy-backing field might eventually bring in sufficient revenue to equal a substantial proportion of the burden of UPI's general communications costs.[38]

The implications of the growth in supplementaries are far from clear. On the one hand it is good editorial and economic sense, in the minds of many managing editors, to rely on only one major news agency service and then to take a supplementary service which offers a more analytical approach. Then, on the other hand, the supplementaries are themselves important new revenue sources for the major agencies, whose communications the supplementaries increasingly use. It might be that some of the supplementaries will become so powerful they will virtually become major agencies, possibly at the expense of UPI rather than AP. Then again, both UPI and AP have increased their own output of feature, commentary and background news journalism. The leading supplementaries are closely associated with the leading newspapers and generally use material that has been prepared for publication in those newspapers. This might seem to weaken their competitive impact. On the other hand, since such services rest on the editorial strength of their respective newspapers, the resources available to them are very varied, but in some cases quite substantial. In the early 1970s, for instance, the *New York Times* had an editorial staff of about 35 in its Washington bureau, while the *Washington Post* had 49 and Gannett had 11. The *New York Times* claimed a total of 15 domestic and 28 overseas bureaux (manned by 42 foreign correspondents); the *Washington Post* claimed 4 domestic and 11 overseas bureaux (manned by 35 foreign correspondents). This is of course much less than each of the major agencies has at its disposal: AP had about 90 editorial staff in its Washington bureau at that time, with 100 domestic bureaux and 60 overseas bureaux. And single newspapers may be more likely to cut back on resources during periods of recession than the agencies. But in so far as even the coverage of the major agencies is very stretched (in Washington they are often able to cope only with the major congressional committees on any given day) there are clear market openings for specialized news services.

The political factor

The relative affluence of the US media market, coupled with a strong tradition of press independence from government, has meant that the US agencies have not, by and large, experienced the same kind of government-agency collusion characteristic of Havas, even of Reuters between the world wars. Nor have they ever been dependent on government revenue. It would stretch credibility of course to suppose that government departments had always conquered the temptation to exploit, albeit surreptitiously, the power of influence at the disposal of the agencies. Certainly there has been occasional recognition of common interest. In 1920, for instance, AP successfully campaigned for lower naval transpacific radio rates, so that it could reduce its dependence on Reuters for news of the East, arguing that the British had the power to shape the image of the US in the Far East and could distort Far East news for US consumption. But the US agencies did not make their wires available for propaganda purposes during World War One. In Mexico, Washington expressly instructed the Committee on Public Information not to proceed with a campaign of subsidies to interior newspapers for AP subscriptions in order to reduce the impact of German propaganda.[39] During World War Two the US agencies did contract to provide news for government global information services, but were not willing to do so after the war, even though they were told these services would be mainly directed at media too poor in any case to subscribe directly to the agencies.[40]

At least one account of the media coverage leading up to the 'Bay of Pigs' indirectly suggests that senior agency personnel were either too trusting of Pentagon sources or had agreed on this occasion to protect the 'national interest'.[41] AP's general manager, reviewing this incident on the occasion of his retirement, was quoted as saying 'Occasionally we have withheld stories for a time in the national interest. When the President of the United States calls you in and says this is a matter of vital security, you accept the injunction.'[42] There is also the question to what extent CIA employment and use of journalists has affected the agencies. CIA director William Colby in 1973 admitted to only 'some three dozen' American newsmen on its payroll at that time, including five who worked for 'general-circulation news organizations',[43] whom in any case the CIA intended to drop. George Bush, who took over the directorship of the CIA early in 1976, promised that the CIA would not enter into any relationship with full-time or part-time journalists accredited to US news organizations, leaving himself the option of recruiting both non-American and American reporters who worked for foreign news organizations. Institutional arrangements were not excluded. A further tightening of CIA regulations in November 1977 likewise failed to allay suspicions. These appeared to exclude CIA recruitment of all news personnel bar non-journalists recruited with the approval of their management, freelancers, and employees of foreign news organizations. But the door was left open for exceptions to the regulations in the event of specific approval of the Director of Central Intelligence.[44]

While correspondents may have contacts with intelligence service personnel in the same way they would with important news sources of any category, to actually work for such services is potentially so damaging to the reputation and credibility of major news services that there is no evidence that they have ever allowed or encouraged it. In fact the suspension of an AP photographer for providing information to the FBI during the Indian occupation of Wounded Knee in 1974 indicates just the opposite. AP president Wes Gallagher explained that whereas journalists, like other citizens, had an obligation to report or to testify to criminal events to the authorities, in this case the FBI sought to use a journalist to gather information which they should have been gathering themselves.

Formal collusion, of course, can be less important than coincidence of value, and there is scope for argument that a government-pursued policy of cold war was eventually successful in shaping the attitudes of agency foreign correspondents, and of the average newspaper editors who received agency services and attended agency conferences. Nevertheless, this is a semi-conscious deep-rooted agreement rather different from government-dictated policy, one which can erode as easily as it accumulates, as it seemed to erode in the early stages of the Vietnam war.⁴⁵ The inspiration of such independence in the case of the American agencies is professional and also in part commercial. Both AP and UPI had argued in the years prior to World War Two that their services were better for the world than those of the European agencies because they were not allied to governments, and because their governments were not in any case imperial governments. In other words, they preached free trade, and believed they would fare best under a free-trade system. And if the government's post-war policy of freedom of global information was sinister in some respects⁴⁶ the agencies' sympathy for that policy did not follow from quite the same reasoning.

In a very broad and long-term sense, and relative to the socio-economic-ideological parameters of the US market, it may be argued that the agencies have drifted towards the political centre, the 'middle market'. At one time there was a clear political distinction between the two agencies. UP reflected the populist radicalism of its founder, E. W. Scripps (though less so than Scripps' NEA which was intended to serve Scripps papers exclusively), and found expression in its celebration of the human interest, man-in-the-street style. Gunther described UP as aggressive, independent, and liberal.⁴⁷ While this image has survived the years, there can be little doubt that a broader market orientation tempered the radicalism, which was in any case as much economic as political.

The conservatism of AP against which UP set itself was not primarily political in origin, although it had political consequences, but had to do with the kind of authoritativeness which certain media organizations attract and encourage, arising from the cultivation of important Establishment sources, superiority of news-gathering facilities, longevity in the field, and the relative socio-economic status of readers or clients. AP's authoritativeness was founded in its cooperative support, and its long-established and continuous status in the two legislative houses, where by 1866 AP rather than the Washington papers was the normal machinery through which routine floor proceedings were reported, until the 1890s when it transferred its attention to committees. As Gunther puts it, 'AP tries to be strictly non-partisan, but was born conservative'.⁴⁸

In recent times it has been common practice for the two major wire services to be lumped together in discussion about the media industry. UPI is still considered a little 'racier', more brash, than AP; but AP provides much the same kind of feature coverage that was considered innovatory before the war. But both services were equally as likely to come under attack, albeit inconsistently and sketchily, by the often leftish-inclined media critics of the 1960s and 1970s. While few US papers declared formal allegiance to a political

Wholesale news and market control: Domestic

party or line, whether Republican or Democrat, those that did were more likely to take AP than UPI, and to rely solely on AP rather than subscribe to both major services.[49] This might suggest that for such papers AP is seen as the more authoritative source on regular national political news. A survey of journalists reported in 1976 ranked AP second to the *New York Times* as the 'fairest and most reliable' source, and as 'a media organization on which journalists depend in their work'. UPI ranked fifth as 'fairest and most reliable' and third as a 'media organization on which journalists depend'.[50] This may reflect the rather heavier allocation of AP resources to in-depth reporting from Washington. In the eyes of Washington news-sources, however, there is no evidence that AP and UPI are treated differently as a rule, or as anything other than the most representative of press organizations. Some professional commentators, for example, would have been happy (before Watergate) to see the White House left to both the major news services, thus freeing some of the newspaper correspondents stationed there for other work.[51]

4
Wholesale news and market control: Foreign

Not all parts of the world can be of equal interest to all the agencies all of the time. Clients in certain areas will inevitably feel that their interests are given less priority, either temporarily or continually, than they deserve. Europe and North America continually attract a substantial proportion of all agency news-gathering resources; on many agency wires, Black Africa continually fails to attract more than the most modest representation. Such disparities of client reaction, objective or otherwise, have formed the basis of a continuing but modest element of insecurity in 'Big Four' entrenchment on certain world markets.

This chapter is concerned with factors that help explain the wide variations from country to country in the resources for news coverage that are committed by the major news agencies as well as variations *between* each of the major agencies in the different world regions.

Factors that determine the location of major bureaux

Whether a country attracts considerable or only modest attention from a global agency is not simply a factor of its geographic or population size, nor even a factor of its political power in the world. These considerations have some but far from determining importance. Otherwise a country like Indonesia, with more than 125 million population, would require a much larger editorial representation than, say, Italy, with much less than half that population. But Italy invariably receives more attention in this sense. Similarly, if political power was a determining factor, Moscow bureaux would be much larger than bureaux in Buenos Aires, but the reverse is generally true.

The survey of major world regions which follows suggests a number of interrelated factors which help explain such differences in the strength of agency representation in different countries, as well as disparities in agency content. The most important of these can be categorized as (i) *historical*, referring largely to the continuing influence of the old agency cartel practices; (ii) *logistical*, referring to differences between countries in their importance as possible strategic or communication centres for coverage of wider geographic regions; (iii) *political* factors arising from controls or restrictions imposed by given countries on visiting correspondents; (iv) more important than these others, *commercial* or *cost/revenue* factors arising out of differences of market-pull between different areas of the world, and differences in the responsiveness of the agencies to the news requirements of different markets; while (v), a category of *'temporary'* factors, relates to news-crises in centres which are not otherwise well represented in agency terms, especially crises affecting the balance of global power, like the Vietnam war in the 1960s and early 1970s.

Bureaux with editorial staffs of between one and five persons per agency are fairly typical in very many areas. Relatively few editorial staff are actively engaged in news-gathering above and beyond monitoring the local media, rewriting and translation – in many places only one or two. There are not many bureaux which employ ten or more editorial staff. Most of those that did, in the early 1970s for example, appear in the sample of bureau sizes in Table 1. In Europe at this time there were bureaux of this size in the UK, France, Italy, West Germany and Belgium. Not all the agencies maintained large bureaux in each of these countries: in Italy it was only the American agencies; in West Germany, only Reuters and AP; in Brussels, only Reuters and UPI. London was important as a market, as a centre for news of interest to the world, and also as a logistical or support base for the rest of Europe, the Middle East and Africa. In the 1970s UPI temporarily shifted its European head office (for Europe, the Middle East and Africa) to Brussels, so naturally Brussels was one of its largest bureaux. Reuters maintained a sizeable staff there because Brussels was an important news-centre, especially so for economic news stories – a special interest for Reuters. France and West Germany were important markets and news-centres; Italy was an important market, but by 1975 was no longer considered to be one of the leading news-centres.

In the Middle East, only the Lebanon, up to the civil war in the mid-1970s, had bureaux of ten editorial staff or more in the case of most agencies. This was because of Beirut's strategic location for coverage of the Middle East conflict story, as well as being a news-centre and a moderate market. There were no bureaux of this size on continental Africa. In Asia, major bureaux were to be found in Japan (all agencies), Singapore (one agency), Hong Kong (one agency and up to the end of the Vietnam war in South Vietnam (American agencies). Japan was both a news-centre for a story of global interest

(Japan's economy) and an important media market. Singapore and Hong Kong were regional communications centres, and modest markets, but did not themselves generate much news of global interest. South Vietnam was of course a major news-centre but almost non-existent as a market or as a communications centre.

In North America, the European agencies naturally maintained sizeable bureaux in New York and Washington, but until Reuters' attempt to cultivate a stronger clientele in the United States, this had not been an important market for them. In South America, the major bureaux were to be found in Brazil and Argentina, where the American agencies in particular had high editorial strength – exploiting the major South American media markets, even though the agencies did not typically consider these to be major news-centres for news of global interest. Within the major world regions there were therefore great differences of emphasis. In Japan, the Western global agencies collectively maintained more than fifty editorial staff; whereas Indonesia, with a 20% greater recorded population and five times the land mass, was host to a much smaller complement of agency staff.

Most countries which had sizeable agency news-gathering teams were also countries the agencies considered to be at least fairly important as revenue centres. There was not necessarily a direct relationship between investing journalistic labour in a country and drawing revenue from it, but interviews with bureau chiefs suggested that it certainly helped to be able to show that local revenue exceeded local cost when it came to requesting additional staff. All the agencies encouraged their bureau chiefs to think in these and similar terms and bureau chiefs had become progressively more involved in business considerations and client-relationships as a result.

Important differences between the major world regions in terms of revenue helped explain the heavy representation on agency wires of news from Western Europe and North America. Western Europe was regarded as an important revenue and news centre by all four agencies – the single most important foreign centre for the US agencies. North America continued to be an extremely important news centre for the European agencies, but for AFP it was far more obviously a cost burden rather than a revenue centre; Reuters had recently increased its sales activity on the North American market so that it represented the second most important market in revenue terms, but this revenue was consumed in the continuing expansion of economic news services in the US. Outside of Europe, AFP's overseas markets were fairly evenly spread through the other major world regions. Reuters was about equally involved in Asia and the African–Middle East regions, but had fewer revenue possibilities in South America than even AFP. The American agencies on the other hand were very strongly entrenched in South America, which was their most important region outside Europe, followed by Asia, the Middle East and, a long way behind, Africa.

Distinctive features in the development of world markets

We have noted the factors that help determine the location of major bureaux. A development analysis suggests a number of aspects of the way in which these factors have interacted over time, which are of considerable importance for an understanding of the contemporary crisis. First, while North America and Western Europe have considerable market pull, the European agencies failed until very late in the day to cultivate the US market for major revenue as well as for news; and even the US agency penetration of Europe was strangely slow in coming about and may now even be on the decline in some respects. Second, coverage of the Soviet Union and Eastern Europe, but especially of Eastern Europe, continues to represent something of a 'black hole' in news which may be more serious than alleged weaknesses in the handling of Third World news. Third, competition between *all* the 'Big Four' agencies is not everywhere of equal intensity, and diversity of available resources is therefore less than it seems, although in many areas it is considerably better than it was before World War Two. Fourth, such diversity is further reduced by the many national news agencies which add the further threat of local news dictatorship to the danger of cultural imperialism in news supply. And within the broad spectrum of client categories, some categories have a seemingly disproportionate importance.

Before examining the major world regions in any detail, it is instructive to look at the pattern of early expansion as a response, at least in part, to shifting economic relations among the great powers. The early pattern of agency expansion reflected a mixture of the imperial, political, investment and trade interests of their respective home countries, interests which would also have motivated the major media and non-media clients for agency services. The most powerful European agencies were agencies of the most powerful of late nineteenth-century imperial countries: Britain, France, and Germany. But of these three Britain was the most powerful, with an empire that covered one-fifth of the land area of the globe in 1900, and something like a quarter of the world population. While trade with overseas dependencies was a surprisingly small proportion of total trade for the imperial countries, it accounted for a higher proportion of Britain's trade than that of France and Germany.[1] Such factors help explain why Reuters acquired such a wide sphere of influence outside of Europe by comparison with its partners in the triumvirate. But in some ways Reuters' expansion in the wake of empire ran counter to the interests of trade and investments. Most of the trade of the imperial countries was with each other and with other industrial countries, precisely those countries where Reuters depended in large measure on news-exchange agreements for news supply, and forfeited revenue opportunities. More than half of Britain's long-term investments in the period 1870–1913 were non-imperial, mainly to North and South America. Yet Reuters agreed that South America should be 'Havas' territory and did relatively little to establish an independent news-gathering presence in the US before World War One. What was the cause of Reuters' preference for imperial, or what would later be described as 'Commonwealth' expansion? Expansion in the directions suggested by trade and investment was clearly not in the interests of other developed countries with their own news agencies, whose services were considered sufficiently reliable for news-exchange purposes. News of the dependencies, however, and other non-industrial countries with which there were special ties, would have received no public coverage had it not been for Reuters: these markets were particularly accessible because of communications and cultural links, and because they were virtually monopoly markets. The overseas long-term investments of France and Germany were much less imperial than those of Britain, much more concentrated in Europe, and otherwise directed largely to North and South America.[2] The concentration of French and German foreign investment in Europe helps to explain why both Havas and Wolff confined their major expansionary efforts to that continent while Reuters soon gave up an independent role on continental Europe (where British long-term overseas investment was a mere 6% of the total, compared with 61% for France and 53% for Germany).

In terms of agency politics, Reuters and Havas should perhaps have paid greater attention to the North American market. But in Britain the climate of informed opinion was mainly obsessed with the consequences of German competition for the British economy.[3] While US manufacturing output was already two and a half times that of the UK's by 1913, US exports tended to be complementary rather than competitive with UK output. American agency expansion meanwhile coincided with the upturn of US foreign investment in the 1900s, which was mainly directed to Mexico and Canada and was not initially perceived as threatening to either the European economies or their respective agencies. But after World War One the US switched from its role as international debtor to that of major creditor; while British and French foreign investments fell by a quarter and a half respectively, US investments abroad were four and a half times those of British by 1930.[4] Moreover, its pattern of trade exports, especially in machinery and motor vehicles, was now much more potentially damaging as competition to Britain's few remaining expanding export activities. As the British economy declined, the imperial market for investment became proportionately more important than it had been before the war, reaching 59% by 1930. Of non-imperial investment, Latin America accounted for well over half, while the US attracted only 5·5% (a slump from 20% in 1913).[5] Europe's share rose. This investment position suggests there were several developing points of danger for Reuters as leading British and world news supplier. Not only was it facing invasion of established markets by the US agencies, but in areas which were becoming more important to Britain rather than less, the primary producing markets. In South America, for instance, British holdings were still greater than US holdings even up to World War Two, but South America 'belonged' to Havas and was the target of intensive US agency expansion, while belated attempts by Reuters to service South American media were given a dismal reception. The role that Britain's investments in the US might once have played in encouraging a stronger Reuters US presence was now greatly diminished by their rapid decline in importance.

New agencies in the Old World

The principal structural feature of agency organization in Europe until well into the twentieth century was an oligopolistic division of the market in which the American agencies played only a relatively small part. The gradual expansion of American agency penetration of foreign markets was triggered in the first place by the competition between them for domestic clients. Their initial progress in Europe especially in the case of AP, was modest, relative to post-World War Two expansion. Expansion was especially rapid and competitive in the immediate post-war period, although the total joint market strength of the American agencies in Europe has arguably experienced a relative decline in recent years. It is of no slight importance that for some seventy years following the establishment of the first major agencies (AP, Havas, Reuters) the national media of most European countries had but one main source of international news apart from their own correspondents. The European tradition in international news supply at point of reception was distinctly monopolistic. This was because the cartel agreements between Wolff of Germany, Havas in France and Reuters in Britain, which were also signed by newly emerging national news agencies elsewhere, eliminated open market competition. Within the larger countries there were a few small alternative sources – like Central News in London – operating outside the cartel system, but these were never of primary importance.

Within Europe, Havas news went to France and southern Europe; Wolff's news was distributed to Austria-Hungary and northern Europe. Apart from a supplemental payment from Wolff, and clients in the Low Countries and some German cities, Reuters' market strength on the continent of Europe was relatively weak. Each of the big three agencies would take news from the other two, and distribute a selection of this news, along with its own, to clients within its exclusive territory. After the First World War, Reuters and Havas divided the overseas markets of Wolff between them:* Reuters became a major supplier in northern Europe; Havas extended its influence in the region that had once been the Austrian-Hungarian Empire.

Up to this time the visibility of the American agencies to European 'retail' media was extremely low. AP news was filtered through Reuters. After the Spanish-American war, AP began to place its own correspondents in Europe in order to supplement the cartel diet, but there was no question of it selling its news service independently, under the terms of the cartel agreements. In 1900 AP had four forwarding stations in Europe, in which its representatives put together cable dispatches from reports supplied by the several European agencies. By 1910 the number of such offices had grown to sixteen. But the major news sources were still the large European agencies. The purpose of the forwarding bureaux was primarily to rationalize the selection of European agency news (and other world news channelled through Europe at that time, including Asian news) for the American market, and to speed up transmission. UP, on the other hand, had no obligations to the European cartel. Almost as soon as it was established in 1907 the agency began organizing a news-gathering and distribution network, primarily in Europe. By 1909 it had bureaux in London, Paris, Berlin and Rome, headed and mostly staffed by Americans. This news was supplemented by arrangements with smaller European agencies, like Extel in London, the Hirsch bureau in Berlin and Agence Fournier in Paris. News exchanges with such agencies helped UP compete with AP's foreign news sources, and gained for the smaller agencies a longer lease of life

* Wolff (WTB) did regain some influence in Europe (e.g. in the Baltic States), and continued to exchange news with other agencies. In Germany it remained the most important channel of official news dissemination. In 1932, WTB's shares were bought up by the Third Reich. In 1934 it combined with another agency, TU, to form DNB. The Third Reich also acquired Trans-Ocean, a wireless agency established in 1919 which grew to service up to 100 overseas papers and foreign agencies in 22 countries with international news (Hohne, 1977).

than they might otherwise have had. There were also exchange arrangements with some of the larger metropolitan papers.

Competition from UP spurred AP to further overseas investment and helped bring about AP's secession from the cartel. Its secession did not begin in Europe – this might have imposed too sudden an increase in news-gathering costs in an area where important news sources were already monopolized by the existing domestic agencies. But the ground for an independent European operation was well prepared by World War One. There has been no factor more powerful than war to explain the major expansionist periods of the agencies. No foreign news appeals to Western media values more immediately than war; war also convincingly demonstrates the dangers of relying on other people's news supply. In South America, moreover, the concern of leading newspapers that the Havas supply of news was anti-German created an immensely important market opening to UPI and then AP. Indeed, it was said that the decision by the wealthy *La Prensa* of Buenos Aires to take UP exerted a profound editorial influence on UP, which learnt to provide the terse, factual reports *La Prensa* wanted rather than the populist, human-interest coverage with which UP had hitherto been too much associated. *La Prensa*'s subscriptions helped pay for the further expansion of UP's network.

When AP formally disassociated itself from the cartel, UP could claim 350 overseas clients, accounting for 20% of income, in Hungary, Spain, England, Japan, and at least a 'dozen other countries'.[6] Sufficient, it would seem, to persuade UP's Roy Howard to turn down an offer from Reuters to take AP's place in the cartel. Instead, the two American agencies mutually pledged never to enter into exclusive agreements with any European agency. UP now boasted thirty overseas bureaux to AP's twenty.

Neither agency did especially well in Europe, with the possible exception of British United Press in the UK, which distributed UP overseas news to the British national press. The main British market share was of course held by Reuters. In Germany, UP acquired up to sixty clients, including TU, one of the major private agencies until taken over by the Third Reich. But generally Europe was a very problematic market. Havas was especially well entrenched in France and had plenty of scope for retaliation against any paper which subscribed to alternative global agencies. In most other countries there were strong national agencies with links to the cartel which distributed foreign news to their respective media clients. They might have had the will to subscribe to alternative agencies, but few were prepared to risk excommunication from the cartel, and it is questionable whether the American agencies could have provided at that time a service of European news that was comparable to that of the major European agencies. Nevertheless, UP in particular did sell to many smaller non-official agencies in Europe.

UP had suffered one particular disadvantage in overseas sales. Because it did not have exchange relations with the major national agencies and the agencies which organized the cartel, it did not have access to their official news – many of them were in any case official news agencies – and it is very important to be able to provide official news, even if it is the easiest to collect, and to provide it at the greatest speed. After AP broke from the cartel it too had to cultivate its own sources of official news. While UP, and later AP, were important sources of American news, the demand for news of the United States between the wars was nowhere near as great as after the Second World War. There was too much happening in Europe. The PEP report on the British press in 1938 drew attention to what it considered the particularly conspicuous inadequacy of reporting from the United States. Only two British papers at that time, the *Daily Telegraph* and *The Times*, had their own full-time correspondents in the United States, outside of New York, and some national papers had no correspondents in America at all.

Like the First World War, the Second brought a new flood of American journalists to Europe. In the immediate post-war era, the American agencies had some strong, though temporary advantages. The new French agency was struggling to its feet, unable to find sufficient media revenue (the 'retail' media themselves had yet to recover fully from war damage) and therefore dependent on state help. And Reuters had suffered considerable war loss in terms of clients and facilities. The major European opportunities were quickly seized. In France the US agencies moved in even in advance of liberation troops. UP had only 3 clients in France in 1939; a year after Liberation it had 46. In Sweden, where AP first arrived in 1943 with 3 clients, it had 24 by the end of the war. In Germany, each occupation authority set up a news agency; the agencies of the western zones were to form the nucleus of DPA, founded in 1949. Whereas Reuters supplied to DPA direct until 1972, the US agencies operated independently. As many as 40% of West Germany's 1,330 daily newspaper editions in 1970 were served by AP, 37% by UPI. In Italy, the Allies initially distributed news through the Psychological War Branch, using news supplied by the major private agencies and Allied government information services. After the liberation of Rome, Reuters and the American agencies successfully pressed for the right to distribute independently, and of the 100 daily papers which existed in Italy in 1946, 75 subscribed to at least one American service.

For a number of reasons, however, the initial advance of the US agencies on European markets was not altogether sustained. In the first place, Reuters and AFP recovered fairly quickly. Reuters moved in swiftly, for instance, to replace some of the old DNB-dominated agreements with national agencies in Norway, Finland, Denmark, Sweden, Holland, Belgium, and Switzerland. 'Watch Reuters!' one US observer counselled. 'This agency will give our big press associations top international competition in the near future'.[7] American media interest in Europe naturally subsided in peace-time conditions. Bureau chiefs told Grossman that they were being obliged to lay off correspondents because of budget reductions and because US newspapers were not printing adequate amounts of foreign news. European interest in America after the Marshall Plan settlement may also have subsided to a more normal level, weakening any special advantage the American connection had afforded AP and UPI. Meanwhile, Reuters and AFP were especially well placed, politically more than geographically, for coverage of the passage from colonialism in Africa and the Indian subcontinent, so far as European media were concerned. To a far greater extent than Reuters or AFP, the US agencies continued to supply *in situ* translation for direct distribution to individual media. This was in part necessitated by the absence of traditional ties between the US agencies and the national news agencies of Europe, which before the war had generally undertaken the translation of cartel-supplied news for national distribution (which also helps explain why it should seem more normal for Reuters and AFP to supply indirectly through agencies). But with declining levels of journalistic unemployment, and a rising standard of living, maintenance of translation teams became increasingly burdensome, until eventually UPI converted to indirect distribution for most European countries, and even AP dropped direct distribution in one or two countries where government assistance to national agencies may have made any other form of distribution unattractive to retail media. As a news-centre, of course, Western Europe is still of very great importance to the American agencies, and in terms of gross revenue is the most important overseas market, although possibly no longer so in terms of growth or profit. The issue of economic news services for non-media clients is a complicating factor considered in Chapter 6.

Eastern Europe

The activity of the Western agencies in Russia and the Russian sphere of influence has always been fairly restricted, so that today Eastern Europe bears no comparison as a source of revenue, or as an important news-gathering centre attracting substantial editorial manpower, to Western Europe. This in turn greatly affects the scope and quality of reporting by the agencies of matters concerning the socialist countries. The national agencies of Eastern Europe help to provide at least a basic source of both official news and revenue; they also represent a number of models for the political control of agency operations which have since been adopted extensively in the Third World. Coverage of Russia and Eastern Europe well illustrates the relative inability of the 'Big Four' to surmount the obstacles which are presented by the division of the world into super-power blocs. The cartel system established by the European agencies provided possibly the very worst background to the formation first of Russian and then of Soviet policy with respect to agency development. One of the predecessors of TASS, the Trade Telegraph Agency (TTA), was established in 1902 by the Russian Finance Ministry in an attempt to reduce Germany's influence over foreign news supply to Russia via Wolff, in whose 'territory' Russia belonged under the cartel agreements of 1870 (shared with Havas after 1894). The following year AP's Melville Stone won a lower press concession for sending news out of Russia. State control had its perfect justification as the only viable means of counteracting the cartel influence. Czar Nicholas II merged TTA with the Foreign Ministry subsidized Russian agency (RTA, established 1893) in 1904, to form the St Petersburg Telegraph Agency. The Petrograd Telegraph Agency, as it was later called, continued to function as a government news agency up to and throughout the First World War and the subsequent revolution, when it became ROSTA, even retaining the same editorial staff until trained Bolsheviks could take over. During World War One, Reuters and AP both maintained correspondents in Russia, until expelled after the revolution. UP relied on available reports from London. Reuters' correspondent in Petrograd was instrumental in helping several editors of the Petrograd Telegraph Agency to escape. UP's Berlin correspondent got to Moscow and persuaded ROSTA to buy UP before he in turn was expelled, to Finland. UP's New York management decided to ignore this contract, and covered Russia for a while from Riga, Warsaw, and Bucharest. But in 1923 UP secured an exchange arrangement with ROSTA, and some of ROSTA's early teleprinters were bought from UP. Then, a year later, UP was dumped when Russia became signatory to treaties in which Britain and France recognized the new régime, and ROSTA joined the cartel. Agency correspondents were now allowed to report from Moscow. AP was allowed to distribute TASS news in the US, and in Moscow had access to Soviet news transmission facilities withheld from UP. From 1933, however (ROSTA became TASS in 1935), the Soviet agency signed separate agreements with agencies, UP included.

Agency representation in Moscow may have improved since World War Two, but the number of correspondents is still restricted. The numbers are negotiated in relation to the number of Russian diplomats permitted in the West. The maximum for each agency in the early 1970s was five, although AP, Reuters and UPI had only four staffers each in Moscow at that time. An interesting development in the mid-1970s was the establishment of a UPI bureau in Leningrad and, reciprocally, of a TASS bureau in San Francisco. TASS subscribes to all the major Western agencies on an exchange basis. As in other communist countries, the Western agencies cannot supply media directly except through the national agency.

Many national agencies of Eastern Europe have their origins in the network established by the old agency of the Austrian-Hungarian empire – K.K. Telegraphic Correspondence Bureau, or Corrbureau, a junior member of the European cartel, with close ties to Wolff. From this were eventually spawned the first national agencies of Hungary, Czechoslovakia, Bulgaria, Rumania and Turkey. During World War Two the agencies of Eastern Europe came under the control of the Nazi agency, Deutsches Nachrichtenbüro (DNB), as little more than translation centres for DNB reports. But resistance movements in Albania, Slovakia and Yugoslavia created their own agencies. The old agencies elsewhere came under communist control in the post-war years. In East Germany a new agency was established under the Soviet occupying powers, ADN, one of the most powerful of the national agencies in the Socialist world with independent coverage of 32 capitals.[8]

Penetration of this area by the American agencies before World War Two was not extensive. In the 1930s, for instance, UP served only three media clients in Poland, two in Austria and a 'scattering' in the Balkans. Principal supplier of foreign news for this region at that time was Havas, whose reports were channelled through the national agencies. In the immediate post-war period the wretched state of the media discouraged active exploration of market opportunities; Czechoslovakia was promising, but opportunity was short-lived. For most of the post-war period these agencies depended heavily on the freely provided services of TASS, while also subscribing to the major Western agencies on an exchange plus cash basis. Yugoslavia's Tanjug has for over a decade made exceptionally liberal use of Western agency copy, which accounted for 45% of Tanjug's foreign news copy in 1970 while only 10% came from the other communist agencies.[9] By 1978, Western agency copy accounted for 37% of Tanjug's foreign news output against only 3% from TASS and other East European agencies.[10] Like ADN, Tanjug has considerable news-gathering resources of its own, recording 46 foreign correspondents in 1978, not far short of the 61 correspondents claimed by TASS in the same ICSCP report.[11] At least one source suggests that other East European agency dependency on TASS is declining.[12]

There are obvious political restrictions on news coverage of the Soviet bloc by Western media, and the unanimous verdict is that a Soviet bloc posting can be a very frustrating experience. Nonetheless, there is at least access to these countries, there are many official and semi-official publications and there are useful diplomatic sources. The story of dissidents in the Soviet Union has been exceptionally well covered, so much so that it has almost become a routine issue that retail media are prepared to rely on agency coverage for. But critics argue that coverage of the dissidents masks the impotence of the Western media to really analyse Soviet politics and institutions; moreover, cold war ideology has convinced most Western media readers that Soviet bloc news is intrinsically dull (especially without Stalin), and there is a correspondingly weak consumer demand. Certainly, the Soviet Union and Eastern Europe do not figure at all prominently on news agency wires. Maximum sizes of bureaux in Moscow are, as we have seen, predetermined, but maximum sizes are not always reached. These bureaux are autonomous, in the sense that they report directly to London, Paris or New York. Other important centres for coverage of Eastern Europe in the mid-1970s (apart from one or two area specialists resident in the London offices) were Berlin and Vienna. Berlin had declined in importance with the political institutionalization of the Berlin Wall, but was still the main centre for coverage of East Germany. Berlin correspondents reported either directly to London offices or via Bonn. By contrast the role of Vienna had much increased, and it had now become the main base from which Bulgaria, Rumania, Hungary and Czechoslovakia were covered. There were interesting variations in the autonomy, in relation to Vienna, of those bureaux actually situated in these East European countries. All the AFP bureaux filed through Vienna. UPI's full-time staff in Eastern Europe filed directly into UPI's computer-controlled distribution system, but copy was monitored in Vienna. The news services of many of the East European agencies were received (in English, a recent development) and monitored in the Viennese bureaux of the Western agencies. Vienna was a convenient location for this purpose, close to the borders of Hungary, Czechoslovakia and Yugoslavia. Barring Russia it had in fact become a communications channel for news flow between East and West. And in interesting illustration of the interdependence of global and national agencies, the Austrian news agency, Austria Presse Agentur (APA), controlled the communications infrastructure that made this possible. Vienna itself was not considered an important news centre, but newsmen based in Vienna might very well spend substantial periods in Eastern Europe, to supplement East European staff. In 1974 the agencies together maintained a total of ten news-gathering journalists in Vienna. They all maintained at least one full-time staffer in the capitals of Poland and Yugoslavia (generally autonomous bureaux) and Czechoslovakia. Bulgaria, Hungary and Rumania were in almost all cases covered either by stringers or by staffers visiting from Vienna or neighbouring bureaux. Albania received barely any coverage at all: access for foreign journalists was not permitted and the country was conveniently not regarded as highly 'newsworthy'. Excluding Russia and East Germany, therefore, the 'Big Four' maintained 21 full-time journalists on East European coverage of whom 10 were based in Vienna. But of course the agencies were competing and the figure of 21 represented considerable duplication of effort. Almost the only clients for 'Big Four' services were the East European national agencies,* who paid part of their way in exchange arrangements and the rest in 'soft' non-exchangeable local currencies which since they had to be spent locally, helped ensure that these bureaux were seen to be paying their way. While the overall coverage of this region, therefore, was perhaps not in too low a profile by comparison with some Third World regions, it does seem low in terms of its political significance, and critics may well argue that political obstacles should not be the excuse for low manpower commitments, but that on the contrary they should be the justification for extra investments of manpower, if not in the region itself (should access be restrained) then in the surrounding area or in centrally based pools of expertise.

Old agencies in the New World

The United States quickly established itself as the world's most affluent media market. Yet for over one hundred years neither Reuters nor Havas/AFP appeared to take an interest in the US for its market potential. When in the 1960s Reuters did greatly increase its US involvement, most of this new attention was devoted to economic news services for non-media clients. AFP's North American presence improved only very slightly.

Perhaps the longest-standing failure of the European agencies was their reluctance to adopt innovatory and aggressive tactics in relation to the United States. This was in contradiction to the general principle

* In Yugoslavia, however, Robinson (1977) reports that individual 'retail' media were permitted to subscribe directly to external agencies from the late 1960s.

that wealthy markets attract the most attention. But strategy in relation to the United States was for long blunted by the oligopolistic control established over that market by the American agencies themselves, and by European reluctance to put up the kind of capital necessary to fight such control. Their failure is both testimony to the advantages enjoyed by an agency on its domestic ground, and also to a certain laziness of mind engendered by the cartel framework of European agency operations before World War Two.

Apart from civil war coverage, Baron Reuter's attention was too much taken up with the initial problems of extending the boundaries of his imperial coverage, and with European affairs, to be too much concerned with American coverage or with establishing his agency in the United States. The agency proved itself willing to learn from US journalistic technique, but stood aloof from the competitive domestic US market.

During the crucial years of AP's internal and external struggles, therefore, Reuters was otherwise engaged. Independent newscoverage was not considered so great a priority then as it is today, as the European cartel and its operations well proved. One reason for this, it must be remembered, was that Reuter, Wolff and Havas had all at one time worked alongside each other. They knew one another, knew how each operated and the limits of their professional integrity. They did not much mind depending on one another's news services because they had reason to think that they could do so with confidence. And it saved money. Hardly surprising therefore that Reuters should expect its main supply of American news to come from a proven American agency, whichever agency emerged least unscathed from the internecine struggles between the US agencies themselves.

There was relatively little supplementation to US agency sources. Even by as late as the 1890s Reuters had only one correspondent in New York, who selected AP and general American news for transmission to Europe. He represented the cartel agencies. Havas suggested to Reuters that they might usefully set up a common agency bureau in New York in 1891, but this did not materialize. Not until 1913 did Havas establish a separate New York bureau. This arrangement seemed to suit Reuters: in the first place, the English agency, acting on behalf of the triumvirate, had great influence. It could and did help determine the course of US agency history by deciding with which of the US agencies it would deal. By offering its service exclusively it won an agreement that AP would not interfere with the established global markets of the European agencies. It is not fanciful to suppose that its influence helped ensure that AP took an interest in providing Reuters with an adequate news supply. Moreover, by virtue of its influence, Reuters could offer concessions to help keep AP in line. Under the treaty of 1893 with AP of Illinois, AP was permitted to share Mexico and Central America with Reuters and Havas, and also to share Canada and the West Indies with Reuters, while handling distribution of Reuter services in those areas. But as AP became more powerful, Reuters' concessions began to look increasingly like appeasement, designed above all to deter AP from leaving the cartel and invading Europe; which is why the concessions began in Central and South America and Asia (Philippines, Japan). Reuters' interests might actually have been better served had it applied a more aggressive strategy very early on in AP's growth after the settlement of 1893: a strategy based on a willingness to threaten the withdrawal of a European news supply, and to switch at short notice its exchange plus cash deals from one to another of the US agencies. The long-term deals characteristic of the European agency settlements were unwise in the protean American market. The American agencies in the late nineteenth century would have found it relatively difficult to establish good relations with official overseas news sources, and it is doubtful whether deals between them and minor agencies would have unsettled Reuters and Havas domestic market dominance. Such a policy might have involved trying to save the old UP, rather than contributing to its demise. By the time AP's role in the cartel had completely collapsed in the early 1930s, it was too late for successful retaliatory action, although Reuters did try – by approaching UP, for example, (unsuccessfully) and by selling news to radio stations which AP and UP would not supply or which did not recognize the Press-Radio Bureau. But by this time both American agencies were secure on their domestic markets, had substantial overseas newsgathering facilities, and were soon to recognize radio clientele in any case. Reuters, now caught by a recessionary world market, was not in a position to offer a real fight.

Reuters' market position improved after World War Two when, Storey says, there was a record increase in US clients. Regional transmission to North American clients began in 1944 for 30 US newspaper clients. Two years later the North American desk in London was first established, and remained there until 1972 when it was transferred to New York. But the 1974 *Editor and Publisher Yearbook* recorded only 28 daily newspaper subscribers for Reuters, most of these being big-city Eastern dailies, justifying the comment in Reuters' company report that the US media market was 'difficult'.

But the media market had become the smallest part of Reuters' operations in the US by this time. In 1967 AP refused to renew the exchange arrangement it had maintained with Reuters since the end of the cartel, whereby AP made its domestic service available to Reuters and the PA was made available to AP in London. The exchange was an equal one, involving no additional cash. By 1967, AP considered that America was too important a news-centre to justify an equal exchange, and said that the provision of AP's domestic service would now cost Reuters an additional £110,000–120,000 a year. Reuters' decision not to renew the exchange on this basis but to establish a fully independent news-gathering team in the US had doubtless been well thought out in advance of the expiry date of the old agreement. If so it must have been related to a parallel decision to break the exchange arrangement it had maintained with Dow Jones, the leading American economic news agency.

Reuters had started selling economic news in the 1920s with its 'American Markets Service' for non-media clients, and this had always tended to do rather better than the media market. Under the post-war 'Comtel' label, it had what one senior HQ executive described as a 'nice tidy little business of about a million dollars turnover'. This service was principally a commodity service – that is, it dealt mainly with prices for metals, cocoa, coffee and items for which there is no major US production but some considerable consumption. For other kinds of economic news, Reuters depended on its arrangement with Dow Jones.

The decision to break with Dow Jones and with AP represented several related strategic factors. It was a clear commitment to the expanding role of Reuters Economic Services. It directly acknowledged that the profitability of the economic services was sufficient to carry the cost of an expanding news-gathering machinery. It implicitly acknowledged the possibility of an integrated general and economic news strategy. The very importance of the US market strategy placed the US executive team in a key organizational role, culminating eventually in the designation of Reuters North America as a separate revenue centre, with separate representation on the executive board.

Reuters immediately began to develop its reporting strength, expanding its leased communications network to link up 450 US cities, augmenting its New York and Washington bureaux and establishing new bureaux in places like Chicago, San Francisco, Miami, Atlanta and Houston. The major increase was in economic news reporters and by 1971 total US economic services staff was forty full-time and forty stringer journalists. New journalists were paid on a scale that competed with those of the American agencies. The increased investment of manpower enabled Reuters to cover more economic news centres, to provide a service of important nation-wide US news to US media subscribers (including the CATV market, and the insertion of general news on economic news wires), and to provide an efficient supply of US news for overseas markets. A far greater degree of integration between general and economic news was sought, at the editorial rather than the reporting level. It was significant therefore that the New York bureau chief appointed in 1972 had previously been posted in Tokyo where an integrated operation already existed, with a single group of editors responsible for general and economic news.

Before the break with Dow Jones, Reuters had enjoyed a good if not exclusive reputation in the field of international commodity news for the US market. But in the US the domestic commodity market, mostly centralized in Chicago, was by far the more important. Until 1968 Reuters had no economic news correspondents in Chicago. By 1973 Chicago was Reuters' editorial centre for both its commodity and financial report, with established offices in the Chicago Board of Trade and the Mercantile Exchange, and with a full-time staff of eighteen. Principal competitor was the Commodities News Service (CNS), established in the 1880s, and with a hitherto near-monopoly on domestic commodity news, supplemented with a general news feed-in from UPI. With its own supply of general news, Reuters argued that it could tailor it more quickly to the needs of the commodity market. A senior executive claimed in interview in 1974 that Reuters had captured as much as 60% of the commodities market.

Success came less readily in the field of financial as opposed to commodity news. Here the major competition was Dow Jones, which until Reuters came along had the entire brokerage market – estimated at around 5,000 tickers in 1967. Dow Jones was strong because it had been *the* financial news agency for so long, and because it was an offshoot of the *Wall Street Journal,* America's most prestigious financial newspaper, whose journalists were primarily responsible for the Dow Jones service. A great deal of Reuters' initial work consisted of eliciting promises from corporations to provide the agency with their quarterly figures. For most corporations there was a particular advantage in going to Dow Jones, because through Dow Jones they hoped for a mention in the *Wall Street Journal.* This was not helped by the fact that American Stock Exchanges initially recognized only AP and UPI as suitable news-gathering organizations to which company figures should be released.

Every subscriber Reuters picked up was either a customer who had cancelled his Dow Jones subscription, or one that Dow Jones would have had before Reuters came along. Furthermore it was not a growing market, but perhaps even a shrinking one. A particular point in Reuters' favour was its pricing system – based on the simple number of teleprinter machines in operation, whereas Dow Jones charged large organizations as if they had a teleprinter in each branch office, regardless of whether they did or not, or needed to or not.

In 1974, Reuters had about 700 installations against a computed total of Dow Jones installations of 3,200, according to Reuters sources, which put its share of the financial market at almost 18% in these terms, still a considerable feat for a newcomer. The fact that it got so far was partly because some large brokerage companies had encouraged competition, believing this would bring down Dow Jones' rates and that competition was editorially beneficial. Although Reuters did sell to companies in the large multi-branch bracket, it did particularly well with one-office clients (which perhaps explained its liberal pricing system), in other words, the smaller companies.

By the late 1970s Reuters had also established a sizeable US clientele for its Monitor (money market and securities) service, delivered via a push-button televisual interrogation receiver. But its invasion of US markets had not been taken quietly. The Reuters break with Dow Jones had brought about a combined AP–DJ assault on overseas non-media finance news markets followed in 1977 by a combined UPI–CNS–UNICOM assault on overseas commodity news markets. By the late 1970s the potential for competition to Reuters' sophisticated televisual services had greatly increased. Nevertheless Reuters' links with the US had played a vital part in RES expansion, not least because of a link-up by Reuters with Ultronics Inc. (controlled by General Telephone and Electronics Information Systems Inc.) which gave Reuters overseas rights to the marketing of Ultronics interrogation display systems on which the profitable Reuters Videomaster service was based. Regardless of Reuters' profits from the US market specifically it was obvious that RES services globally depended considerably on a reliable input from the US, and this the rapid expansion of the US operation provided. In 1973 it was estimated that 60% of all the reporting costs for RES were incurred in the US. One day's analysis of all RES files in 1971 showed that about 40% of the world financial service came from the US, according to one Reuters' source.

The expansion in the US had in any case provided sufficient manpower to encourage innovation in many directions, not all of them successful. The Reuters Audio service, started in 1972 with a studio base in London, had its most important client in the US Mutual Broadcasting Corporation. But the audio service was scheduled for discontinuation by the late 1970s. Provision of news services for CATV systems with direct electronic feed-in of words on to screens

Wholesale news and market control: Foreign

(a technique initially ahead of AP and UPI) helped secure a respectable slice of the US CATV market. Reuters also ran the Times Tower electronic news ticker.

By contrast with Reuters, AFP did not sever its exchange relationship with AP but agreed to pay cash (1972 rate was $200,000 p.a.) for a service which had been its most important source of domestic US news since 1949, and in whose offices in New York its own bureau was still based. AFP had few possibilities of establishing a US clientele. For a while in the 1950s INS distributed a selected and translated file of AFP news to its US subscribers. From 1961, AFP tried to sell where it could on an independent basis, but not until 1967 did it transmit its own English-language service to the US. Its single major breakthrough in the 1970s was a contract to supply the *Washington Post–Los Angeles Times* news service, partly in reward for AFP's remarkable scoop in 1973 on the Munich Games assassination story. But otherwise for AFP the US continues to be an expensive news-gathering centre, where few of the costs can be offset against sales. Despite sizeable New York and Washington bureaux of twelve and six editorial staff respectively (and three sub-editors at the UN) in the early 1970s, the AP domestic report was the backbone of AFP's American coverage.

Backyard empires: South America

The interest of the 'Big Four' in Third World markets is not everywhere equally intense. This can have positive functions for the maintenance of the system: low revenue markets continue to promise some yield in conditions of only moderate competition. The divisions of interest reflect the combination of old cartel influences, and contemporary politico-cultural affiliations. The emergence of new agencies complicates but does not significantly alter the prevailing pattern. The dominant feature of the South American market is the predictably strong presence of the North American agencies. The much weaker position of the European agencies in media markets, especially of Reuters, is nevertheless a factor of some interest. The cartel agreements of 1870 onwards to 1933 recognized South America as Havas territory, although AP had achieved concessionary entry well before then. Of the European agencies, however, Havas had established itself as a 'Latin' agency, since the cartel agreements also recognized southern Europe as Havas territory, and in Spain the agency Fabra actually came to be known as 'Agence Havas, Madrid'. Havas was news supplier of Latin America for Europe. Full-time representation did not begin until 1874, following completion of the first cable communication between Brazil and Europe:

a Havas correspondent in Rio de Janeiro and a Reuters correspondent in Santiago covered for both agencies jointly until 1876 when Havas assumed entire responsibility. A Havas bureau in London was established to receive telegrams from Brazil (and a small Latin-American desk has survived in the AFP London bureau into the 1970s). Havas correspondents manned Santiago, Rio, Montevideo, and Buenos Aires. Services to papers in those cities were very brief and very expensive until in the 1900s Havas rented its own cable network from the Western Corp., increasing traffic and reducing costs. The First World War however very nearly eliminated the French interest. Three-quarters of the agency's personnel were conscripted; censorship in Europe prevented the transmission of dispatches from Germany to South American clients, many of whom were pro-German or at least neutral; the US agencies were willing to supply the gap; many existing Latin-American clients defaulted on payments. Two factors kept Havas inside South America after the war. The first was radio-telegraph, which cut communication costs considerably, so that by 1923 Havas could again claim to be in the black on its Latin-American service. Using shortwave PTT transmission it temporarily recaptured *La Nación* of Buenos Aires from AP and *El Mercurio* of Santiago from UP. This alone would hardly have been sufficient inducement had it not been for the very active insistence of the Quai d'Orsay that Havas should stay. The Quai d'Orsay offered to cover any deficits incurred on the Latin-American service. This in turn reflected the growing interest of all the major powers in the potential for propaganda, an interest aroused by the experiences of World War One and fanned by the extraordinary flexibility of radio transmissions. Partly for this reason Reuters in 1927 sought entry to South America and negotiated parallel concessions to Havas on the question of access to Asia in order to obtain it. In 1931 Reuters started a radio-telegraph service to South America, and allowed Havas to do likewise for the Far East. Hardly by coincidence the Prince of Wales in his address to the Manchester Chamber of Commerce that year spoke of the need for Britain to follow the example of the US in putting its 'goods across' by sophisticated advertising. 'One of the first things we need to do is to improve the present very inadequate British news service to South America'.[13] In his tour of South America that year, the Prince of Wales mourned the fact that nearly all news of England in South America was transmitted by non-British agencies, and proceeded to secure the cooperation of *La Nación* and of the *Buenos Aires Herald* in establishing the Reuters news service from London. Reuters' European general manager explained to the Post Office that 'it was most desirable from the national point of view that the dissemination of British news in South America should be fostered at the present time in every possible way'.[14] He had good reason to press a sceptical Post Office for lower rates: between June and November 1931 Reuters paid the Post Office £3,619 for Rugby World Service radio transmission, and took in the sum of only £335 in receipts from clients. But the Post Office would have needed convincing that there was a strong likelihood of a sharp increase in traffic to South America.

There was little room for Reuters in South America. Even as early as 1922, for example, nearly every paper in Mexico was a member or subscriber of AP. In 1933 Benet's *Fortune* article alleged that 95% of the important South American papers which could take and pay for a news service received UP. Competing as a European agency, Reuters also had to contend with Havas, which had fifty years' experience of this market, suitable 'Latin' and Catholic affiliations, ten years' experience of radio transmission to South America, and a Spanish-language service. Havas also enjoyed direct government subsidy, which Reuters did not.

By 1934 the Buenos Aires transmissions were suspended and, as one observer noted, 'South America is little better off in the matter of British news, and world news carried through British channels, than it was ten years ago'.[15] By contrast, Havas transmitted a substantial 15,000 words a day. Transmissions did resume in the late thirties, but with no more success. One disappointed client complained to the London manager that AP and UP were able to send their copy at greater speed, and at less cost to clients, and that the Reuters wireless service was 'spasmodic and restricted':

> In these days of slackness in Argentinian trade and of high paper costs we are forced to cut down expenses in every direction and sentiment falls by the wayside.[16]

The US agencies had superior transmission facilities, helped by special rates conceded them by US telegraph corporations in the promotion of US business in South America. Because they were much closer geographically, they could afford communications by cable. In 1936, press rates from South America to Europe were almost twice as expensive per word as rates between North and South America.

During World War Two, the Reuters position improved temporarily. With the German occupation of France and the disappearance of Havas, Reuters took over the management of eight Havas bureaux in South America, and received heavy government backing to pay off existing Havas debts.[17] This subsidy was withdrawn after the war. Meanwhile, AFP's predecessor, AFI, cooperated with British information and Reuters in a world distribution of a French news service. After the war, Reuters' general manager, Christopher Chancellor, then handed over to AFP this old network of Havas bureaux and contracts. Within seven years AFP had restored its prewar position and even improved on it by opening new bureaux in Colombia, Venezuela and Peru. But Reuters' media market position deteriorated rapidly. Even in Argentina, it had relatively few clients. For a while it did supply the wealthy liberal paper, *La Prensa*: when Peron temporarily shut down the bureau of UP in 1944, *La Prensa* lost its major agency service and Reuters stepped in, offering its service free of charge for an initial period. A few years later, in 1951, in another phase of Peron's battle with *La Prensa*, the paper was nationalized. While UP, in protest, refused to supply its service to the new government-approved management, Reuters continued to supply. In retaliation, the publisher, Gainza Paz, when he was eventually reestablished, cancelled the Reuters contract.

By 1958 the British agency withdrew from general news supply to South America. In the period immediately prior to this withdrawal, Reuters had only eight clients in Argentina, and of these seven used the service only as a supplementary, in addition to American and French services, and paid rather less for it. Reuters in fact had never transmitted the same volume of news to South America as other agencies. In 1950, for example, while it filed 12,000 words a day to Argentina, AFP's wordage was 20,000, AP's 30,000 and UP's 60,000.[18]

For an agency *not* to have a foothold on the Latin-American market might have seemed to some to disqualify it from 'world-wide' status. On his accession as general manager, in 1964, Gerald Long determined to restore a Latin-American connection. In the event this was achieved indirectly with the negotiation of an arrangement between Reuters and a group of leading conservative South American newspapers which wanted to establish a cooperatively based continental agency.[19] Reuters agreed to provide the new agency, Latin, with technical and administrative assistance. Latin became an important news source for Reuters, supplemented by a small team of half a dozen independent Reuters journalists, and it also took the Reuters service, translating portions of it into Spanish and Portuguese for local distribution. One recent source[20] suggests that 'Reuters remained closely linked to Latin, administratively and financially; the Reuters manager for Latin America was, in effect, the manager of Latin, according to private evaluations by executives of the two agencies'. By 1977 there were twelve newspapers which had governing 'member' status in the new agency, and 'scores' of other non-voting subscribers. Latin had twenty-one South American correspondents of South American nationality, but it was clear that it depended largely on Reuters for survival. In 1978 the reporting networks of both agencies, Latin and Reuters, were integrated, and at the same time Reuters share in Latin increased from one-sixteenth to almost half. These developments represented a significant increase in Reuters' Latin American involvement. Latin served 106 newspaper and broadcast clients in South America at that time (less than half of AFP's total subscribers, media and non-media). Latin has at least increased the diversity of foreign news sources in South America, but with little indication as yet that the dominance of the US agencies has been seriously threatened. The character of some of Latin's early founder members and Reuters' earlier role in the *La Prensa* affair may have given the new agency an unfavourable conservative image in some quarters. Reuters' economic services for non-media clients on the other hand have prospered, although in 1977 these were still limited to teleprinter installations. Improved communications facilities to Rio in 1978 carried Reuters' Quotation Retrieval Service to Rio Stock Exchange, which distributed it locally.

Of the two European agencies, AFP was still the stronger on media markets by virtue of tradition, a Catholic connection, relative continuity of service and a reputation for good football coverage. In the 1970s it had a Latin American desk in Paris, manned by thirty editorial staff who translated the service into Spanish and tailored it for the market. This was only ten persons fewer than the English-language desk which serviced the rest of the non-French speaking world. But AFP's role in South America is diminished by the services distributed from other European-based agencies, and in particular those of the Spanish agency, EFE, which since 1972 has supplied international news to the Central American agency, ACACAN. Whereas, before World War Two, Havas was in a far stronger position – and it owned Fabra, then the Spanish agency.

The American agencies had too many natural advantages in South America to be seriously threatened, in the 1970s, by the European agencies. Innumerable sources for all South American countries clearly indicate that AP and UP – but especially UP – were the dominant agencies from the 1930s, if not before. Just previous to Reuters' withdrawal in 1958, UP had a total of 487 clients in South America, including clients to its controversial Special Services, but before the link-up with INS. This had increased to 654 in 1963. AP's development of the South American market had lagged behind UPI's earlier start, but in the 1960s it waged a determined battle of redress. Constant references in the AP annual reports for the 1960s made mention of new client acquisitions in South America. AP's

World Services vice-president Stan Swinton claims that AP passed UPI as early as 1963.[21]* Certainly AP added to UPI's troubles. In the 1960s to 1970s AP bureaux were increased from four to eleven, exclusive contracting was suspended (but note how long it had been retained on an international market, by contrast with the changed legal position at home), some stories were filed only in Spanish to speed up retransmission, Spanish writers were installed in London, Paris, and Rome, satellite distribution was introduced for five regional services. By the mid-1970s one source put AP's Latin-American clientele at 650 to UPI's 400[22] but a 1980 AP source refers to 430 AP clients; a 1979 source refers to 500 UPI clients. AP's improved market position may have been aided by the passage of generations, as long-established publishers gave way to sons who wanted change and diversity. While US agency strength in South America is indubitably stronger than any other source of foreign news, it is vulnerable to charges of neo-imperialism from nationalists and leftists alike. Much the most passionate complaints about dependence on foreign agencies have come from South America, and this has made it all the easier for governments to restrict foreign agency activities.†

* Beltran and Cardona (1979) quote a UN-Ciespal study (1975) as showing that of twenty Latin American countries surveyed, UPI served sixteen, AP fourteen. They quote studies by Rangel (1967) and Ciespal (1967) as showing that AP and UPI were contributors of 72–80% of foreign news in samples of Latin American newspapers. In the Ciespal study, UPI was source of 50% of foreign news in 29 dailies, AP for 30%.

† In a highly critical account of the Spanish-language services of the US agencies, Massing (1979) alleges, on the basis of interviews with agency journalists and executives in New York, (i) that the Latin American desks in New York had come too much under the influence of groups of Argentinians; (ii) that the services focused disproportionately on matters concerning Argentina; and (iii) that the major function of the desks was one of translation, together with relatively 'cosmetic 'changes (often in a conservative direction, some of Massing's informants maintain); (iv) that neither desk had been adequately controlled from executive level; (v) that little attention was given to news concerning the Hispanic community in the US, whose media were also subscribers to these services. (Cf. Massing, M.: 'Inside the Wires' Banana Republics', CJR, Nov/Dec.) In replying to these allegations, AP's Stnaley Swinton (CJR, Jan./Feb. 1980) gave many examples of enterprise reporting by AP's 'LPA' staff, including stories concerning the Hispanic US community; he argued that US Hispanic coverage was the province of domestic US bureaux, not that of the LPA; and that the term 'comestic' was highly misleading. UPI's 'Chester' Spanish desk's supervisor, Enrique Durand, argued in the same issue that the size of UPI's Argentinian contingent partly reflected the fact that UPI had for decades run a large national service in Argentina that was a natural source of candidates for the Chester desk; that Massing had given undue weight to 'unsubstantiated gossip'; and that he had generalized from an internal UPI content survey conducted at a time when Argentina and Chile were close to war. UPI's Adolfo Merino (CJR, March/April 1980) referred to many

Backyard empires: Africa and the Middle East

Had there been strong national agencies in South America from an early date, Havas might have maintained a stronger foothold; the US agencies would not have found it so easy to pick off individual clients, and a national agency would have been less likely to dispense with a European service altogether. In Africa, the relative scarcity of media and the indispensability of national agencies has provided a limited but welcome degree of market security, the benefits of which have been mainly extended to the European agencies on the basis of old imperial and continuing cultural and economic ties. As in South America, there is an overall tendency for market strength to vary in proportion with news-gathering resources. To a considerable extent the US agencies left non-crisis coverage of Black Africa to the European agencies: there were relatively few AP clients, and at one point in the 1970s UPI ceased to transmit services to West Africa altogether in retaliation for defaults on payment. Thus North American agency coverage has been especially crisis-oriented. Up to the post-war wave of independence AFP maintained local bureaux in most French African colonies, and these bureaux later formed the nucleii of national government-controlled agencies, sometimes with little change of staff or mode of operation. Of eleven national news agencies in former French Africa in 1969, all but two, Guinea and Mali, were started by AFP. Most of these agencies depended on AFP as their primary source of international news, even where Reuters and UPI services were also taken.

Even Reuters is relatively new to much of Africa. British colonial officials did not encourage foreign correspondents and for their news supply could rely on official services or on the BBC. What services Reuters did provide were of the most basic kind: even in 1945 the major Nigerian client received but 500–800 words a day, in morse. North Africa had figured in agency networks for some time: Havas and Reuters operated Egyptian bureaux from the 1860s; Havas had correspondents in Tunisia, Algeria and Madagascar from the 1890s. But Reuters had the advantage of one very strong client in South

---

UPI stories which could certainly not be regarded as favourable to dictatorial regimes. *CJR* editors commented in the Jan./Feb. issue that, early in January, Durand had moved from New York to Washington, where he would serve as diplomatic correspondent. Readers may like to note that in his original article, Massing claimed that UPI's Spanish wire service in 1978 produced 13·3% of UPI's $80m. revenue, while incurring only 9% of its expenses. This impression is at variance with the 1977 figures quoted on p. 37 from Righter (1978), suggesting once again that a great deal depends on accounting procedures and on different ways of interpreting them.

Africa, the South African Press Agency (SAPA), founded in 1912 by Reuters' representative and later owner Sir Roderick Jones. SAPA became independent of Reuters' control only in 1938, and it is still a main supplier of news of South Africa and Rhodesia to Reuters, distributing Reuters' news in both countries.

With the independence wave of the 1950s – 1960s it became evident that Black Africa was likelier to be a more important news-centre than hitherto. A survey by Reuters' Patrick Crosse in 1960 showed that extra costs of news-gathering could be recouped to some extent from the provision of an international news service specially tailored to local requirements. Failure to have seized this opportunity might also have left the doors of Anglophone Africa wide open to AFP which was already providing a regionalized service to clients in Francophone Africa. There followed a major expansion of Reuters' news-gathering staff and a willingness to cooperate with and foster the development of national news agencies in a way which AP, for example, might have found inimical to its tradition of direct distribution.[23] By the early 1970s, Reuters had approximately 22 staff correspondents in Africa as against AFP's 24. The American agencies each had approximately half a dozen staff correspondents.[24] In the late 1960s Reuters' services were received in 39 African countries, AFP's in 33, AP's in 14 and UPI's in 19. TASS was distributed free of charge to 19 countries.[25] By 1977, while the number of countries receiving Reuters' services had remained constant, AP went to only eight countries and UPI to only five.[26] Reuters and AFP each distributed a larger number of specialized services to the different major regions of Africa, in English and in French, than the other agencies provided. While Reuters and AFP had made some inroads on to one another's territories, there was still a clear tendency for the ex-imperial agency to be the dominant news source, receiving the highest subscription fee. And this remained the case where US agency services were received. But for all agencies the 1970s represented an ominous period as an increasing number of African countries veered towards the Soviet block; these and others imposed a variety of restrictions on access to 'Big Four' newsmen. One of the most powerful of Black African countries, Nigeria, had denied residential access to representatives of Reuters, AP and UPI for several years, perhaps obliging AP, for example, to rely more on a news exchange agreement with the new Nigerian News Agency in 1979 than it would normally have liked.

In the Middle East there has been a surer transition from dependence on European agencies to dependency on European and American agencies, supplemented by the growth of relatively strong national agencies and other media systems. Up to World War Two,

Havas had a news monopoly in Syria and the Lebanon, territories over which France was assigned mandates by the League of Nations. Rates were modest, and the service was not suspended if editors did not pay. Iraq, Transjordan, Palestine and Egypt were under British mandate or occupation and Reuters was the leading agency. Both these Havas and Reuters markets were opened up after the war. By 1953, for instance, AP and UPI served 11 of the 32 dailies that then existed in Cairo and Alexandria. Post-war media activity centred mainly on Cairo, and then, after France and Britain fell from Egyptian grace over Suez, Beirut. Beirut progressively became a more convenient communications centre and listening post for coverage of Cyprus, the Arab–Israeli conflict and oil politics, until civil war in the Lebanon in the mid-1970s served to scatter agency resources more widely. In the early 1970s both Reuters and AFP each had something in excess of thirty clients for their news services. Reuters had had only one Beirut client in the 1940s.

After World War Two, Reuters was distributed throughout much of the Middle East by the Arab News Agency, first established during the war under the control of Hulton Press in London and renamed Regional News Service in 1956. Most of its employees were Arab (many Palestinians), top management was British. Indirect subsidization from the British government was commonly suspected. In some places (e.g. Baghdad), ANA initially distributed free of charge. Reuters continued to gather most of its own news at first, but came to rely more and more on RNS in time.

The Arab–Israeli war of 1967 highlighted the region's increasing political centrality and the benefits of a direct news supply. Reuters did not renew its contract with RNS after 1969, which effectively brought about the disbandment of that agency and the subsequent re-employment of many RNS journalists by Reuters. Following a survey of market possibilities along the lines of the Crosse survey of Africa in 1960, Reuters introduced a regionalized Arabic news service largely compiled in Beirut (but dispersed to Amman and Cairo in the civil war), transmitted to London and from there distributed to various client centres in the Middle East as a substantial part of the overall daily service. AFP likewise introduced an Arabic service, translated and distributed by the Egyptian news agency, MENA.

The Arab–Israeli conflict also increased US representation, while oil money proved an inducement to all the agencies to sustain a reasonably comprehensive area coverage. By the early 1970s Reuters, AP and UPI maintained total full-time staffs of 30, 16 and 8 respectively (of whom between a third and a half were strictly editorial). In Cairo, AP's full-time bureau strength of 15 was greater than that of

Reuters (9), AFP (6/7) and UPI (5). UPI's smaller bureau reflected the UPI policy of distributing only in English and French. AP also had the largest agency representation in Israel with a full-time journalist staff of 5, followed by Reuters (4), UPI (4) and AFP (3). This was a remarkable increase by comparison with the period preceding the 1967 war, when no agency had more than one staff correspondent covering Israel, and in some cases Israel was not even that correspondent's sole responsibility. In the early 1970s both Reuters and AFP bureaux were headed by Israeli bureau chiefs. Reuters and AFP tended at that time to have a better scattering of full-time representatives in other Arab capitals, and Reuters was most heavily used of the news agencies by the Saudi Arabian broadcasting network.[27]

'From Bombay to Yokohama'

The most striking feature of agency development in Asia has been the shift from an almost complete dependency on Reuters as supplier of international news up to a few years before World War Two to a rather wider subsequent spread of dependency. For Reuters in particular the increasing competition, and more importantly the intense political changes experienced by all countries of the region during the twentieth century, demonstrated the danger if not the impossibility of relying indefinitely on international media markets for survival. Major factors of change included the rivalry between the US agencies and consequent breakdown of the European cartel, the diplomatic and propaganda ambitions of the agencies' home governments, and the rising tide of Asian nationalism.

By 1872, Storey tells us that from Bombay to Yokohama Reuters was becoming another British institution in the East.[28] In the very earliest exchange agreements between the European agencies, Asia, like North America and Africa, had not figured at all: these territories were considered inaccessible to the agencies and no communication line went beyond the extreme east of the Mediterranean. But all this had changed by the 1870 treaty, which recognized most of Asia as belonging to Reuters for market purposes. The major cable routes to and from the Far East had now been laid, mostly by British cable companies. Reuters and Havas agreed that the markets of Australia, the East Indies and the Far East generally, with the exception only of Indochina, would be reserved for Reuters. And because British communications dominated, Havas was even obliged to pay heavily for communications to and from Indochina.

Reuters' communication advantage was as marked with respect to Havas as to the American agencies. Communications between North America and the Far East remained very expensive for a long time to come. In 1936, for example, when the cost of communication from New York to Europe was just 5 cents a word, the cost from San Francisco to Shanghai was as high as 25 cents and to Manila from 6 to 12 cents. At the urgent rate, a message from Tokyo to San Francisco cost $2.16 a word! The American agencies grew accustomed to receiving most of their Asian news via London.

In India the *Bombay Times* received Reuters news by mail from 1860, but the first Reuters bureau came only in 1878, its principal function to supply market quotations to commercial houses and merchants. As in England and many other parts of the world therefore it was only on the back of the finance and commodity markets that the news service was broadened out into a regular supply of foreign news summaries for Indian newspapers. Newspapers would typically furnish a greater supply of telegrammed foreign news than telegrammed Indian news. The gathering and distribution of national news was rationalized by the formation of the pro-government Associated Press of India (API) in 1910 and the Indian News Agency, both founded by K. G. Roy, which affiliated with Reuters before World War One under the credit-line of API and with the encouragement of the colonial government. Referred to as the 'Royist gang', and favouring the Anglo-Indian press, these agency reporters were the only ones along with *The Times of India* to have lobby passes for parliamentary coverage. Basic subscription income was substantially supplemented by the sale of 'exclusives' for special rates. These 'exclusives' and 'scoops' were often manufactured by the simple device of sending certain stories to some papers but not others, palming the rest of the news on to the less fortunate subscribers. The same stories might also be written for different papers from different angles. The basic agency reports, however, would be 'routine, sequential, inanimate, and dull, with neither highlights nor low lights', in order to make the 'exclusives' all the more appetising by contrast. This description by Sahni[29] well illustrates the dangerous cosiness of some pre-war affiliations with approved national agencies, which inevitably generated rebellion. In this case smaller and non-capital dailies of India began to send in their own staffers for parliamentary coverage and to subscribe to alternative agencies. One of these, the Free Press of India, founded in 1925 by an ex-Reuters employee, S. Sadanand, was a clearing-house for news of nationalist movements from all parts of India and Burma which obtained a supply of world news from Reuters' smaller London-based competitors in 1932 (but not, significantly, from UP – reliable coverage of the imperial capital was too important). The colonial government closed down the agency in the following year for 'seditious reporting' and alleged lack of press support. The Calcutta editor of

Free Press then set up United Press of India, which employed many Free Press journalists. United Press survived for some time, but had no foreign agency connection nor teleprinter transmission and was therefore weakly constituted to offer serious competition to API before World War Two.

Reuters continued as dominant foreign agency well into the postwar period. In 1948 it established a special relationship with the new nationalist agency and successor to API, the cooperative Press Trust of India (PTI), which was brought into the Commonwealth ownership structure of Reuters instituted at the end of the war. PTI was assigned a zone of news coverage from Cairo to Singapore for which it was responsible to Reuters in return for the continued provision of the world news service.

PTI maintained correspondents not only in South East Asia, but also in the Middle East, Washington, Geneva and London. In London, PTI journalists situated in the Reuters office selected the world news they wanted for transmission to PTI, a privilege Reuters had only previously conceded to South African and Australian media and which for a time was extended to some allied European agencies. The Reuters–PTI relationship survived only four years, and was then terminated at the initiative of PTI. Instead, an exchange arrangement was signed with Reuters in 1953, but PTI had to contribute an additional cash payment.

Independence opened the India market to other global agencies, although these were obliged by law to distribute via Indian news agencies. UP had first penetrated the Indian market in 1942; after the war it sold to the '*Express*' group, until in 1960 it was obliged to distribute only through a national agency, going to the Indian News Service established by the *Express* and *Times of India* groups, and, when that closed down in 1961, to PTI. AP sold to the *Times of India* group until 1960–61. AFP served the second Indian national agency, United Press of India, but this closed down in 1958, having made heavy losses over a number of years. In 1960, two companies combined to set up an alternative, the United News of India, which had its own teleprinter network and substantial press support.

In the 1970s PTI subscribed to Reuters, UPI and AFP while AP distributed via United News. United News was a cooperative of eight dailies, with less than a quarter of PTI's clientele and many fewer correspondents. PTI's own foreign representation had declined steeply from the days of its Reuters partnership and in 1973 it had foreign correspondents only in the UN, Cairo, Moscow, Kuala Lumpur and Tokyo. It claimed to pass on some 50% of the international material received from the major agencies – significant, because PTI distributed and still distributes mainly in English and no translation is required. PTI had no facilities for photo-transmission, and here the US agencies could operate directly, hindered only by poor communications and the free information and photo services of foreign governments, including those of the US and Soviet Union. During the period of 'Emergency Rule' under prime minister Indira Gandhi, 1975–7, PTI, UNI and other smaller agencies were forcibly merged under the umbrella of a new national agency, Samachar, a decision taken by Indira Gandhi on the basis that one agency was easier to control than two or more,[30] and effected by threatening to demand the immediate repayment of long-term government loans and by forcing India's broadcasting organization (AIR) to cancel its contracts with PTI and UNI.[31] The Union Cabinet of the succeeding Janata Government subsequently dismantled Samachar and AP once again distributed via United News. A Ministry of Information committee report in August 1977, however, proposed that there should be a tripartite agency structure, established by parliamentary charter, comprising one English-language agency and one Indian-languages agency, which together would control a third agency whose task would be the exclusive handling of incoming and outgoing foreign news.[32]

Beyond the British Empire there was greater scope for US agency penetration from an earlier date and a more obvious justification for encouraging diversity of news supply. While there were a great many contenders for international influence, it was the 'Big Four' of the between-the-wars period which mainly prevailed under conditions of free choice, and not so much the barefaced propaganda machines of Nazi Germany or Fascist Italy, for example. Media may have been poor but they were plentiful. There were 358 daily papers in China in 1925, and 910 by 1935. And for Reuters the market in the supply of commercial information remained a staple. Had the Chinese market survived, indeed, the general balance of world news flow might have been very different. Both US agencies increased their journalistic strength in China from the 1920s and UP established its first sale with a brief news report to some Peking newspapers in 1925. Supply of US news was facilitated by concessionary US Navy radio press rates and a UP deal with RCA for the reduction of Pacific wireless and cable rates for China. Although UP quickly extended its report to Shanghai, Hankow, and Tientsin, UP's historian, Morris, records that by the late 1920s it was still to be 'several years before important progress would be made in opposition to the powerful Reuters agency'.[33] By the late 1930s, however, one US journalist source concluded that 'the North American journalistic position in the Far East is as strong and perhaps stronger than the British, although the dependence of the East upon Reuters for commercial figures is an important item in any assessment'.[34] But, perhaps because their services were too heavily Western in content, or because their ground strength in China was unrealistically slender and depended too much on dubious stringer sources such as diplomatic personnel or religious missionaries, it was possible for one seasoned correspondent to record in *Journalism Quarterly* (1931) that press association coverage in China 'was far from satisfactory, especially from the Chinese point of view'.[35] If so, then all the more reason why by the early 1930s the climate was receptive to the establishment of a national news agency. Although the Central News Agency (CNA) was founded in 1924 it was one of several nationalist enterprises, and did not become prominent until a decade later, subsidized by the government and faithfully imitating 'the propaganda methods about which all Chinese, government officials included, complain so bitterly in the conduct of the foreign news agencies operating in this country'.[36] The need for a better supply of China news and possibly the lack of adequate market support for all the global agencies then operating, helped promote the development of CNA into a strong national agency, first in the East to secure exclusive rights of distribution to major foreign agency services. Following the exposure of a link between CNA and the German agency Trans-Ocean, Havas was to join Reuters and the US agencies in the competition for Chinese interest. CNA's first pact with one of the 'Big Four', however, was with Reuters as early as 1932. Reuters was evidently happy to have CNA worry about distribution to the newspapers, while it retained the lucrative commercial market. The following year Nash recorded the installation by Reuters of teletype machines in several banks and other business offices in Shanghai to 'facilitate the rapid transmission of one of its specialities, commercial and financial news'.[37]

Further pacts were signed by CNA with Havas in 1933, Trans-Ocean in 1936 and UP in 1938. INS also wanted to deal with CNA, but the plan was blocked by UP which claimed the exclusive right as American agency to exchange news with a Chinese agency. AP had only a news-gathering presence in China before the war. Reuters was therefore first to do business with the agency of the nationalist government, and the American agency UP held out until last. But despite the alliance they both appear to have done their own translation, and resorted to employing an increasing number of Chinese journalists. (In Nanking and Canton, Reuters' bureau managers were Chinese.) This may have been to minimize distortions by CNA or a way of subsidizing an allied agency.

CNA's pacts were exclusive – the agencies could not distribute independently. On the other hand, despite claims to nine divisional bureaux and twenty news bureaux within China (and a body of employees which included many university graduates from the US), CNA seems to have had little if any overseas representation. Its dependence for such news on the foreign agencies was therefore almost total, though one competent observer asserted his belief in 1939 that the Chinese reading public was not satisfied with the service from foreign sources.[38] That year CNA followed Chiang Kai-Shek to his emergency mountain headquarters of Chungking in the south-west, from where, much later he was to retreat to Taiwan. There, in the following decades, CNA built up a powerful overseas network of correspondents and clients, especially among the expatriate Chinese communities of South-east Asia. The agency of the communist forces, established in 1929 as the Red China News Agency, and renamed Hsin Hua in 1937, was to become the only agency of mainland China.

Not until the mid-1950s had both European agencies re-negotiated a return to the Chinese mainland, and in 1956 Hsin Hua subscribed to Reuters' general and commercial services. Despite the internment of Reuters' correspondent Anthony Grey during the cultural revolution of 1968, representation was subsequently uninterrupted. China coverage by the US agencies was much more restricted. Until 1959 the US State Department forbade the entry of American newsmen into China. When this ruling was lifted that year a UPI reporter, a Chinese national born in Shanghai, was arrested on spy charges. Other US correspondents had trouble getting visas, and there was no continuous representation of US agencies in mainland China between 1949 and 1979. While the Nixon visit of 1972 raised high hopes that the US agencies would be allowed to establish Peking bureaux, it did not in fact come about till 1979, after the visit of the Chinese premier to the US. From 1972, however the US agencies formally exchanged news services with the Chinese agency. Otherwise the US agencies up to 1979 managed much of their China coverage from Hong Kong, important also for the European agencies, who had not been allowed more than two correspondents each in Peking and were subject to the customary news-gathering restrictions of communist countries.

Japan: Asian prize

Up to World War Two developments in Japan followed a similar path: initial control of the foreign news supply by a single global agency, an opening up of the market by the American agencies and propaganda services of other countries and then a diminution of real diversity as a strong national agency buys up the exclusive rights of distribution within its territory. As in China, it was Reuters which lost the most ground because it had the most to lose. The post-war Japanese development was very different from the Chinese, and as in Germany the Allies sought to establish real diversity of foreign news supply and news distribution. In Japan as in Germany the success of this initiative owed much more to the native affluence of these media markets than to any innate magnetic appeal of the principle of diversity in itself.

The leading national agency in Japan before World War One was Kokusai, founded in 1914, and linked to the European cartel through Reuters, whose service it distributed exclusively. In 1926 Kokusai became a cooperative of national newspapers and changed its name to Rengo, and in the same year Reuters bowed to the inevitable by allowing AP, at that time still a member of the cartel, to enter into a separate exchange arrangement. Japan was of even more importance to AP and to the American government than China; it was concern for the American image in Japan in particular and the quality of news coming from Japan which led the government to open up Navy traffic to press users. Kokusai was eager to establish relations with AP: it was frustrated by Reuters' hold, and sought to break from it by turning into a cooperative styled on the AP pattern. The real inspiration came from Japanese businessmen who saw no future in the British connection. An alternative agency, which dated back to 1901, was Dentsu Tsushin or Nippon Dentsu, which now subscribed to UP. From 1931, Rengo was also supplied by Havas, following agreement on mutual concessions between Havas and Reuters. In 1936 the two major agencies, Rengo and Dentsu Tsuchin, merged together to form Domei, the leading official Japanese agency until the country's defeat at the end of World War Two. Domei subscribed to all the leading agencies, including AP and UP. Reuters' position was therefore more quickly and more effectively challenged in Japan than in China.

Domei grew to be one of the leading national agencies of the world, rivalling Germany's DNB, and like DNB it was a government agency. By the year 1937 it had bureaux in eleven major world capitals, and by 1942 had three zonal bureaux and twenty-eight branch offices in the Far East alone, while in China during the Japanese invasion it maintained 500 correspondents. Its New York bureau was especially important: it was housed in the AP building where it received AP, UP, Dow Jones and Reuters Commercial Services. The New York bureau remained in operation right up to the declaration of war between Japan and the US. European news to Tokyo went via Domei's New York office. At the beginning of the European war, but before Pearl Harbour, there was a heavy representation of

Domei newsmen on European war fronts. Because the Allied European censors were particularly lenient in dealing with the flow of news to North America – as part of a policy to persuade the US to join the war – Domei correspondents also benefited, and through them perhaps, the Axis powers. When, in September 1945, General McArthur instructed the Japanese government to eliminate its control over the press, no preferential treatment was accorded Domei. In reaction Domei's board of directors voted the agency's dissolution, which was effective 31 October 1945.

Two new agencies emerged to replace Domei: Kyodo and Jiji. Kyodo was cooperatively owned by the Japanese daily press, and Jiji was a private company. This pattern was inspired and encouraged by the Americans who believed Japan would benefit from a competitive situation similar to that of the US, where the leading agencies were also one cooperative and one private company. In practice it worked out rather differently. Jiji began to specialize in economic news; Kyodo in general news. This was a partial return to an earlier pre-1936 pattern, when Dentsu Tsushin tended to specialize in economics and Rengo was major source for general news.

In the 1970s, Japan was the single most important market within the Asian region for all the major agencies. Reuters employed a Tokyo staff of 35 in 1973, of whom 11 to 14 were journalists. All but two of these were bi-lingual Japanese. The Tokyo bureau was the sixth largest in the agency's network, beaten only by New York, Washington, Paris, Beirut and Singapore. AP at the same time had a staff of 16 journalists and 54 support staff, putting this bureau in third place amongst the agency's overseas bureaux, behind London and Paris. UPI's bureau had ten journalists, the fourth or fifth most important UPI bureau in its foreign network. AFP placed rather less relative importance on Tokyo, assigning some eight journalists to this bureau, which ranked only ninth in its overall foreign network.

All 'Big Four' agencies sold to Kyodo in the early 1970s, but they each also had direct media sales. In 1973 40% of Kyodo's foreign news supply derived from its own foreign correspondents,[39] and the percentage was increasing over time, indicating a general trend towards self-sufficiency of Japanese media in international news coverage. Kyodo maintained 37 correspondents overseas at that time, about the same number as the *New York Times* (Asahi had 25). 43% of Kyodo's overseas report derived from Reuters, AP and UPI, while an extra 8% came from AP–Dow Jones, the economic news agency. Kyodo was making increasingly less use of incoming agency reports: it did not undertake exact translations, but extracted precise summarized reports. The 'Big Four' agencies had reduced the volume of their supply in response to Kyodo's need for swift, convenient copy handling. Fears that Kyodo might become totally self-reliant were tempered by the fact that only a third of its foreign correspondents were based in the US and Western Europe, while most of the rest were based in Asia; moreover, 55% of its foreign news was news of the US and Western Europe, indicating the need for continued reliance on Western agencies, either by Kyodo correspondents in the field or by editors in Tokyo. Kyodo executives interviewed in 1973 claimed that Kyodo did not intend to try and become a global agency, given the language difficulties – even in Asia English was the regional lingua franca.[40] However, Kyodo's own overseas news coverage had become less dominated by narrow Japanese 'angles', and better able to compete with 'Big Four' coverage. Reuters and AFP also sold to Jiji, the economic news agency, and Jiji had the right of distribution for RES teleprinter services in Japan. But AP–DJ had become Kyodo's most important source of economic news. UPI distributed a special local economic service for Tokyo papers, banks and business firms. The 'Big Four' agencies also sold directly to national retail media. AP sold to two of the three Tokyo giants, Asahi and Yomiuri, Reuters to Asahi and NHK, UPI to Mainichi and NHK, AFP to NHK. Provincial media mainly took their overseas news from Kyodo. The possibility that the importance of the Japanese market in Asia might threaten the balance of 'Big Four' resources too much in its favour seemed to be contained first, by the increasing self-reliance of Japanese media; second, by the high cost of maintaining correspondents in Tokyo and of communications, which made it preferable to locate regional agency headquarters in Hong Kong (UPI, AFP) and Singapore (Reuters); third, by the continuing economic character of the prevailing Japanese 'news story', unlikely to obliterate the more sensational political character of other major 'stories' in the Far East (Indochina, China).

During the post-war period therefore, there has been a trend towards equal representation of all the world agencies, supplemented by intra-regional news exchanges between domestic news agencies. There was still a tendency for general news subscriptions in some countries to reflect old imperial, political and cultural affiliations. In Hong Kong, for instance, Reuters was the main supplier of overseas news in 1973 to Government Information Services (which distributed to 67 clients), and claimed 22 clients for the general news service (including the *South China Morning Post* and the *Standard*, which also took the other world agencies). Its total staff of 45–50 (mostly RES) surpassed that of UPI and AFP, both of which maintained regional bureaux in Hong Kong. Reuters' general news regional centre in Singapore, employing a total of

60 full-time staff (15 editorial), also far surpassed the bureaux of other agencies. Reuters was a leading supplier of foreign news in 1973 to the *Straits Times* (Singapore), which also subscribed to UPI, AP photos, *New York Times* News Service and the *Los Angeles Times-Washington Post* news service. In Thailand, however, AP had 14 teleprinter clients, against Reuters' 7, but Reuters' bulletin services went to 33, against AP's 4 and RES services sold to a further 120 private clients. Staffing figures were similar, at around two news-gathering journalists per agency. In some other parts of the region, the American agencies had a very clear lead. In Taiwan, for instance, AP and UPI both leased office space from CNA in Taipei with full-time staffs of six and three respectively, and their services were distributed through CNA communications to leading media. Reuters and AFP sold only to CNA and maintained only one correspondent each in Taipei. In the Philippines the US agencies had a longer and less interrupted history than the European. In 1973 the European agencies each had only two editorial staff; Reuters sold its general news service to only two teleprinter clients, AFP sold only to private clients. RES services for non-media clients however went to some 400 clients. The US agency bureaux were considerably larger: UPI, for instance, employed a staff of a dozen, including three journalists and three photographers. They sold to most of the leading metropolitan media. AFP's own special sphere of influence in the Far East, inherited from the days of the cartel, had been Indochina, but whatever influence it had enjoyed was severely shaken by the political developments of the 1960s and 1970s.

Towards the Asian vernacular

The agencies in Asia in 1973 distributed, wherever they were free to distribute as they wished, to the wealthier media who could afford to take them. The English-language press, for example, was a relatively lucrative market in the 1970s because it went to élite readers, attracted high advertising revenue (often from the multinational corporations, or handled by multinational, especially American, advertising agencies), and printed a relatively high volume of foreign news. In general, English-language papers were charged more than leading vernacular papers, even when their circulation was less, because their ability to pay was often so much greater. A study in 1965 found that of 30 English-language papers in this region, 27 credited an average of 3·4 news agencies and 2·0 special news services per paper a week.[41] The English-language dailies had 25% of the newspaper reading population.

Vernacular papers tended not to print much foreign news, perhaps in part owing to the absence of suitable international news material. This material was often not available outside the capital cities, in which case there was complete reliance on truncated versions provided by national agencies; or, in the absence of national agencies, on the free provision of domestic and foreign government information services, or the monitoring of overseas broadcasts. USIS, for example, concentrated its news activities in areas not served by the American agencies for lack of commercial viability. Any reduction in this kind of official provision might actually increase undercover political pressure on the agencies to perform the kind of function traditionally performed by official channels.

The vernacular press was generally very poor. An IPI study in 1968 showed that of 149 Chinese dailies published in Asia outside mainland China, only 10 were making substantial profits, and the rest were working on a shoestring.[42] A survey of 36 Hong Kong Chinese papers in 1966 showed that only 9 owned their own equipment – and for international news they tended to use agency dispatches of larger papers without crediting them. There were news editors in Hong Kong whose jobs consisted entirely in rewriting AP and UPI copy from other newspapers.[43] The leading vernacular papers usually had to pay for the cost of translating agency services from English.

The world agencies were the most important sources of international news. Most Asian countries had national agencies which took the bulk of their foreign news supply from the global agencies. Alternative sources included other national news agencies and foreign broadcasts, but much of this material did in any case originate with the global agencies.

The global agencies tended to concentrate their manpower and office facilities in a few leading capitals of the economically most advanced countries, namely, Tokyo, Hong Kong and Singapore, the few profit-generating centres in the Far East. Of course staff from these centres could be deployed in other parts of the region, and often were – but on a 'news crisis' basis. The agencies also maintained some degree of representation in most countries where access was permitted. They preferred not to depend too heavily on 'roving' correspondents. Such individuals ranked too highly on prestige and were a threat to the bureau-chief system of authority precisely because they were more mobile, and in any case were soon pilfered by newspapers and news-magazines once they had established themselves.

Considerations such as these were of interest to media of the developed world concerned with the adequacy of Third World news coverage, but such concern was rarely articulated in more than cursory fashion. For Third World media, on the other hand, they had a much more immediate relevance, raising very practical questions as to the extent to which the 'Big Four' agencies really were indispensable and if they were not, what other forms of news provision could be cultivated.

5
National news agencies: the unstable nexus

The world agencies do not control the distribution of their own product to all their 'retail' newspapers, broadcast and other clients. An important intermediary in many countries and for at least some clients in most countries is the national news agency, and nowhere is this more the case than in the developing countries of the Third World. Where dependence on the global agencies is already great, therefore, the scope for news selection by the individual retail media organization is further reduced by the intervention of a third party.

A national agency typically collects news items of its country, selects items of foreign news from one or more world or intermediate agencies, and distributes the resulting national and foreign news service to media and non-media clients of the country in question. Some national agencies employ their own foreign correspondents, generally very few in number and posted in a few capitals of special political, economic or cultural relevance, who concentrate on news of specific interest to their country. Few national agencies have significant overseas or foreign sales, although many have exchange arrangements with other agencies and offset a percentage of the cost of their world agency subscriptions by their provision of domestic news services to these organizations. National agencies, especially in the Third World, are very often government agencies run by or heavily subsidized from ministries of culture or information, perhaps with management participation from client media. National agencies are very often virtual monopolies in the supply either of domestic or both domestic and foreign news to their retail clients, either because governments have decreed that they should be monopolies, or because monopoly is the inevitable outcome of market conditions. In many countries, smaller and more specialized agencies exist alongside the national agencies.

These then, are some of the component characteristics of 'typical' national news agencies. Some agencies are less elaborate; others more so. Some, for example, can hardly be said to have domestic news-gathering functions, either because there are hardly any media and therefore little news demand, or because the media are metropolitan rather than national in outlook, or simply because the infrastructure required for an efficient domestic news-gathering operation is not made available. When this happens, agencies exist primarily to redistribute international news collected from international news agencies. International news represents 50% or more of the total news output of a great many national agencies, large and small.

At the other end of the scale there are the national agencies which employ sizeable corps of foreign correspondents who do not confine themselves to reporting events of interest only to their own country and which also sell news to some other countries. In the Introduction these were described as 'intermediate' agencies as opposed to 'world' agencies.

Any study of the world agencies must also account for the role of national news agencies. National news agencies are the source of a good but unknown proportion of the world agencies' total overseas revenue; and through the national agencies the world news services are distributed to media which otherwise would not or might not receive them. The national agency is in a sense a convenient revenue device, whereby revenue is assured the global agencies from media which individually might be unable to afford global agency services, but which collectively, or through government help, can afford them. For that reason many national agencies have emerged in close relationship with one or more world agencies. But the unequal character of the relationship causes its own resentments and has led many national agencies to seek ways of doing without, competing with, or at least reducing the influence of the world agencies.

The growth and resource distribution of national agencies[1]

In 1971 there were national agencies in 90 sovereign countries, a 76% increase on 1950 when there were national agencies in 51 countries. There were still as many as 40 countries without national agencies, and of these 25 had populations greater than a million. In 56% of all cases the national agencies were state-controlled; most of the others were corporate newspaper endeavours or public corporations established under state auspices. Of the news agencies founded pre-1915 which survived into the post-World-War-Two era, most were European. In the period between the wars, only just under half of the agencies established were European, the rest were mainly Asian, African and Arab. But over two-thirds of all existing agencies have been established since World War Two. As many as 27 agencies were established in Africa and the Middle East in the period 1939–62, a third of the total, and almost as many again in Asia. By 1964 agencies of Africa and the Middle East accounted for about one-third of all agencies; Europe accounted for another third; the rest were mainly Asian. Most subsequent national agencies were in the Third World, and by 1971 some South American countries, like Brazil, Argentina, Colombia, Chile and Venezuela, now had strong agencies, many of them privately owned and in competition with other private agencies. In 1971 there were still 13 African and 5 Asian countries without national agencies, but there were further establishments in the 1970s including the Caribbean News Agency (CANA), the Central American news agency, ACACAN, Sri Lanka's Lanka Puwarth, Angola's ANGOP, and the Nigerian News Agency (NNA), among others. Some nine out of ten agencies in the 1960s were purely domestic agencies. The number of domestic bureaux maintained by such agencies varied widely, as high as fifty in the case of agencies such as PTI of India but as low as four or fewer in the case of approximately one-third of all agencies. National agencies of the developed world claimed far more manpower resources per head of population than agencies of the developing world: Canada's two principal domestic agencies in 1966, for example, claimed some two hundred full-time journalists between them for a population of some 20 million, whereas PTI of India employed about the same number of correspondents for a population of 483 million. In Japan, Jiji and Kyodo employed about six hundred journalists for a population of 55 million. (The poor resourcing of many national agencies in the Third World is one important cause of problems associated with the 'imbalance' of world news flow, since national agencies are generally important news sources for the world agencies; but of course poor resourcing merely reflects the basic problem, which is the non-existence or impoverishment of local markets in most Third World regions.) However, countries with competing agencies were not necessarily the most affluent: they included, for instance, Turkey and Indonesia, as well as the US and Japan. The daily wordage provided by these agencies varied enormously in volume from a few tens of thousands to hundreds of thousands in the case of some agencies of the developed countries. Of 29 agencies which supplied estimated percentages of the importance of foreign news in their overall news files (in UNESCO surveys of the 1950s and 1960s), 21 claimed to give 40–60% of their total wordage to foreign news, and in the case of some African agencies the percentages were as high as 75–80%.

Overall there have been large increases in the total wordage supplied by world and national news agencies. Amongst the smaller Third World agencies there were also signs by 1971 of a growth in personnel. But many agencies were still very modest affairs: the

Colombian Ultra Prensa had an editorial strength of only 8 persons; the total staff (all categories) of the agency of the People's Republic of the Congo was 46 and of Dahomey only 26. Many of these small Third World agencies still distributed by bulletin. One interesting feature of growth in most parts of the world by 1971, however, was a great increase in the number of other agency services received by any given national agency, either through subscription or, much more frequently, through news-exchange arrangements or freely distributed services. But world agencies remained by far the most significant news suppliers. A 1971 study of the four Scandinavian agencies, for example, showed that Reuters and AFP accounted for 72% of ingoing foreign news material (the US agencies delivered direct to subscribers at that time), and two-thirds of the material was actually used.[2] Main suppliers to the Afghan agency Bakhtar in a 1968 study were Reuters, AP and DPA, and Reuters and DPA accounted for half the foreign news output.[3] Principal suppliers of international news to the Senegalese news agency, APS, in 1977 were AFP and Reuters;[4] likewise for the Ghana News Agency.[5] Even in the case of Tanjug the 'Big Four' agencies supplied 52% of ingoing and 37% of outgoing foreign news material.[6]

News flow as news exchange

The concept 'imperialism' denotes an imbalance of power relationship between nations. The first agencies emerged among the great imperial powers of the nineteenth century and their relationship with agencies of other countries was and is to some extent still a reflection of the imperial balance of power.

It should be understood, however, that this imbalance was not often completely unidirectional. The agencies did not everywhere impose their own news-gathering and distribution machinery. Rather, they established relations with local independent agencies. The essential characteristic of this relationship was the principle of *news-exchange* it embodied, although the exchange was rarely equal.

The flow of international news therefore involved and still involves a multiplicity of distinct organizations and the absence of one single overall locus of editorial control. Despite this fact, the weaker members of the network could not act with sufficient unanimity to place countervailing pressure on the stronger members and thus achieve a lasting equilibrium of influence. The great possibility – creation of a truly international news organization, acting as a single body with no concessions to particular national interests or pressures – was never realized.

Instead, cooperation between agencies has tended to reflect both 'economic necessity', sometimes at the cost of effective editorial control over the use to which news is put and the quality of the news which is received, and the state of diplomatic relations between the nations of the agencies which are party to the agreement.

Inequality of exchange arrangements was evident even in the relations between the dominant agencies of the nineteenth-century cartel. The first significant agreement was signed in 1856, by Reuters and Havas, and was confined to news of trade and stocks. The agreement was widened to include Wolff in 1859, and in subsequent years incorporated general news and identified those geographical areas which would be regarded as each agency's exclusive markets. For Havas these were to be France, Spain, Italy, and the Levant, South America and Indochina. Wolff's part of the agreement involved news distribution to Germany, Russia, Scandinavia and the Slavonic countries; Reuters had its own Empire and most of the Far East.

The primary purpose of the agreements was to reduce the cost of foreign news-gathering (since the agencies tended to confine their news-gathering activities to their own exclusive markets except for major stories or news centres) and at the same time of course to protect markets. The partners to the post-1870 agreements were to sell their news services only in what by common consent were their own spheres of influence. Outside these spheres they would provide news only to the other partners. But relations between agencies of the triumvirate were not in fact equal. Reuters was able to benefit from the special advantages offered by Britain's incomparable global influence and the leading role of British capital in the expansion of cable communication routes. It was Reuters which controlled the reception and distribution of news from the American agencies. In Europe, Reuters was for a long time able to maintain some of the affluent non-Prussian German clients acquired before agreements signed with Wolff (maintaining services to Hamburg even up to 1900), and it ceded to Wolff's monopoly rights in 1870 only by demanding that Wolff should pay an annual cash sum to Reuters and Havas in addition to supplying them with news of its sphere of influence. The international influence of Havas, while potentially greater than that of Wolff, was severely weakened by the consequences of the Franco-Prussian war. Reuters facilitated Havas' recovery by a 'joint purse' arrangement under which all profits from all sources were to be shared, but then broke the spirit of the agreement by presenting Havas with a bill towards the cost of an overambitious telegram operation between South and North America, the West Indies and Europe. Otherwise the world might have seen the creation of a truly private internationally-owned news agency.

Changing diplomatic interests of Britain and France further

removed the chances of a lasting partnership of the kind envisaged in the 'joint purse' agreement. Disraeli's aggressive Near East policy in the mid-1870s onwards, for instance, brought about renewed struggle for the markets of Turkey and Egypt, where before the agencies had acted on a joint basis. As British influence was established in Egypt, Reuters became its leading internal agency. Havas was later (in 1900) to withdraw from Egypt in return for financial compensation from Reuters and the promise that dispatches would still be headed 'Reuter-Havas'. This was but one aspect of the imperial scramble for Africa which further intensified the identification of agencies with the policies of national governments, at least in the eyes of many observers. Precisely because Germany was not the most active participant in the scramble for overseas territories, perhaps, Reuters was now inclined to move closer to the German than to the French agency. In 1887 Wolff and Reuters signed an 'offensive-defensive' alliance providing for joint action in case the renewal of the 1870 agreements, scheduled for 1890, could not be accomplished. In the same year as the alliance, Francesco Crispi, the Italian premier, discussed with Bismarck how the agencies of the Triple Alliance powers – Stefani in Rome, Wolff in Berlin and the Korrespondenz-Bureau of Vienna – could combine to crush the dominant position of Havas in continental Europe. Although Reuters' first reaction was to avoid such polarization, for fear that the conflict would cut it off from its primary source of continental news, it evidently considered enmity with Wolff a more serious possibility. The success of the pact depended on the joint operation by Wolff and Reuter of bureaux in Rome and in Paris, since neither could expect any cooperation from Havas. Stefani in Rome had initially been an ally of Havas, but now sided with Wolff.

Except in the very early days, when Reuter himself had worked with Wolff in the Paris office of Havas, there had been no experience of such close cooperation between the German and British agencies. The joint offices were not successful. Crispi did not in the end permit the cooperation of Stefani, for fear of retaliation from Francophil interests in Italy; while in Paris the alliance agencies could not hope to compete for news with Havas on its own ground.

The pact failed, and the 1870 agreements were renewed after all by the original triumverate in 1890. The renewal merely confirmed each agency in the 'territories' it had already acquired. This was despite an unsuccessful bid for the Russian market by Havas, reflecting an emerging accord between Russia and France. But the alliances between the agencies were not quite as fickle as those of their home governments; and markets once gained were not readily relinquished. One consequence of this state of affairs, as we have seen, was the promotion of state backing in Russia for a single national agency to counter the dependency on Wolff for foreign news, and this in turn laid the foundations for what was later to become TASS.

The 1890 agreement was further renewed in 1900. The essential news-exchange character of the triumvirate survived therefore for most of the second half of the nineteenth century, and continued up to the First World War in its original form, with consequences that lasted at least until World War Two, and in some respects until today.

The satellite agencies

The smaller European agencies allied themselves to members of the triumvirate. There was little choice if they were to survive as credible news organizations; there was nowhere else to go for a comparable supply of foreign news if they lacked resources to cater for themselves.

The triumvirate both nourished and contained these smaller agencies. The typical pattern of news exchange was already established before the 1870 agreement. Havas, for instance, had a special relationship with the Turin agency, Stefani. Under this arrangement Stefani signed over to Havas the world monopoly on its Italian news, and undertook to transmit it directly to Paris and, if Havas so required, to Germany, Switzerland and England as well. It agreed to maintain correspondents in Rome, Naples and other major Italian cities. It would also transmit Havas news to subscribers of the French agency in the Levant. In return, the Stefani agency had an exclusive right to all Havas news, which meant that Stefani was sole distributor in Italy of a world news service. Alliance with the triumvirate therefore automatically conferred a monopoly status on a smaller agency within its domestic market, an extremely attractive political and commercial proposition.

In Spain, Havas and Reuter signed an agreement with Nilo Maria Fabra, director of an agency founded in 1865 under the title 'Bureau de Correspondance'. This functioned for several years under the common name 'Havas–Reuter', and when Havas' superiority in southern Europe was formally recognized, as 'Agence Havas, Madrid'.

Wolff's most important ally was the Korrespondenz–Bureau of Vienna, founded in 1859, although this agency did sign separate news-exchange agreements with the other agencies from 1869 to offset the consequences of internal disputes within the triumvirate. The Viennese agency acted as point of transmission between the Baltic States and Middle Europe, one of the most febrile areas of the world for much of the period leading up to the First World War. It maintained offices in the countries that were later to be known as Bulgaria, Rumania, Hungary and Czechoslovakia, and with the development of national groupings within the Austro-Hungarian Empire, these branches were to become the head offices of new independent national agencies. One of these was the Hungarian agency, MTI, founded in 1881. The Czech agency, CTK, was formed after the First World War out of the old offices of Korrespondenz-Bureau in Prague and Brünn (Brno).

Perhaps in no case was the importance of the triumvirate to smaller agencies more apparent than in its relationship with the American agencies. Membership of the triumvirate was the deciding factor in the successful establishment of the Western AP in its eventual victory over the old UP. This postponed the development of a major rival agency in America, and when the second United Press was formed many years later it had to struggle in a domestic market in which the AP was clearly to be the dominant competitor.

Reuters was the most active in its encouragement or sponsorship of new agencies in this period. In the period before 1870, Reuters was first to approach Ritzhaus agency in Denmark, oldest of the Scandinavian agencies, founded in 1866, and one of the first national agencies. Reuters also took the main initiative in purchasing control of a local agency in Amsterdam, founded by Alexander Dalamar. Dalamar's brother Herman took charge of the Reuter-Havas office later established in Brussels. A Swiss agency founded in 1895 maintained similarly intimate relations with Reuters and Havas. These two agencies together also helped establish the Ottoman Telegraph Agency for news of Turkey in 1911.

Reuters was no less active outside Europe. Before World War One it took control of the Eastern News Agency in India, formed on the basis of two previous domestic agencies. In Japan, Kokusai, founded in 1914, was at first little more than a foreign distributing centre for Reuters. After the failure of an indigenous venture by British newspapers in South Africa, Reuters established the South African Press Agency, in which it held a controlling interest until the inter-war period.

Since one of the most important functions of any given national agency was to distribute international news, it was inevitable that it quickly tied in with the existing arrangements of the triumvirate. The resulting relationship of inequality was sometimes expressed in the part-acquisition of the agency by a major one; or a major agency would establish its own satellite in competition with an existing local agency. Since the triumvirate agency needed an office in any case, to collect and if possible distribute news, it was an easy alternative to set up a local 'front' agency, and in that way to secure a foothold on the local market.

More commonly the relationship remained indirect: as a condition of the news exchange, and the domestic monopoly position it bestowed, the national agency was usually forbidden to sell its service to other agencies outside the cartel. After 1907, 'other agencies' increasingly came to mean UP, AP and the German Trans-Ocean agency. UP tended in consequence to deal with some of the smaller domestic rivals of the triumvirate agencies, such as Central News in the UK or Extel, or Fournier in Paris.

Because the world agencies did at least half the job of these smaller agencies by collecting and providing international news, they very deeply influenced the character of local agency services. The smaller agencies could not have called on a fraction of the resources they would need if they were to provide for themselves what they could buy from the European triumvirate. Even if they could have found the resources, say from state coffers, they would still have been at a severe disadvantage in news-reporting in comparison with the larger agencies. The political-economic character of the period would have demanded as a matter of the utmost priority an excellent service of news from the parliaments, governments and stock exchanges of Britain, France and Germany, and similar news from the territories those countries controlled or greatly influenced. It would have been impossible to compete meaningfully on the domestic ground of even one of these three. Wolff and Havas enjoyed privileged relationships with their own respective governments. Wolff and Reuter found it impossible to compete successfully against Havas in 1887–90 to maintain a joint Paris office. So what chance would a smaller agency have had? Reuters was less close to the British government perhaps, but it had what was, all things considered, a respectable relationship and status which no other agency – especially a foreign agency – could conceivably have won. In British territories it might have been easier to displace the position of Reuters, but only with at least an equivalent service of British economic and political news, which a smaller agency would have been unable to obtain. Even UP could not displace Reuters, or the other partners of the triumvirate, in their colonial markets before World War Two. This agency was able to get as far as it did partly because of its sizeable home market. Reuters' early experience of handling the world agency–local agency nexus may have influenced its attitude at home to the formation of the Press Association. Here, Reuters managed to have its cake and eat it: not to be encumbered with the problems of domestic news-gathering and provincial distribution, yet to derive a considerable share of its total revenue both from the London press and the PA acting on behalf of the provincial press.

World agency promotion of new satellites

This close involvement of global with national agencies has continued throughout their subsequent history. Actual global agency involvement in the setting-up of national agencies has been a characteristic of post-colonial times as much as it was of colonial days. There has usually been no question of an ownership interest; rather the involvement has been considered in terms of an investment by news organizations of the developed countries in ensuring an improved future supply of news from the developing countries. The world agencies most active in this context have probably been Reuters and AFP, although some of the 'intermediary' agencies have also established aid programmes (e.g. DPA).

AFP was heavily involved in both an advisory and material capacity in the French African territories when these became independent. The national agencies which emerged in these territories were usually the old branch offices of AFP, and were often staffed initially by the very same journalists who had staffed the old AFP bureaux. The special relationship was also represented by the heavy consumption of AFP news files by the new national agencies, though such dependence became less considerable when both Reuters and AFP in Africa established inroads into one another's ex-colonial territories. But it remained the case that revenue was usually greater for the ex-imperial agency. That is, a Francophone African country would use AFP as a primary foreign news source and pay it a higher subscription, and use Reuters as a secondary source, paying a much smaller subscription. (*Mutatis mutandis* in ex-English territories.) Like AFP, Reuters has been an active consultant to the governments of many countries of the Third World in the setting up of national news agencies, in giving technical and editorial training and assistance, and lending out its own highly-qualified personnel for such purposes. In 1978, for instance, Reuters was providing free development assistance (excluding actual hardware costs) to as many as thirty-four agencies on a bilateral, confidential basis.[7] In 'some two dozen' countries it also handled the transmission of public information from Third World governments to their embassies abroad. (This kind of activity has also been of some considerable revenue importance for the new breed of 'international intermediary' agencies such as IPS, ACACAN, and Latin, which serve groups of countries, but in the case of Reuters it is offered as assistance in return for the right to use the information carried for its own news services.) Its own research and development in the areas of transmission and receiver technology has been of great benefit to many Third World agencies. Although much of this general developmental effort has concentrated on Africa and the Middle East, Reuters was actively instrumental in helping to establish, for example, the South American agency Latin and the Caribbean news agency, CANA. In the case of Latin, Reuters selected and trained the journalists, set up the communications and administrative structure and managed the new agency, supplying its own world service. Reuters has a 49 % share in the ownership, and appoints the chief executive. The case of CANA was somewhat different, in that Reuters had found it increasingly difficult to maintain its regional Caribbean service without requiring much higher subscriptions than local media were prepared to pay, and its regional operations formed the nucleus on which the new regional agency was initially based, while Reuters has continued as major provider of world news. Since Caribbean media were a mixture of government and private (including some Western-owned private organizations, and Rediffusion in particular), the new agency emerged as a privately based cooperative, which was nevertheless dependent for its continuing viability on the willingness of regional governments to buy the service for their respective ministries of information or foreign affairs.

A seeming paradox in the kind of advisory relationship between global and national agencies thus outlined is the fact that most of the agencies in receipt of consultancy assistance are government owned and in some respects often subscribe to different norms of news-gathering and news-distribution than those professed by the world agencies.

But a new national agency is a new client, and as such it contributes to the continued survival of the global agencies. A new national agency may also mean the introduction of improvements in the infrastructure of national news-gathering. Where there are few newspapers or other media, or where the existing media are also the media of the capital city serving only the urban population, a national news agency may represent the beginning of a geographically much more widespread coverage. This is sometimes best done by the government if in the absence of provincial media or even of provincial literacy it is probably only the government which has something to gain in the short term. It would be too pessimistic to rule out the possibility that in the long run the very existence of an adequate technical facility for news-gathering might help generate the needs and pressures that also stimulate the growth of non-government or at least critical media. In short, as the global agencies themselves might argue, some news is better than no news: helping a government-owned agency may be the only means of generating a regular news supply from some countries.

Governments must also be well informed to govern well. They need to be well informed about international news, and about their own country. The world agencies can claim to be helping them do just that through their programmes of assistance. A very substantial part of the activity of the world agencies is associated with the transmission of news about governments, and governments are among their most avid consumers. It might also be said on the other hand that the world agencies indirectly help support certain kinds of repressive government. But they do not help exclusively the same kind of government. The instances include one-party as well as multi-party states. They rarely, if ever, include communist agencies, but those agencies have help from elsewhere. The kind of assistance offered is in one sense infrastructural, in that its usefulness is not dependent on any particular policy. It does not extend the influence of the content of the world agencies, since their files would be available to these governments in any case. What it does represent however is the very considerable adjustment of world agency activities to the political constraints which many Third World countries impose on news-gathering by foreign media, so that in some senses the major part of world agency activity in Third World news-gathering is to do with the transmission of news already 'gathered' and selected by or with the approval of Third World governments via their controls over the respective national agencies. This in turn underlines the rhetorical character of much of the Third World complaint about the world agencies, although of course the global agencies are still not obliged to disseminate all or any of the approved news with which they are provided. But the possibility of critical news is much reduced. That the world agency news files still do not adopt a specifically Third World perspective in their treatment of news, or that they give far less play to all the issues and views which Third World governments might consider important, is still a source of grievance. But it is a sign of major change when an agency like AP, which has hitherto sought to avoid precisely the kind of concession which this seems to entail, enters into news-exchanges with agencies like TAP of Tunisia, the Nigerian News Agency, or Prensa Latina of Cuba, in order to secure at least a basic news supply from areas of the world to which Western access for the purpose of news-gathering has become highly arbitrary if not impossible.

General character of the agency nexus

The relationship between the world and national news agencies is of enduring significance to both parties. National agencies are invariably regarded as important sources of news by the global agencies; if they are not so regarded then that state of affairs is associated with a state of grievance by world agency journalists, mixed with a sense of professional (and cultural) triumph – a national agency which is not important as a news source for a global agency, the implication is, has no right to be a national agency.

Wherever there is a national agency, it is common for the bureau of the world agency in that country to subscribe to it, but in some cases the national agency service may not be received in the country itself. Most Eastern European national news agencies, for example, are not received by the global agencies at the points of origin, but are picked up in Vienna. At the height of the Cold War it was difficult to get correspondents into Eastern Europe at all, and so there was not always a local bureau at which local news services could be received; but it also suited the Eastern European governments to have their services picked up outside their own territories – it removed the apparent need in their eyes for correspondents actually to set foot in the countries they covered. And since Eastern Europe does not rank high in the news priorities of the world agencies, it is not uncommon for these countries to be literally considered as a 'block' to be viewed and covered from one perspective. Where national agency services are received by the world agencies outside the countries concerned, it may also be because it is cheaper for the world agencies to maintain a team of service monitors, and perhaps translators, at a point which is central in their own network. This is possible if the outgoing signals of the national (or international) agencies are sufficiently strong. To maintain an editing team in the capital of origin can sometimes be slower, especially where communications for global agency transmission to the nearest regional centre or to head office are inferior, or where agency dispatches must pass through a censor's office.

There are cases where national agencies do exist whose services are not taken by the global agencies. UPI, for instance, ceased in the mid-1970s to subscribe to some national agencies of French North Africa, which were not considered sufficiently newsworthy or trustworthy as sources, and did not always pay for the world services they received. In some cases national agency services are not taken because they are allied with world agency operations and therefore considered to be direct competitors. In the 1970s Reuters did not subscribe to AFP's domestic French service, for example, but it did have arrangements with smaller French agencies. Nor did Reuters subscribe to the domestic services of the US agencies or, in Germany, to DPA's domestic service. Needless to say, it would usually be possible for a world agency bureau to gain access to domestic services through its own clients or contacts if the need arose.

What can a world agency expect from a national agency? This varies considerably. The most comprehensive national agency services are those of the Western developed nations, which include the PA of Britain, Germany's DPA, and Italy's ANSA. The relative adequacy of these agencies, in the eyes of the world agency journalists, reflects the high development of print and broadcast media in such countries. This implies, therefore, that the best national agencies exist in countries where there are already sufficient alternatives to these agencies as news sources.

Where necessary, therefore, world agencies can survive in the absence of competent national agencies, because other media will normally be available as news sources. In other countries, however, the only reason for doing without a local national agency would be that it was thought to be too bad, not because there was any alternative. But were this to happen a world agency would not generally have the local resources to provide an adequate alternative for itself.

Governments may sometimes prefer to use broadcast media as national news outlets, and this may mean that the broadcast media will act as primary news sources for the world agencies. The usefulness of broadcast media in practice is often low by comparison: a national agency provides an immediate written record of an announcement or an event, whereas a broadcast station has to be monitored by the world agency, which must arrange to tape key bulletins. This consumes extra manpower, although both agency and broadcasts may sometimes be monitored. Radio may be more important than other media for a government which is communicating directly to its people, many of whom may not be reached by any alternative media-form; but in communicating with its own media or with those of other countries, a government will often find a national news agency to be a more sophisticated policy-communicating instrument.

A national news agency is an important news source in a number of different ways. In the first place it is a source of national news. 'National news' in many countries refers principally to news which refers to events of nation-wide significance or relevance. Thus the activities of a central government are as a general rule matters of national significance. Some national agencies in fact cater mostly for news of this kind only. Concentration on national news suits the world agencies admirably. Their focus is on news which is international in character, or on the salient 'national' events, news which reflects the nation-state character of international political divisions. There may be other suitable media (including national broadcast networks) which the world agencies can use as sources. But the chances are strong that the agency will be a primary source. The local broadcast station or the national newspaper frequently do not have as extensive a network of news-gathering resources as the national agency. But national agencies often fail to meet standards of competence as defined by professionals in the US and the UK for instance. But this does not necessarily make them useless as sources. If the national agency is a government agency, for example, and its news distribution is government controlled, it is still very often of value to the world agencies as a reliable source on government policies and activities and has the advantage of often being used as the initial channel for such communications. This is true of many countries, whether the agency is controlled or not, since it is sometimes easier for a government to talk to one rather than all media, especially on certain routine kinds of announcement.

And as Third World countries tend less and less to grant automatic access to Western media, it is a fact of life that national agencies are becoming increasingly important (though not in every case increasingly credible or competent) sources of news. In some instances the 'Big Four' agencies must evaluate the usefulness to them of maintaining bureaux in countries where, although formal access to the country is possible, practical access to news *sources* is withheld. Or they must increasingly weigh the advantages of maintaining a residential correspondent in a Third World country against those of relying on a national news agency and trusting that access will be granted to visiting reporters in the event of a news-crisis. If the national agency has been the benefactor of a world agency's consultancy or training programme, then the decision might be an easier one to take. Frequently, all these and other more strategic considerations are relevant. Examples of national agencies which play a very significant role as basic news suppliers to 'Big Four' agencies include the Ghana News Agency, which Reuters originally helped to develop and which was so consistently the major source of news in practice that Reuters ceased to maintain its own staff correspondents in Ghana and related to the national agency *as* its correspondent. The agency receives Reuters service messages for instance, which may carry requests or suggestions for further information on developing stories. Similarly, Reuters has a special relationship of this kind with the news agency of Zaire.

National agencies may be important to global agencies not only for news. In some countries they may employ a good proportion of all trained journalists, who can feed news to Westerners in a style and at a speed which resembles what many Western professionals tend to regard as journalism. Precisely for that reason they may be of more immediate or personal use to world agencies as stringers, or at least as news-contacts, than as representatives of a national agency. This may be the case where the agency is both quite strong and is also tied to the political machine, so that agency journalists enjoy high status as civil servants or party members. Their job means that they are quite well informed, whilst at the same time it also indicates they have a good deal of contact with other journalists, including foreign journalists. In some countries, especially the less developed nations, journalism is not seen as the distinct profession it is regarded as in the US or in UK but more as a way of life for a certain sector of the élite, where the frontiers of journalism with literature, art and politics are not clearly defined. In such a case the national agency journalist, especially at the senior level, might also be a potential dissident – his artistic aspirations, his close understanding of but not his direct involvement with the political élite (many members of which may be personally known to him), and his exposure to Western developments and ideas, all contributing to this possibility. A further indirect function of the national agency in its partnership with the world agency is its role as a location for local expertise in communications technology.

The national agencies are also of very great importance as clients or subscribers to global agency news services. Most national agencies pay considerably more to a global agency than they receive from a global agency for the sale of their national news services. The difference can be as much as 800%. In some cases, where domestic news-gathering operations are primitive or non-existent, the national agency exists for no other purpose than to receive and distribute to local media or government offices the edited versions of global agency services. It increasingly happens that the national agency is the only organization allowed by the government to receive the services of the world agencies. Sometimes the global agencies have no choice but to accept this arrangement, which occurs in countries where news is rigidly controlled and the national agency doubles as distributor and censor. It also occurs in countries where the local media are underdeveloped and cannot afford to take the global agencies singly or where there is severe shortage of foreign exchange reserves. Often they do not want the services of global agencies even if they could afford them because they do not want to handle that volume of wordage, or to employ monitors to watch the teleprinter for up to eighteen or twenty-four hours a day, and prefer a national agency which will distil the news for them. Even in the developed nations there is a tendency for national news agencies to distribute world agency services for provincial or non-metropolitan newspapers – this being a valuable market in bulk, but one which it would be difficult for a world agency to cultivate by itself. The national agency may also undertake the translation, if needed, into local languages, and if the revenue possibilities of a country are not particularly high then a world agency may prefer not to take responsibility for such a task.

It goes without saying that the world agencies are of considerable importance to the national agencies. The national agencies invariably distribute world news as well as domestic news, and their main source of world news is one or more of the world news agencies. This applies to the strongest national agencies just as much as to the weaker: strong national agencies of the intermediate kind may maintain sizeable overseas reporting staffs, but these are not exhaustive enough to substitute for the world agencies. DPA, for instance, in the late 1970s had bureaux and stringers in 80 countries and an overseas clientele of 144 clients, including 45 agencies, but took world news and photos from UPI. The primary reporting function for the intermediary agencies, and of course for the national agencies, is reporting for their home markets (a more singular requirement than in the case of the world agencies' relationship with their respective home markets), and whatever overseas markets they have are relatively small – the international news they cover is intentionally inclined to be filtered through national eyes. Second, they do not cover the world as comprehensively as the world agencies. Most tend to concentrate on the Western developed nations, or on particular regions of the world, and their foreign staff numbers are modest.

National agencies can and do use alternative sources to the world agencies, by monitoring foreign radio stations, for instance. In this case there is still an indirect dependence on the world agencies because the foreign radio stations will also take *their* news from the world agencies. Foreign radio is an original news source only for news of its source country, as a rule, although in some cases it may act as a useful source of news about events in neighbouring countries, and no national agency would be able to, or would want to, monitor all the radio stations of all the major powers when it could subscribe instead to a world agency service. However some of the major broadcasters like the BBC sell digests of monitored foreign radio programming. Another supplemental source is represented by other national news agency services. But these tend to share the same disadvantages as radio: they are good news sources only for news of the countries they individually represent, sometimes not even very good for that; and their foreign reporting strength in no way compares with that of the world agencies, is often hampered by lack of skill or government control, and the task of monitoring so many disparate sources is rarely considered worthwhile. However the development of cooperatives of national news agencies, as we shall see, represents a different kind of alternative.

Resistance and alternatives

The power of the world agencies has not altogether rested on the willing compliance of all the smaller agencies. Resistance to their power has been a common theme in the history of the world–national–agency relationship, and it is within this perspective that recent Third World ventures should also be seen. But resistance has rarely succeeded in establishing a viable alternative, and the degree of success seems closely related to the political power of the country or countries in which the contending agencies are based. The most striking examples of success have been the American agencies. AP challenged the dominance of the European triumvirate because its competitive edge on the home market was threatened by the independent foreign operations of its chief rival, UP. The prominence of these agencies on the world scene was truly established only after World War Two, in the wake of America's role in political and economic reconstruction of the Western world and the containment of communism, so that the American agencies joined the world agency 'club'.

The other notable examples of agencies which have achieved some substantial measure of independence from the flow of information provided them by the global agencies are those of West Germany and Japan, DPA and Kyodo respectively. These are the agencies of the two principal losers of the Second World War, countries which before that war had also maintained news agencies that had struggled for their own sphere of influence and which since the war have ranked among the economic giants.

The story of AP's disaffection is vividly described in Kent Cooper's book *Barriers Down*. AP joined the European cartel because it was an extremely convenient mode of foreign news collection, conserving the agency's resources for its primary objective, to satisfy the appetites of its domestic members for domestic news, while giving it an initial advantage in the competition with its domestic rivals.

These advantages were not permanent. The US rapidly developed its own cable networks across the globe and the cost of foreign news-gathering came to seem less onerous; the domestic competition,

UP, having to rely solely on its own foreign news collection, could argue that it was truly independent editorially whereas AP was not. For this very reason AP had to engage in its own reporting of overseas events, but was unable to recoup foreign news-gathering costs by foreign sales.

AP's main complaints against the cartel, then, were that it kept it out of foreign markets; that the European agencies could present American news disparagingly if they wished even though their clients had no access to alternative sources; and in any case they did not report enough American news, while they could present news of their own countries favourably.

AP's unhappiness was both commercial and diplomatic. It began to recognize that in a free trade situation it would do very well overseas, and one way to exploit this situation was to stress how the cartel system worked against the diplomatic interests of the United States and the interests of other countries dependent on the cartel.

AP's role in the breaking down of the oligopolistic system occurred first of all nearer to home than Europe – in South America. Its interest was excited by UP's success in signing up the Argentinian paper *La Nación* as a client, even though this paper had first of all approached AP whose chief, Melville Stone, soon to be replaced by Kent Cooper, had not reacted. UP's initial success was partly due to the distrust of some South American newspapers in the reporting of the opening of the European war by the French agency Havas. Since Havas and Reuters had the advantage of access to transatlantic communications which were under Allied control, the German agency could not distribute its own version.

When *La Nación* again approached AP after the war AP decided to approach Havas and negotiate for limited entry to the French agency's traditional South American market. Havas agreed, on condition that it received compensation for any financial loss, and in return for the use of AP's own service. Havas was banking on being able to maintain sales, while AP would be taken as a 'second' agency, and on being able to undercut AP rates if necessary, with the backing of the French government. In the meantime, access to AP's service allowed Havas to compare the respective performance of the two agencies. AP accepted these conditions because it did not want a clean break from the cartel: it still needed the cartel's supply of news of other parts of the world (especially those European countries of the cartel agencies), and did not want to provoke a battle with Reuters at this stage. AP also took over the news service for South America which previously had been run by the American Cable Co., at that time cooperating with the State Department to enlarge cable traffic with South America.

While in favour of breaking with the cartel, AP, like UP, had no objection to signing up deals with other agencies. In the Far East it won an exchange arrangement with the Japanese agency, Rengo, in defiance of Rengo's earlier agreement with Reuters. UP had already signed up a number of opposition agencies throughout the world and AP was possibly anxious not to lose out on the available supply. Reuters tried to dissuade AP from leaving the cartel by threatening to sign an alternative agreement with UP, thus reversing the tables between the American agencies. UP briefly considered the idea and then turned it down.

A 'free market' in news was formally achieved in 1933 with Reuters' reluctant but powerless consent; in Europe, as we have seen, neither American agency could make much headway in the domestic markets of the major European agencies. On a global scale, AP was a long way behind UP as news distributor. The real consequences of the pre-war victory were not to be evident until after the war.

Shifting centres of resistance

Leading centres of resistance to the global agencies before World War Two were primarily those agencies of countries which had pretensions to major political status in the world. The overseas activities of the German agency, Wolff, or Continental, had been restricted by the Allies after Germany's first defeat. But the Nazis created their own international news machinery: Trans-Ocean, which disseminated by radio, and DMB, which was a forced merger of previously existing agencies, notably Continental and TU. These affected Reuters and Havas in two ways: they distributed free of charge or at extremely low rates for propaganda purposes, and with the aid of state funds; and they deprived the old European agencies of subscriptions, thus further weakening them financially. Much the same was true of the Italian agency under Mussolini. In the Far East, the new Japanese agency Domei further encroached on already overcrowded markets to the added discomfort of Reuters. Even in friendlier regions, Australia, Canada, and South Africa, there were growing signs of media dissatisfaction with news services that seemed to reflect the interests of the British Empire rather than strict journalistic norms of impartiality. CP resisted attempts to oblige it to distribute Reuters in Canada; South African newspapers took over SAPA, which became an independent agency.

The efforts of the Fascist agencies were doomed to eventual failure, of course, because of their defeat in war. Elsewhere there was no serious attempt actually to do *without* the global agencies altogether: even TASS continued to exchange news for the services of the Western agencies. Then as now, the most common forms of attempting to control the influence of the Western agencies were, first, using a national agency (which if it did not exist was set up for the purpose) to distribute world agency services locally; and second, to threaten a change of allegiance from one world agency to another.

After the Second World War, the centres of resistance shifted to the Third World: Africa, Asia and South America, but with no notable success initially except for the New China News Agency, which developed its own foreign news-gathering resources, but continued to subscribe to or exchange services for Western agency news. Unlike TASS, the New China News Agency did not collect quite as loyal a string of client agencies as the Russian agency collected in Eastern Europe after the war. Its service was very likely to be only one of several sources of communist news for those national agencies depending mainly on such sources, but in its own country Hsin Hua became every bit as powerful as TASS.

Attempts to counteract dependence on the major agencies in the post-war period have taken a number of forms. The road to self-sufficiency in foreign news-gathering, as we have seen, has been seriously attempted only by agencies of the more affluent countries, and in practice all continue to receive one or more of the major agency services. By far the most common attempt to counteract the power of the major agencies has been to concentrate the reception, editing and local distribution of their services into the hands of one national agency. This has detracted still further from the opportunity for editorial diversity without adding very much in its place except the possibility of national political censorship. Censorship of course rather than diversity has increasingly been the issue and the aim, its justification couched in language of discontent concerning the sins of omission and commission of the Western media with respect to the non-Western world. Nationalization of information flow, it has been alleged, facilitates developmental goals and political stability.

The response of some Third World countries to questions of news supply, however, has become a great deal less negative in recent years. There has, for example, been an enormous increase in bi-lateral news-exchange agreements between national news agencies. Of potentially greater significance have been those attempts to establish regional news agencies, based on one strong or at least ambitious national agency, or, more frequently, involving cooperation between news agencies of the region. The Ghana News Agency, founded in 1957, for example, attempted under Nkrumah to develop into a Pan-African news agency and established bureaux (often in embassy buildings) in several African capitals, London and New

York. This ambition did not overcome neighbouring suspicions, nor did it survive internal political instability. But it did help establish GNA as a relatively powerful national agency, and as an important local news source for the world agencies. In the wake of the Non-Aligned News Agencies Pool, the Pan-African idea has more recently been adopted by the OAU, under whose auspices a secretariat for the establishment of such an agency was established in Kampala in 1977 to organize regional pools of news. This was a parallel development to the setting up of the Nigerian News Agency, without which many felt that a Pan-African agency would not be feasible. Formation of the Pan-African agency was said by Nigeria's agency director in 1978 to have been obstructed by the lack of proper telecommunication links.[8] In Latin America and Asia, meanwhile, the establishment of the non-aligned pool gave further force to longstanding proposals for regional inter-governmental news agencies, reiterated at UNESCO conferences in the late 1970s. In South America, where regional news agencies already existed for the Carribean and the Central American republics, the existing regional agency, Latin, was too closely associated with conservative publishers, some critics argued, and with Reuters news agency, and not sufficiently adaptable to national developmental objectives. In 1979, however, ten Latin American and Caribbean nations formed ASIN (Action by National Information Systems) to provide daily interchanges of information, and to be the base of a hemisphere-wide news agency. In Asia the completion of the Asian satellite Telecom Highway, connecting fifteen countries from Iran to Indonesia, certainly seemed to pave the way for greater agency coordination. In the Middle East, Egypt's news agency, MENA, had made a bid under Nasser to become a regional news agency (as its name implies) and established bureaux in several African, Asian, Middle Eastern and European capitals. Although this foreign representation was later reduced the agency became an important news source for other agencies in the region and for the world agencies, with whom it established fairly cordial relations (for example, translating AFP's service into Arabic). In 1977 it described itself as a clearing and distributing house for all the Arab news agencies.[9] The following year it sponsored a proposal, in association with Cairo University, and the Edward R. Murrow Centre at Tufts University, backed by a US media foundation, the Twentieth Century Fund, for the creation of a Multinational News Agency (MNA) to improve reporting from Third World countries.[10] In this choice of alignment MENA appeared to place itself in the camp opposing attempts from within UNESCO to legitimate government nationalization of information flows. But MENA also cooperated with NANA. MENA is founder member of the

Arab News Agencies Federation,[11] the African News Agencies Federation, and a member of the Islamic News Agencies Federation. While these titles might suggest a status not commensurate with their actual achievements, such federations have grown in number in recent decades, existing to review common policy objectives in such matters as telecommunications, technical developments, training and news-exchange.

Indeed, one of the strongest of such regional alliances is the European Alliance, sometimes known as 'Group 39'. This originated in 1939 out of an agreement between the agencies of Finland, Sweden, Norway, Denmark, Holland, Belgium, Switzerland and Austria, in an effort to set up an alternative source of news to the agencies of the major powers. After the war it expanded to include Spain, Portugal, France, England, West Germany, Italy, Yugoslavia, Greece and Turkey, and in 1970 it included some of the Warsaw Treaty countries, namely Bulgaria, Czechoslovakia, East Germany, Poland, the Soviet Union and Hungary. The significance of the group does not depend primarily on news exchanges. Such information is only infrequently of help to other member agencies, who can obtain their normal diet of European news from the global agencies. The alliance is helpful sometimes when a member wants special coverage of an event in the country of another member, but there is little consistency in the speed with which a request of this kind will be met or the quality of coverage, since each member agency is generally fully employed on coverage of its own country for domestic subscribers. More significant is the agreement between the agencies to cooperate in technical developments involving communications, and in protecting their joint interest in the free flow of information between their countries.

It is quite apparent, therefore, that the idea of cooperation between national agencies to reduce dependence on the world agencies, to supplement their news diets and to promote mutual aid and discussion is hardly a novelty in either the developed or the developing worlds. The excitement temporarily generated by the establishment of a non-aligned Pool in 1976 at the non-aligned countries' summit, had much to do with the simultaneously developing (but formally unrelated) struggle in UNESCO on the issue of the 'free' flow of information: by attempting to become more self-sufficient it was feared that Third World countries might be even further encouraged to restrict news access for Western journalists. The director of the Pool's most active participating agency, Tanjug of Yugoslavia,* has argued that without the 'Big Four' agencies, 'the

* Tanjug's expansion of its foreign coverage in the 1970s and its active role in the establishment of the non-aligned news agencies' pool may be seen at least in

Yugoslav press and every other news media could never provide the scope and detail of international news coverage that it does, regardless of the development of its own foreign correspondents and its bilateral news exchanges with other national news agencies'.[12] But in the same article he went on to say that 'our vision of the new information order does not mean *simply* replacing the existing world-wide wire services or *merely* improving the balance in their news products, *albeit this is a welcome first step*. What is needed is to elaborate a complete system, at the bilateral, regional and multilateral levels, for enabling a multidimensional news flow'[13] (my italics). But at the time this article was published the survey evidence suggested that only seven countries contributed 60% of the total news pool content.[14] Like most of the post-war attempts to reduce dependence on the 'Big Four' agencies, the Pool is clearly limited by its inter-governmental character, with its implications of political fragility in instances of tension and conflict, and government sensitivity to whatever is transmitted and redistributed. While almost half of its content is of developmental relevance, it is important to determine more precisely what is meant by developmental news and to investigate the most appropriate modes of collection and dissemination of such news in relation to the audiences for whom it is intended or from whom there is either an explicit or implicit demand. Stricter specification of what is meant by developmental news might also help generate improved supply, from both existing 'Big Four' agencies and from regional exchange pools.

But apart from the kind of innovations represented by the non-aligned Pool and other regional exchanges, there have been other important, though maybe more familiar, features in the world of international news in the mid to late 1970s. These have included the considerable number of consultancy arrangements between 'Big Four' agencies and national news agencies; the generally very high national agency consumption of 'Big Four' news, by comparison with their consumption of news from alternative sources; the endeavours of Western media foundations, governments etc. to help sponsor aid projects for media of the developing world; and continuous improvements of 'Big Four' operations that go some of the way to answering some of the criticisms from the Third World.

---

part as a response to a declining domestic influence in the early 1970s. This arose because domestic media were allowed to set up their own teams of foreign correspondents and to subscribe directly to external agencies. But because they tended to concentrate their correspondents in the capitals of the more developed countries, they were especially reliant on Tanjug for news of other regions. One way of fostering the growth of such news was through the encouragement given to the principle of news exchange between non-aligned countries.

While the long-term market interests of 'Big Four' agencies have not been seriously affected, the overriding concerns of these agencies (whose revenue from the Third World is slight in any case) has been the problem of access to Third World countries, and the price they have had to pay in terms of news quality to secure and maintain such access. These problems may do greater eventual damage to the agencies' reputation in the developed world (as sources of world news) than they have yet suffered in the developing world. In the meantime the prospect of any privately owned venture rivalling the 'Big Four' in scope seems very distant, even on a regional base. But two unusual experiments require a mention.

One of these was the short-lived Asian News Agency (ANS) whose demise in March 1973 after eighteen months' operation as a teleprinter-distributed general news service is instructive of the difficulties involved. The agency was run and staffed by Asian journalists, and produced some remarkable editorial copy. The reasons for its demise were principally economic: insufficient capital to cover losses in the first few years, and insufficient executive experience. But there was also a shortage of interested newspaper clients. The papers which most needed ANS were perhaps the very papers which found it so difficult to pay for such a service – the poor vernaculars, rather than the wealthier English-language and Western-oriented papers of the major Asian capitals. Communication costs were considerable. Since ANS leased its wires from Reuters, it could not hope for priority at a time of news crisis, but a time of crisis was precisely the time it needed to be able to demonstrate its capacity for speed as well as for hard copy. Another difficulty affecting speed was that the language of the service was English, the lingua franca of the region, but English was not the first tongue of the correspondents, who could not therefore operate quite as smoothly in it as Western correspondents. Finally, some correspondents did entertain nationalistic prejudices which seemed to affect the agency's image in other countries.

A more successful venture has been the Inter Press Service, established in 1964 for the reciprocal transmission of development information between Latin America and South European governments.[15] When many of its contracts were suspended in the late 1960s and early 1970s as support for reformist change declined, the agency, cooperatively owned by its journalists, developed a more coherent and oppositional ideology involving support for Third World democracy, social and internal justice, and 'real national sovereignty over national resources, including such cultural resources as information and communication'. Its primary revenue source appeared in 1979 to come from Tanjug, which distributed its Spanish report to Latin America through IPS, and similar arrangements with other agencies, including the Cuban agency Prensa Latina. It distributed non-aligned Pool material from the Tunisian agency, TAP (North African regional centre for the Pool) to Tanjug, and the material of the Venezuelan agency, Venpress, and Iraqi agency, INA, to other Pool members. It also received and distributed the material of the agencies of Mozambique and Libya. But IPS remained predominantly a Latin-American and Spanish-language agency. Whereas its Latin-American centre at Buenos Aires transmitted 48,000 words a day, the European centre in Rome distributed only 18,000 words a day. Most of the bureaux were based in Latin America. Whereas the Spanish-language service was distributed for sixteen hours a day, the English and Arabic services were distributed for only five hours a day each. Most of the countries linked with IPS and most of its four hundred clients were Spanish-speaking. And of the Spanish transmissions, two-thirds were written by IPS journalists (it claimed two hundred full-time journalist staff), and one-third by national news agency sources. Its clear espousal of the Third World developmental cause, and its links with some of the leading socialist members of the news Pool, have predictably limited its impact on the spot-news oriented 'Big Four' agencies and Western media.

Experiments such as those represented by ANS and IPS suggest that major improvements with regard to the Third World news issue, outside any improvements adopted by the 'Big Four' agencies themselves, may come from the growing number of specialist feature agencies, not in direct competition with the 'Big Four' and not actually dependent on as sophisticated a distribution system (although IPS distributes by satellite to teleprinter outlets for its major services). Agencies such as London's Gemini news services for the Third World, or the development-oriented DepthNews service of the Asian Press Foundation, are other instances. But one source of further competition here could be among the range of freely-distributed government information services of the major powers which have wide experience and relatively generous support for such activities, and which also enjoy the ironic advantage of at least being known quantities so far as their ideological and material interests are concerned.

6
New markets, new methods, conflict and risk

The news agencies are commonly associated with newspaper markets in the public imagination: it is only through newspapers that most members of the public are likely to see agency credits. Since newspaper interests have a controlling share in the ownership and management of three of the 'Big Four' agencies, and of the management of the fourth, such an association is very reasonable. But all the agencies are also deeply involved in other markets; indeed, for one agency the newspaper market itself initially represented a form of diversification. Diversification is fundamentally of three kinds: providing services for news media other than newspapers; non-traditional kinds of service for newspapers; and non-media client services. Total reliance on traditional services for newspaper markets was clearly unsatisfactory: left to themselves newspapers were volatile clients, highly cost-conscious, potentially weak in 'brand' loyalty. Competition between the agencies stunted revenue growth in relation to costs. For these reasons the agencies early on strived to retain clients and restrict competition by news-exchange and cartel practices, by which means they at least secured their affluent domestic markets. The breakdown of the cartel system hastened the necessity for diversification. But with the development of alternative news media and the relative decline in newspaper growth, intra-media diversification would have happened anyway. The competition between AP and UPI in the US and the relatively unfettered growth of US broadcast media led the American agencies to concentrate their attention on this market sooner than the European agencies. The European agencies, on the other hand, with more limited domestic newspaper markets, became from a much earlier date involved in non-media diversification – economic services mainly in the case of Reuters, and advertising in the case of Havas. The discredit which the advertising activities earned for Havas severely restricted the formulation of a constitution for its successor, AFP, forcing it further into the cushion of government support, itself a different kind of non-media diversification. Reuters, by contrast, having toyed with the idea of a government connection, and experienced the limited benefits of media ownership, came to rely increasingly on the finance market for economic services. In recent years the American agencies have become more attracted to this particular non-media market, while the European agencies, especially Reuters, increased their activity in the area of intra-media diversification.

The distinction between media and non-media markets lies firstly in the nature of the clientele, not the service. The same service may go to both media and non-media clients; for instance, a basic news service may be taken by both an independent newspaper and a government department. But increasingly, with the sophisticated specialist economic news services backed up with equally sophisticated systems of delivery hardware, the distinction is reflected in differences in the nature of the service provided. It is also reflected in the use to which the respective client groupings put the service. A media client typically takes the service with a view to retailing it, in some form or other, for mass markets. A non-media client on the other hand buys the agency service for its own private use, distributing it for the use of its own employees/clients. Both groups may employ the service for their own organizational or individual gain, although in the case of a government department the gain is less likely to be commercial. However, while the basic distinction is useful, it is not exclusive.

The most common example of an organization that is both media and non-media is the government-controlled news agency or broadcast station. Such instances will differ in the extent to which that control is direct. But it is of significance especially with the development of both news agencies and broadcast media in the Third World, whose very raison d'être is formally couched in a vocabulary of collectivism, the need for national ideological and socio-economic growth. This means that increasingly the 'Big Four' agencies in their Third World markets are negotiating with organizations whose survival is dictated not by popular taste but by acquiescence in government-conferred objectives, a completely different model of operation. This enormously heightens the overt political context of 'Big Four' agency operations, and may have the effect of requiring 'Big Four' agencies to increase costs in servicing Third World markets without corresponding increases in revenue, which must add to the pressure of formulating survival strategies in the markets of the developed world.

There have been four major categories of non-media client in the history of the agencies: finance and commercial institutions; advertising agencies or advertisers; government ministries and departments; and 'private' clients. Again, these clients are not mutually exclusive. Governments can be advertisers, governments can control banks. Finance and commercial institutions can also be advertisers. But the usefulness of the category 'advertiser' in the case of the 'Big Four' agencies is restricted largely to the experience of Havas, which was related in Chapter 2, and serves as a reminder of the potential use of agencies as machines for propaganda. Even today, some critics imply that the agencies, in devoting a considerable proportion of their news-gathering resources to the routine coverage of government activities, largely dependent on government sources, do assist governments in the fulfilment of their objectives in ways which belie the agencies' formal claim to neutrality. The category of 'private' client is a residual category covering not just individuals, but hotels, clubs, educational institutions, collectively not as important as the other categories. Intra-media diversification covers both the introduction of significantly new kinds of service to newspapers, and the development of services to media other than newspapers. Within the newspaper market the most important developments have concerned the sophistication of delivery systems, from regular teleprinter delivery to digital transmission and computer-based television outlets with keyboard facilities for on-screen editing (agencies were among the first big media adopters of such technology). Well before this the American agencies pioneered sophisticated systems for the automatic transmission of photographs for newspaper subscribers, which by the late 1970s included a laser-based transmission system and on-screen photo-editing. The agencies have also greatly increased the extent to which they provide access to their communications facilities for their newspaper and news agency clients. For their broadcast clients they have introduced not just tailored teleprinter services, but also voicecasts and news-film or video for television.

While intra-media diversification does raise problems of conflict of interest, these are not so fundamental as with non-media diversification. The development of broadcast markets initially seemed to conflict with the interests of traditional newspaper clients, who feared the competition of broadcast media. The development of a large government-based clientele clearly involves broader issues that reflect on the credibility of the service itself, and the agency's pliability in face of pressure from news sources.

The important feature of the American domestic market was that the media were plentiful and affluent enough not to tempt the agencies in this direction. Reuters was able to find an alternative non-media solution. Overseas, avoidance of dependence on government-based revenues is less easy, which is one thing to be said in favour of high dependence on domestic non-government sources of revenue, again possible in the case of the US agencies. Diversification in the direction of finance institutions, as in the case of Reuters, poses somewhat different problems, which have to do with the allocation of organizational priorities and how this affects the development or the maintenance of the general news service.

The economic news services: Reuters

The agencies define their activities in the rhetoric of service, and they quite clearly perform an enormously important public service. But this should not be allowed to obscure their concern for revenue. In the early days of the agencies it was not the spirit of service that prevailed so much as the spirit of business enterprise. It is necessary to see the European agencies therefore as the inventions of entrepreneurs, and their expansion as the application of business acumen and the shrewd eye. This is manifest in innumerable ways: the personalities of the founders, the first location of their offices, the character of their first clients, the stress on the gathering of economic news, and the general character of their entrepreneurial activities.

Reuters and Havas were conceived as business operations, and the origins of both lie in the demand for financial intelligence from an increasingly international European business community. Charles Havas had a background in contracting and banking before he started his agency, and business clients were among his most important in the first eight years of the agency's life. First location for L'Agence Havas was close to the Bourse de Commerce in Paris. Julius Reuter worked in banking before establishing his first service of commercial news in Paris and his first London office was established in the Royal Exchange Building (Stock Exchange) where he installed one of his first correspondents. For the first seven years of the agency's history the most important clients were financiers and merchants, who took a service that was primarily economic. Dr Bernhard Wolff first specialized in commercial news to brokers and businessmen, and later added general and political news; Wolff's agency (Wolff's Telegraphisches Büro–Corti Nachrichten Büro) was supported by both the Prussian government and banking houses. The first exchange agreement in the history of the three major European agencies was for an exchange of news of Bourse and trading activities.

Economic news generated more speed in the activity of journalists in those days than anything else except war. Competition in the sale of economic news was intense: it was the reason why Reuter left the continent of Europe and came to London. Even as the relative importance of non-media clients for economic news declined, he expanded the agency's involvement in alternative revenue-promoting fields of only incidental relevance to general news-gathering. Economic intelligence was also one of the agency's major attractions to the English press. One reason why *The Times* was last of all Fleet Street papers to subscribe to Reuters was because it had its own service of market prices; one of the first advantages of a subscription to Reuters that attracted *The Times* was the possibility of an American money service. Reuters' most important and earliest groups of clients in Eastern Europe, India and South America were generally merchants. Before South America was signed over to Havas, Reuters ran a commercial service between Rio de Janeiro and the main continental markets. In Australia the market for economic news and the private telegram service was more profitable than newspapers. Much later, when Reuters switched to radio from cable, the first wireless services dealt in commercial news, followed by general news services some eight or nine years afterwards.

All this raises the question: why did Reuters move into general news at all? The requirements of financial and economic news clients also favoured a general news service, since the two were not always to be distinguished. General news was a means of public legitimation for a German national who was sometimes considered with suspicion by the London Establishment although he had already converted to Christianity. Newspapers were an obvious secondary market; and they were an excellent advertisement. They were also rather more exciting and prestigious. One of Reuter's early colleagues, Sigismund Englander, who did much to build up the continental service and who had a reputation as a political radical, encouraged Reuter to take political news seriously. Finally, growing interest in general news was encouraged by cheaper telegraph rates, which allowed for wordier dispatches.

Baron Reuter had other business interests. One of the most successful of these was the private telegram business. The agency created its own codes to allow for exceptionally cheap transmission of private messages. Other ventures were not so successful: he bid for a concession from the Shah of Persia to build a railway from the Caspian Sea to the Persian Gulf, and to operate it for seventy years. Otherwise ill-fated, this venture had one favourable outcome. In satisfaction of his claims for indemnity for his initial outlay in the railway project, Baron Reuter was given the right to found the Imperial Bank of Persia, of which he was to become one of the directors. In 1891 this bank advanced a large loan to the Persian Government and was to play an important part in stabilizing the country's finances before the First World War. One especially blatant instance of the Baron's shrewdness in business dealings occurred in 1870, when he secured the exorbitant sum of £726,000

New markets, new methods, conflict and risk

from the state for his sale of the Norderney Cable – which had cost him £153,000 in 1866.

Neither Reuter nor Havas, Storey tells us, were above accepting a few subventions to help pay the costs of communication. For twenty-five years, each agency received a thousand pounds a year from the Khedive of Egypt towards the expense of cabling messages to and from the Egyptian government. The Viceroy of India used to pay Reuters the transmission costs for some of his speeches to be telegraphed home to England. In turn, Reuters was of quite considerable importance to some of the telegraph companies. A report of the Indian Telegraph Administration of 1888 during the Afghan war said that its increased revenue was due mainly to 'the length and frequency of Reuter messages'.

Although Reuter tried and failed to purchase a share in Havas agency in 1874, he later set up a comparative venture to offset mounting deficits in the general news operation. But the Reuters Advertisement Branch, established in 1891, had little success. The telegraph remittance operation, however, which involved the cabling of money, compensated for the losses incurred by the advertising venture, and contributed greatly to the overall profitability of the agency. In 1912 a Reuters' Bank was founded – the 'British Commercial Bank'. Capital from this venture was also employed in the setting up of a Reuters Financial Publicity Department, which met with strong opposition from both the press and regular advertising agents, and was later closed. The telegram traffic department also closed down in 1915 after a prohibition which applied to all private cabling codes. This jeopardized the bank by rendering unstable Reuters' main source of profits at the time, and created the conditions in which a new private company, inspired by Herbert Reuter's successor, Roderick Jones, was formed to take over Reuters. The company was later bought by Roderick Jones, who in any case put in much of the capital, and the bank was sold.

Commercial news continued to be important after the First World War, although the agency's image was much more bound up with its general news services. The principal non-media activities after all had folded; and under new ownership, the agency's strategy changed. It sought security through respectability. This took several forms, most important of them being the fostering of good relations with the government by placing at its disposal the agency resources for a service of Allied communiqués and official news to neutral countries, British Empire and Allied troops. The service was financed by the government, which paid transmission costs at the rate of £120,000 per annum. The second cornerstone of the new strategy was to involve the press more closely in Reuters' activities. Roderick

Jones initiated a scheme which brought the Press Association into part-ownership of the agency in 1925.

Security lay in Reuters' future as an accepted part of the British Establishment while retaining its reputation for impartiality: a difficult course to steer, and not a successful policy. Although it may have compromised its independence in relation to the government, Reuters was not able to benefit from huge subsidies, as the continental agencies had done, without alienating its newspaper clients and weakening its credibility. Yet overseas clients, perceiving the pro-imperial bias, assumed there was a massive government subsidy. Had there been one it would be difficult to explain just why Reuters lost ground so calamitously during the inter-war period in most parts of the world where before it had been dominant. There were some government connections of course, and a great deal of government sympathy, which might have threatened to become substantial had not World War Two and the British national press intervened. The policy of having the agency's costs underwritten by the British and Commonwealth press, in its turn, was unsatisfactory. These newspapers did not make that amount of money. To rely on government support was inconceivable, both to Reuters staff and to the British press as a whole, and probably not desirable even to the government. What in fact emerged was a partial return to the original supremacy of the economic services.

The place of the economic services as an important revenue earner had been displaced by the comparative but temporary success of the private telegram and telegram remittance activities which, according to Fleetwood May, were the 'bread and butter, while the revered news service was the marmalade'. They disappeared after World War One. The commercial service, meanwhile, 'continued to exist, but only in an extremely under-privileged condition'.[1]

The essence of the commercial service was the reporting of market quotations, evidently not considered an especially noteworthy exercise, and situated up a spiral staircase in the roof of the Old Jewry office, 'looked down upon, despite its elevated position, by the literate on the news desk'. Then as now the commercial service actually embraced a number of different packages for different markets. For instance: the Commodities Service concentrated on rubber prices for Singapore, wheat for Sidney and cotton for Bombay; there were also services in trade, American markets and foreign exchange, and there was a wireless commercial service. The first use of wireless by Reuters was for the commercial service. It was no coincidence that the head of Reuters Commercial Service in the 1920s was also wireless manager.

Well before the Second World War, therefore, the economic

services had developed considerably, and in directions related to current structure, but they later came to have even greater significance; partly because they became more important in revenue terms, but also because they became more respectable. Pre-war fears about conflicts of interest were now actively set aside. The economic services were seen instead as the vital contribution which maintained Reuters as a truly independent news organization. The post-war years were therefore ones of intensive activity in this sphere, in part matching the growing interest of media in economics news but mainly in response to the huge demand for economic information in the non-media market.

Post-war expansion began with two important developments that greatly broadened the international character of Reuters' commercial news-gathering operations. In 1946 Reuters bought up a specialist economic agency in Latin America – Comtel – by which name the economic services were to be known until the mid-1960s. This was the main product of Reuters' activity in the old Havas markets in Latin America during World War Two. One of the principal figures responsible for the development of Comtel under Reuters was Alfred Geringer, who later founded his own profitable commercial service in London – Universal News Services (UNS). After Comtel came a joint operation with the new West German agency established in 1949, DPA, for German economic news. Third partner in this operation, Vereinigte Wirtschaftsdienst (VWD) was the German Federation of Industry.

Expansionary activity increased greatly in the early 1960s, after the succession to the position of general manager of Gerald Long, who firmly believed in the importance of the economic services. He believed it was necessary for Reuters to adopt an explicit marketing strategy, in opposition to its reliance on the old 'service' image.[2] This way it could fend for itself without resort to direct or indirect government support, or dependence on a national press which itself was entering a time of financial difficulty.

Coincident with the expansion of economic services was an extraordinary increase in communications capacity as a result of the introduction and exploitation of the telephonic cable, and multiplex lines. Not only did communication capacity increase but the relative cost of communication per unit message was tending to decrease in real terms. This was an excellent time for increasing existing service volume, if desirable, or for creating new services.

Another sign of the rising star over economic services was the Reuters deal in 1964 with Ultronic Systems, an operating unit of the General Telephone and Electronics Information Corporation (GTE) of New York. The deal gave Reuters the world rights outside of the

H

United States to Ultronic's market quotation interrogation and display systems, and it marked the entry of Reuters into the field of computerized services.

Comtelburo was renamed in 1966 as Reuters Economic Services (RES), identifying the economic services closely with the Reuters trademark. Economic services were no longer to be considered an embarrassing sideline. With 'Stockmaster', a product of the Reuters Ultronic deal, and similar offerings, the character of these services greatly changed in image. Stockmaster was described in the advertising literature as a 'desk-top unit which at the push of a few buttons provides the subscriber with an up-to-the-minute quotation of any one of the more than 10,000 stock or commodity prices on the main United States, Canadian and some European Stock and Commodity Exchanges'. A client could ask for a particular market price, or the maximum or minimum price of a stock in the previous 24 hours' trading. Interrogation possibilities became progressively more sophisticated. Further computer-based services, such as Customprice and Videomaster, were soon added. Videomaster, which began in 1969, introduced the principle of video-display of stock and commodity exchange quotations on world markets. It was a typewriter-sized information display and retrieval unit combining keyboard and videoscreen. It could give eighteen pieces of information about any selected stock simultaneously, or monitor the last sale price of up to eighteen chosen stocks, or give warning when a particular stock reached the high or low price limit the subscriber had set on it.

The growth of computer services was accompanied by an equally rapid development of teleprinter services in the economic field: e.g. the Reuter Commodity Report, covering speculative American commodities; Reuter–Agefi in Europe, in partnership with the French financial paper Agefi (Agence Economique et Financière); and, in Switzerland, the Swiss Bourse ticker, designed to meet the needs of Swiss banks for domestic financial information. All this was in addition to 'basic' RES teleprinter services which included a mixture of comprehensive commodity and finance services for different world markets.

Depression in the early 1970s affected the economic services and may have reduced their rate of growth as activity on stock markets declined drastically. But at least one new service was designed to offset even this obstacle to profit. The innovation was the Monitor Service, launched in the summer of 1973, on the strength of a Eurocurrency facility of £800,000 raised from Reuters' principal bankers. Reuters' Monitor provided immediate and direct access to the money market rates of leading world banks. The service was unique in the sense that whereas stock and commodity markets had centralized dealing floors, this was not true of the money market – in a sense the Reuters' Monitor was the dealing floor. In the mid to late 1970s, the Reuters Monitor Services proved the most spectacular growth area, followed by other video-display economic services such as Videomaster. Growth in teleprinter services was not as rapid. Media markets (apart from CATV in the US) were the most sluggish. By greatly increasing the number of Reuters' overall foreign subscribers the new economic services also greatly increased the extent to which Reuters was aided by the effective depreciation of sterling against such currencies as dollars, deutschmarks and Swiss francs in which a high percentage of business was done (although the pound rose high against the dollar in 1979). Most of the expansion in editorial strength around the world in this period took place in the economic service.

The introduction of computer-based services and the general development of the economic news field had several important features. First of these was the extremely rapid rate of adoption of these innovations, heralding a period of development, structural change and a new dimension of executive decision-making in the agency business. Stockmaster was introduced to the leading countries of Europe within its first two years; by 1967 it was in Asia and South America. The number of Stockmaster units in service increased from 2,000 in June 1969 to 12,578 in 1971. The number of Videomaster units increased from 300 in 1969 to 24,000 in 1974. Reuters' Monitor Service reached 500 subscribers in 1975 and 1,738 in 1977, and acquired a further 3,400 clients by 1979.

Expansion involved *increasing interdependence* with other agencies, economic news media, and finance institutions. Much more than in the general news field, RES expanded through the development of exchange agreements for the purpose of distribution, greatly increasing and complicating its institutional links with the very nerve-centres of capitalism. The 1964 deal with Ultronics was the first major example. The expansion of Customprice was another: it was made available through Extel's Focus Service in the UK, the Boersen–Daten–Zentrale (BDZ) in West Germany, Investors Management Services (IMS) in North America, and Nihon Keizai Shimbun in Japan. These organizations sometimes allowed Reuters exclusive distribution of their services on the world market, in return for exclusive rights to the distribution of Compustat. Some of the leading agencies and institutions directly associated with Reuters through the distribution of RES services included Cosmo in Switzerland, owned by Reuters; VWD in West Germany (up to 1978), ANETA, the Dutch national agency which also serviced Belgium and Luxemburg;

Comtelsa in Spain, a joint venture with the Spanish economic news agency; Radicor, a subsidiary of the Italian national agency, ANSA; and the national agencies in the Scandinavian countries. Reuters developed similar arrangements with associate agencies in India, Pakistan, Burma, Cambodia, Indonesia, South Vietnam, South Korea, Japan, Australia and New Zealand, Egypt, Turkey, and others. Needless to say, some arrangements, such as those with Cambodia or South Vietnam, have been affected by political developments since.

Expansion also tended to increase *concentration of activity in the developed world markets*. The character of these developments in RES inevitably confirmed and increased the extent to which news-gathering and news-distribution functions were concentrated in the developed Western world. The two most active markets for RES services were North America and Europe in the early 1970s. An earlier chapter examined the role of RES in establishing Reuters as an independent force in North America. By 1969, RES was trading in every European country with the exception of Albania and Iceland. Three main European profit centres were the UK, France and Switzerland (France accounted for about 10% of all RES revenue). Even then, computerized services accounted for 55% of RES profit in Europe. Other important revenue centres included the wealthiest countries of other world regions, notably South Africa and Japan. Although RES services consumed a great deal of technical and routine editorial activity, the number of real news-gatherers for RES – journalists who literally go out to get the news – was relatively small, amounting for instance to only ten or eleven in continental Europe in 1971. Most news-gathering, as opposed to news-processing, could be done by general news journalists, or was fed into the computers electronically from source. In some major bureaux where economic news was generated in as much volume as general news, the activities of general and economic news editing were closely integrated. Such editorial integration was one reason given in the advance notice of the transfer of Reuters' Asian general news centre from Singapore to join the RES centre in Hong Kong in 1980, and in December 1979 the integration of all economic and general news activity outside North America was formally announced.

The main data centres for Reuters services in the mid-1970s were located in the US, Europe, Australia, the Far East and South Africa. Of 25 stock exchanges covered by Videomaster in 1974, 12 were located in North America, 5 in Germany, and the others were in London, Paris, Milan, Amsterdam, Brussels, Zurich, Tokyo, and Sydney. The growth of personnel as a result of RES expansion therefore tended to occur in those centres which were best covered by the general news services in any case, and thus intensified the structural imbalance in favour of the news requirements of the Western world.

Most clients were non-media clients, because these services were not designed for media consumption. Clients included corporate treasurers of multinational companies, commercial banks, government treasuries and foreign exchange dealers and brokers. Banks were the single most important type of client for RES services.

The system was extremely flexible in catering for specific regional needs where necessary. In the Far East, at first, Stockmaster services had to be regional in content. World-wide services were not sufficiently in demand, nor was there sufficient communications capacity. The consequence was the development of regional economic service teams, based in Hong Kong and Singapore. But in 1978 editing of international economic services was reorganized to allow control of the operation to move between Hong Kong, London and New York according to time of day. The teleprinter services were also greatly regionalized.

Growth of RES brought about a *change of relationship between economic and general news services*. Development of the economic services increased the size of RES in terms of personnel, and accentuated its importance in relation to the general news division. In 1966 a new RES bureau was opened in Chicago, anticipating the break with Dow Jones, and preparing for a massive commodities newsgathering operation in North America's largest commodities centre. Expansion of economic services in North America was the main impetus behind the opening of Canadian bureaux for the first time in 1975. New bureaux were opened in Australia – Canberra (1969) and Perth (1970) – where previously AAP had been the main news source (but AAP distributed Stockmaster services in Australia). There were nine staffers covering Australian markets in Sydney and Melbourne, and further expansion was expected. By 1973 some 70% of the agency's revenue could be traced to economic services, and a large proportion of this was from non-media clients; this had increased to 85% in 1978.

The rapid growth of RES changed the structure of the British agency, and employee perceptions of it. In particular, the growth of RES was related to the expansion of Reuters in North America, with the result that in 1974 Reuters North America became a separate division.[3] The revenue generated by RES made the general news service look very unprofitable by comparison, even if it did contribute to RES output. So in the new alignment of 1974 general news became a 'cost centre' (with the title of Reuters World Services – a major input for the 'profit' centres, which were North America, media services, economic services – but which was not itself considered in terms of profitability). In this way, it was hoped, the traditional image of the organization and the centrality of general news journalism would be restored. But world services (general news) remained a relatively 'no-growth' area by comparison with RES. A contraction of the executive board in 1977 meanwhile removed specific representation of the World Services and the Economic Services (leading to the resignation of the World Services chief editor Jonathan Fenby), with the effect of weighting the board in favour of those directly concerned with issues of cost and profitability, but was accompanied by the appointment of an Editor-in-Chief (Michael Reupke) in charge of all editorial operations, directly responsible to the Managing Director.

The success of the economic services was partly based on the development of a technical infrastructure at Reuters, a *research and development orientation*, able to adapt and innovate in the area of computer technology, whose existence represented a continuing commitment to self-generated innovation, with all that it implied for future directional unpredictability. The key to this infrastructural capability was the data-processing section of the Technical Department. Economic services benefited most because the media market was not sufficiently wealthy to be able to pay for computer-based services to the same extent as the non-media market; the general news function was in any case far more fluid and its product less amenable to computerized presentation. The numerate quality of economic services also allowed for great flexibility in distribution according to market requirements, although by the late 1970s digital-based transmission systems seemed likely to weaken this ground for distinction.

The major application of computers in the general news field was the so-called 'message-switching' centre introduced in the 1970s, which greatly speeded up the process of selecting different news items for different major news markets, while reducing the amount of editing and repunching that was necessary. The system, known as ADX in Reuters, was introduced in 1969. Significantly the organization's own data-processing department did not advise on the ADX system: its own time and energies were consumed with the expansion of RES. And after the reorganization of 1974, data-processing was almost entirely concerned with the economic service field. Even so, the North American division had its own research and development subsidiary, Information Distribution and Retrieval (IDR Inc.), which was largely responsible for the technical development of the separate North American version of the Reuters Monitor. But IDR was funded from London, and its decisions could be vetoed by London's

Technical Department. Both general and economic news divisions benefited from the introduction of video-display editing units in many leading bureaux from the mid-1970s, although union opposition to their introduction in London greatly delayed the pace of change at headquarters level.

Intensification of competition

The enormous development of the economic services seemed to involve Reuters increasingly with the inner mechanics of big business and high finance. This was what made possible the continued survival of a non-government, surplus-producing and non-American agency. But with what security? While the system might be vulnerable to severe and continuing economic depression, there were at least certain services for which there might still be great demand, at least in the initial stages of a depression where there was both extreme volatility of markets and available investment funds. More important, while Reuters had made great headway in economic news for the global market, how long would it be before such a lucrative activity encouraged new competition and how could Reuters sustain its hefty market share?

Within the US the interest of American agencies in economic and financial news had been almost exclusively a domestic media interest, although a fairly sizeable one, involving staffs of some forty persons per agency. In some respects the development of each of the 'Big Four' agencies exhibits remarkable parallels. In 1964, for instance, when the Reuters deal with Ultronics became operational, both AP and UPI had just computerized their commercial and financial services for the domestic US market, while the leading economic news agency of the US, Dow Jones (operated by staff of the *Wall Street Journal*), also began the computerization of its own news system. This was significant since when in 1967 Reuters cancelled its exchange arrangement with Dow Jones to go it alone in the US, Dow Jones and AP set up a joint news operation overseas for gathering and distributing economic news. Two basic services were provided: the Financial Report, designed mainly for overseas brokers and bankers, and the Economic Report, designed primarily for newspapers. The Economic Report added informed commentary pieces to data dissemination suitable for general readership. Initially the Economic Report alone was offered in some parts of the world, such as the Far East. While AP and Dow Jones remained separate in the US (Dow Jones had had a near monopoly in non-media financial news services, but sold to only 33 newspapers in 1973) a partnership in overseas operations seemed a sound venture. AP had a well-established international communications and news-gathering system, which was especially geared to the needs of the domestic US market. It had the general news service which could blend neatly with a broad economic service for overseas newspapers; while at the same time its name and its interests, like those of Dow Jones, would especially recommend themselves to American banks, brokers and multinational corporations operating outside the US. It also became a relatively cheap way of expanding both the Dow Jones and the *Wall Street Journal*'s overseas coverage, although at first the service did not involve very much additional recruitment. Before the formation of AP–DJ, the Dow Jones company had about four full-time correspondents in Europe and two in the Far East; by the early 1970s AP–DJ maintained some twenty-two overseas full-time correspondents.

The joint venture represented a counter-thrust to Reuters' own expansionary activity in this area; but with some important differences. AP–DJ catered for both media and non-media markets, whereas Reuters' development of economic news did not directly benefit its media services to the same degree so far as content was concerned. Thus AP–DJ economic commentaries in many leading newspapers also helped spread its name. But the AP–DJ services focused on economic and financial news but not so much on commodities, since in the US it was not Dow Jones that lionized the commodities market, but CNS in Chicago, and CNS had a long-standing relationship with UPI, to which service it subscribed. This prompted UPI and CNS to develop an international commodity news service in the mid-1970s, along similar lines to, but much smaller than, the AP–DJ operation, with a London headquarters, and mainly distributing via teleprinter services. AP–DJ did not initially adopt the same sophisticated hardware dissemination technology, but kept to teleprinter services. This may have reflected something of a rather modest initial blueprint for the agency: an operation which could depend largely on existing manpower and capital. And this factor may certainly have hindered its growth. One side advantage, however, was that when later it did go fully electronic it would benefit from a more up-to-date technology. Finally, the new agency did not begin with as fully regionalized an economic service as Reuters.

For AP the venture was attractive because it offered a lucrative opportunity of exploiting the greatly increased communications capacity allowed by developments in telephonic cable technology. It was also a means of furthering sales, of spreading the name and prestige of AP, and thus helping in the competitive fight with UP and Reuters. It fitted into current thinking about the correct competitive strategy in the general press fight against television, namely, the development of specialized fields. And it was another response to the problem of relatively saturated newspaper markets.

AP–DJ was designed as a two-headed structure. AP's responsibilities were mainly to do with technical maintenance, communications and sales, and these functions were initially centred in London, which also gradually took from New York more responsibility for newsgathering and editing, as cable breaks and the desirability of having some of the editing for European markets based in London impressed itself on the new management. London took over from New York eight hours a day while the London Stock Exchange was in operation. Staff were recruited either from AP, Dow Jones, or externally. In New York, Dow Jones took full responsibility for editing.

Progress was uneven. Sales were exceptionally good in Japan, for instance, where possibly it was Kyodo's interest in such a service that led to the introduction of the economic wire in the Far East (at first only the economic media wire was offered in the Far East).* Kyodo at that time was expanding further into the economic news field in competition with Japan's second agency, Jiji, which had always specialized in economic coverage. Kyodo's use of AP–DJ reports from certain major financial centres was often much higher in the early 1970s than its usage of Reuters or AP general news reports. But in Europe the problems were more severe, where AP–DJ faced rather greater resistance than Reuters had faced in the US. In the largest European market of West Germany, AP–DJ set up a teleprinter distribution system through a leading German financial paper, *Handelsblatt*, to compete with VWD (partly owned by Reuters). It offered 6 possible teleprinter services in finance, but VWD had a total offering of 22 teleprinter services and already sold to 550 clients. AP–DJ, which had initially sought a deal with VWD, had only 12 clients after its first year of operation in West Germany with *Handelsblatt*, and reckoned that some 250–300 were needed to become profitable. Yet by the late 1970s the situation looked very different. AP–DJ had signed an exchange agreement with VWD for five years, giving VWD the exclusive rights to market and distribute AP–DJ in West Germany. The relationship between Reuters and VWD was scheduled to be discontinued at the end of 1979.† VWD complained that Reuters did not share its revenues from the lucrative Monitor service, only from teleprinter sales. AP–DJ had greatly improved its data base meanwhile by linking up with one of several

---

* In Asia, AP–DJ's market strength was very likely boosted by the establishment in 1976 of an Asian edition of the *Wall Street Journal*.

† But Reuters continued with its one-third shareholding in VWD, and increased its contingent of staff in West Germany, which reached a total of 116 in 1978 of whom 37 were journalists.

competing US information systems, Telerate, a US equivalent to the Monitor, thus providing it with hardware similar to Reuters' own. Also courting VWD was a different source of competition to Reuters: Telekurs, a Zurich-based operation owned by Swiss bankers anxious to curtail Reuters' success on their own territory. Telekurs had developed important links with many data sources, including that of Bunker-Ramo (US competitor to Ultronics, Reuters' data partner) and also a supplier to AP-DJ. UPI-CNS also hoped to supply VWD with its own US commodity service. It became clear that links of this kind could begin to erode Reuters' dominant position in West Germany and elsewhere, at a time when one commentator wrote that 'the electronic possibilities for financial markets already appear to be far in advance of what the financiers will accept',[4] although for the time being it seemed likely that Reuters was still able to offer the neatest combination of services.

Wirephoto to newsfilm

Exhibiting increasing interest in international economic news markets in the 1970s, previous AP and UPI diversification had nevertheless occurred predominantly *within* the media markets through the development of new technologies. Most significant of these for the printed press was the development of photo distribution by wire and by radio. Despite vigorous opposition from both Hearst and some Scripps–Howard newspaper members, whose interests were better served by seeking to delay improvements in the quality of news-photograph dissemination, AP launched its 'wirephoto' service in 1935, based on a technology developed by Bell laboratories. The increased subscriptions meant that the service was at first of primary benefit to the larger metropolitan dailies. Even as late as 1957 AP's US wirephoto clients numbered only 523, less than half the domestic daily membership, and UP had 679, of whom half had been acquired in 1951 when UP took over the photo agency, ACME. Internationally, the growth of radiophoto distribution was not a major factor till the 1950s when UPI's newspictures division, for example, began to develop regularly scheduled services to South and Central America, Europe, Asia, and Australasia. But UPI's radiophoto for Japan was not introduced till 1963. Newspicture circuits for land-line distribution were still in the process of introduction in Europe in the early 1960s, and did not reach Austria, Spain or Hungary until 1963. A picture network was established in Portugal for the first time in 1968. Much the same was true for AP, which in 1963 introduced wirephoto for Russia and Poland (which before had been served by long-distance phone); in 1966 the European wire-

New markets, new methods, conflict and risk 235

photo network reached Spain, the sixteenth country to be hooked up. Its US wirephoto network was extended to Mexico in 1969, and the same year its European network was extended to include the Czech, Hungarian, and Rumanian news agencies. A photocable to Johannesburg was leased in 1973.

Newspictures have meant a very major expansion of resources and activity for the agencies. Even one-correspondent bureaux of the American agencies overseas generally have an additional photographer-journalist, if not full-time then on a regular fee-paying basis. This new development has inevitably changed the whole pattern of press and agency resource distribution, as one early commentator was quick to point out:

> Telephoto system will begin to operate before fall 10,000 miles of leased wires in the United States. Because of its expense it will have a profound effect upon the fiscal structure of the daily press, diverting a considerable portion of expenditures from editorial employees to wire services.[5]

What is not clear, though, is whether the development of photo distribution has really worked out to the US agencies' advantage. It is highly significant that neither Reuters (nor AFP in any very big way) attempted this market internationally. The pressure was primarily domestic: if one of the two US agencies did not attempt it, the other would. In the US most daily papers are what in Britain would be considered local or provincial. In Britain the national papers, which commanded the lion's share of circulation, had their established foreign networks of sources and correspondents on which to base photo provision. Competition between the US agencies in photo technology has been intense, involving huge financial commitments to research and development. AP for example, pioneered 'Laserphoto' in 1974, which used laser beams to transmit photos by wire and the 'Electronic Darkroom' (1978) which developed a technology similar in function to the cathode ray tube editing terminals, only applied to photography. But while photographs may represent an extremely important activity for the US agencies,[6] AP's service operated at a loss in the late 1970s.[7] But AP's service did make money in some countries, for example, where there was a big news magazine market, as in Brazil; and it also benefited from the more flexible opportunity for tailoring photo services to local market interests than in general news. The global dissemination of many of the latest technological innovations in photo distribution, because its profitability is limited, may be unlikely to occur for some considerable time.

The technological innovations pioneered by AP represent a further instance of the ways in which AP in the sixties and seventies sought to eliminate market leads which UPI had established in certain areas, like the sale of news photographs, broadcast services and radio voicecasts. This competition between the American agencies, with AP's continuing assault on UPI's lead in 'marginal' markets, is a prevailing feature of the 'diversification' theme in recent agency history.

The development of services specifically for broadcast clients was also initiated in the teeth of considerable press opposition. The broadcast wire services offered by AP and UPI in the 1970s were distinct services, with their own teams of editorial, but not reporting, staffs. But the technology was essentially teleprinter-based, and what the agencies were in fact doing was reshuffling existing material to suit a specific set of clients, with appropriate attention to special needs for regional and local news (which grew in volume and proportion from the early 1960s), and this mode of diversification in a country which permitted such considerable free enterprise in the construction of broadcast networks was certainly more profitable in relation to costs than news photography (which had higher cost elements in terms of staffing and development). Existing research seems to indicate, first, that radio stations in the US are heavily dependent on the wire services for news material even at the local level, which is the least well-provided-for by the agencies. Radio stations that rely only on the radio wires of the agencies probably receive much less information than they would if they subscribed to state and/or trunk wires as well. On the other hand, a subscriber to the trunk wire would possibly gain only marginally in information terms by a subscription to an agency's radio wire; but the radio wire would of course afford him much greater convenience.

In 1958, shortly after its involvement in television news had begun, UPI introduced the 'audio' service of voicecast news reports, which by 1977 served 900 stations as against AP–Radio's 537. In addition to special reports, clients in 1965 received an average of 65 voice stories a day from UPI's radio centre in Chicago; in 1974 the agency instituted 'continuous' broadcasts with over 20 newscasts a day. Only in that year did AP initiate a similar 24-hour service which put out hourly five-and-a-half minute newscasts, each with open spots for a 60-second and a 30-second commercial break (and pre-edited specialist or feature packages). Voicecast clients were often contracted on an exclusivity basis, reintroducing a phenomenon that had been outlawed in the general newspaper field. Audio news was seen as fairly lucrative by AP in 1978.[8] It was AP which first decided to begin the experiment with satellite distribution specifically to radio clients, possibly in order to increase its audio clients at UPI's expense. But AP's Stan Swinton predicted, in 1978, that overall the proportionate revenue importance of the broadcast services would remain constant, since some stations had dropped news altogether, while others took their news and other programming on tape from their respective network centres. Overseas, AP did not distribute voicecasts, but UPI maintained voicecast studios in London and Hong Kong (mainly to transmit news back to the US). UPI voicecasts were sometimes used by UPITN.

Reuters, like the US agencies, was initially hostile to the radio medium in defence of its established press clientele. From the early 1920s it joined with other British press and agency media to restrict its provision of news to the newly established BBC. Sir Roderick Jones took the view that the BBC should neither collect nor arrange its own news, and this view was supported by the Post Office. The Post Office established in its talks with the BBC's constituent companies that no news should be broadcast which had not previously been published in the press. This was intended to prevent the wireless companies from becoming competitive with the news agencies, 'as considerable capital is invested in those undertakings, and a large amount of Post Office revenue is derived from them'.[9] The PA went further and said it did not want the companies to transmit even that news which had already been published for fear that broadcast stations might take morning newspaper news to use in competition against local evening papers. Roderick Jones demanded that the power used for transmission of radio be low enough to prevent the possibility of foreign countries picking news up free (and thereby defrauding the agencies of their rightful revenue).

Such restrictions were gradually resisted by the BBC, and during the Second World War its reputation as an independent source of news first came to be established. Nor did Reuters ever follow the US agencies into provision of special broadcast wires, perhaps because the radio market at home for so long consisted of just the one organization, and overseas the extra problems of translation would have been too formidable. In 1972, however, Reuters did follow UPI in the provision of voicecasts (the 'voice services'); its most important client possibly was a US radio network. Increase in the number of BBC local radio stations and of independent radio at home seemed to produce more incentive by 1975. But by 1979 the Voice Service was scheduled to close, and in retrospect the move seems to have been an ill-fated attempt to follow up Reuters' expansion of economic services in the US with new media services. However it did continue to provide electronically-fed news to US CATV stations, a field in which it was technologically superior for some time, and one in which both US agencies were very active, UPI serving 275 clients in 1977, AP serving 247. Meanwhile, the 'Big Four' agencies continue to distribute regular print services to broadcast media throughout the world, and in some areas radio clients outnumber newspaper both in numerical and revenue terms. In Germany, for instance, Reuters in the mid-1970s was primarily established in the broadcast side of the media market, and in Britain the BBC was AFP's main client.

The newsfilm agencies

The supply of newsfilm (and now video) for television as a major form of diversification for the news agencies is one that to date appears principally to have benefited Reuters. AP put its toe in the water in the late 1940s, too soon, and INS began distribution of feature news film from 1950. But in a 1975 article, John Mahoney,[10] then ITN foreign editor, credited United Press Movietone Television (UPMT) as being the first television newsfilm agency, followed by CBS Newsfilm Syndication in 1953. The UPMT arrangement was for Movietone to supply the film, while UP moved it across the world, a partnership that lasted ten years till in 1963 UPI decided to go it alone as UPI Newsfilm Inc., described in the agency's presidential address for that year as a 'multi-million dollar operation' (in 1968, the annual expense of operating UPITN was $4,500,000). But not only did UPI now have to rely totally on its own capital, but it also had to face stiff new competition which included one of its own clients, the BBC. The British Commonwealth International Newsfilm Agency (BCINA) was 'created in a conscious effort to counter the early American monopoly'[11] in 1957. BCINA was mainly controlled by the BBC and the Rank Organization, with smaller shareholdings among the broadcast organizations of Australia and Canada and, from 1965, New Zealand. Reuters took a small shareholding (one-sixth) from 1960. The operations of the BCFA were sufficiently limited for the BBC to continue to take UPI Newsfilm until 1967, by which time (in 1964) the English agency had adopted the less imperial nomenclature of Visnews. These developments may have precipitated the link-up of UPI with Independent Television News (ITN) which serviced Britain's commercial television network with national and international news bulletins. The new organization was known as UPITN, jointly owned on a fifty-fifty basis between UPI and ITN. ITN paid UPITN for its newsfilm, and UPITN paid UPI for the communication and other facilities provided by the agency.

The idea of a link-up with UPI, an American agency, seemed the kind of brash inspiration that had already made independent television one of the most culturally troublesome phenomena, in the eyes of the British establishment, since the arrival of cinema. ITN had until now run a small film distribution system of its own, as well as a joint television film syndicate operation with CBS (US). The syndicate had been ITN's solution to the problem of covering North America within a reasonable budget – CBS would provide the North American film needed by ITN in exchange for ITN's world film. UPI's activities on the other hand were far more extensive geographically than those of CBS in the news field, and there was not the same danger that competitive interests would some day upset the partnership.

Reuters' share of Visnews meanwhile had now increased dramatically from about a sixth to about a third of the total. The Rank Organization had diversified into commercial television through its acquisition of part of Southern Television (UK), which meant that it had interests both in Visnews and, indirectly, in ITN (which of course provided Southern Television with its news and was partly funded by it). Rank was obliged to withdraw from Visnews for fear of contravening the ITA's charter. Visnews now came to be mainly owned by the BBC and by Reuters, each of whom held about a third of the shares, while the remaining third was divided between the broadcasting networks of Canada, Australia and New Zealand in approximately equal parts.

Both Visnews and the international division of UPITN were London-based. In the early 1970s both agencies were especially concerned to secure as adequate and as cheap a supply of news as possible from the US, an exceptionally expensive but major news source area. It may not be coincidence merely that the obsession of both Visnews and UPITN with cheap US film supply chanced to peak in the Watergate era. (The relative importance of North America seemed to have declined by the late 1970s, and in an analysis of Eurovision news for 1977 – Eurovision being the major showcase for agency newsfilm – North America had fallen behind Europe, the Middle East and even Africa.)[12] Visnews had secured an exchange relationship with NBC and then in 1973 with Television News (USA) and took a small percentage of the holding. TVN capital came from the Adolph Coors Company of Golden, Colorado, in a bid to establish a conservative opposition to the 'liberal' major networks through the means of an independent wholesale news distribution system. Visnews supplied the international news. This in turn prompted a similar experiment by UPITN, also in 1973, which linked up with Paramount Pictures Corporation to begin electronic news feeds to US television stations. But in 1974 UPITN–Paramount sold out the American experiment to TVN, and for a while UPITN–Paramount even took US newsfilm from TVN for international distribution. Yet in 1975 Visnews–TVN also folded. Visnews now resumed its reliance on the NBC exchange arrangement, in addition to its own US coverage. In the spring of 1975 the Paramount share of UPITN was bought up by the Sacramento Union Corporation, owned by John P. McGoff. McGoff was the conservative president of Panax Corporation, which in 1975 owned eight US dailies, twenty-eight weeklies and interests in commercial printing, typesetting, printing, machinery sales. McGoff's 50% share (but only one-third in terms of editorial control) was to prove an embarrassment in 1979 when McGoff was alleged by one witness to the South African Erasmus Commission, in its investigation of the so-called 'Muldergate' scandal, to have sought financial backing of over $11 million from the South African government in order to purchase the *Washington Star* and to buy in to UPITN. The *Washington Star* scheme fell through, and it was alleged the money was used to buy the *Sacramento Union* newspaper in California. But McGoff was able to buy in to UPITN for $1·35 million.[13] McGoff said later that no foreign government had ever had an 'interest' in any of his media involvements.

ITN now purchased McGoff's holding and for the first time in the agency's history controlled 75% of the enterprise, much greater than the BBC's share in Visnews. For its supply of US film the new UPITN could depend partly on an exchange arrangement signed with ABC, which involved the exchange of ITN film for all ABC film from its US and ten overseas bureaux.

The BBC's operational involvement in Visnews is contractually organized and involves the supply of newsfilm to Visnews and BBC access to Visnews material. Reuters supplies its own news service and its communications network on a commercial basis. Informal cooperation also occurs in the field between members of the different organizations. The extent of UPI's operational involvement in UPITN (but not in terms of ownership) seems proportionately greater than Reuters' involvement in Visnews, in that it provides not only the news service and communications but also administers and manages UPITN's overseas bureaux.

The 1970s saw a number of important developments in agency newsfilm operations. From the mid-1970s there was a significant shift to electronic feed-in even for non-European clients. By 1978 Visnews had daily satellite transmissions for the Middle East, North and South America, and Asia. Satellite to Asia went via Australasia, Japan, Singapore, and Hong Kong. Lateral distribution of videocassette also occurred from these points to stations with video technology. However, air-freight was still important and even clients who received news electronically also used air-freighted film for once or twice weekly 'background' or 'feature' material. Whereas the newsfilm agencies used to deal mainly in 'international' (non-language) sound accompaniment to film, Visnews was increasingly employing English-language commentary. In Asia, for instance, there were two sound networks, one for 'international' sound, and one for English-language. Film was also increasingly colour film. Visnews, finally, has diversified considerably on its own account. By 1978, for instance, it had made a hundred documentary films for various sponsors; it provided location services for other film-makers, as well as commercial processing and printing services. Especially significant was the range of its consultancy activities, involving advice, supply, installation, maintenance and training. This activity was parallel to Reuters' consultancy services to some Third World national agencies. By offering such services to Third World broadcast organizations Visnews could hope to raise the quality of newsfilm received from them. So that in the long term it could depend more completely than at present on their output for its own world distribution, a direction which would suit most Third World governments. While this might also seem to threaten a further decline in independent news-gathering in Third World countries, it is true that the difficulties of independent and uninvited filming in Third World countries are even more imposing than the difficulties of news-gathering for print services.

In certain respects patterns in the production and distribution of newsfilm exhibit imbalances very similar to those described in the case of the print agencies. It may be that the potentiality for client-specificity in newsfilm is much greater: there are fewer clients, there are fewer stories, and the service is daily, but not continuous. Clients make known what general kinds of news they are interested in (or definitely do not want). But content analysis of 1976-7 film provided on the all-important Eurovision circuit suggests that the demand for Third World news among the developed countries most likely to 'set the agenda' was still fairly low: 30% of all items originated from Latin America, the Middle East, Africa and Asia, but almost half of these came from the Middle East (important for its oil significance). While Europe accounted for 57% of all items, Latin America accounted for 2% and Asia for 6%. But Africa accounted for 11%. Political news heavily dominated the news exchanges in terms of content: 61% of all items exchanged, followed by sport (27%), 'general' news (12%) and economic-social news (6%). The low figures for 'economic-social' suggest fairly low concentration on development-type issues for European clients.* But Eurovision

* Golding and Elliott (1979) reported dissatisfaction among journalists of Nigerian broadcast news media with the Western orientation of newsfilm agencies, as exemplified in selection of items and language of commentaries. They

film also feeds into Middle Eastern and South American exchanges.[14]

Communications

News transmission is an unpredictable commodity in volume terms and it is uneven. Development of services relayed by various forms of digital communication at great speeds increases that unevenness. In order to cope with such unevenness it is in the interests of agencies to maintain a level of leased communication facilities surplus to current requirements at any given time. This in turn has generated in recent years the practice of making agency communications available to other media organizations. In order to avoid restrictions on sub-leasing by the PTTs, what happens technically is that all news carried on agency wires actually 'belongs' to the agencies. In Britain n 1975 for instance (and these arrangements are flexible) Reuters reserved a permanent transatlantic open line for the *Financial Times*; likewise for *The Times*; while the *Daily Telegraph* used an AP line. These 'élite' papers were also more likely (than the populars) to use agency facilities for 'piggy-backing' their copy from important news-centres on a semi-regular basis; that is, they would often send news copy through the agencies' communications rather than their own.

---

found that, of the newsfilm supplied by Eurovision in Nigeria, dominant subjects were international politics, military events and sport. About half the items concerned events located in Western Europe, North America, USSR/Eastern Europe. In the case of Visnews, content was dominated by domestic politics, international politics and military events. One-third of the items concerned Western Europe and North America, 2·5% USSR/Eastern Europe, while the Middle East accounted for 10·5%, Africa 16%, Asia 23% and Central and South America 4%.

Varis (1977), quotes research showing that in the mid-1970s one half of all items offered to Eurovision by the agencies came from Africa, Asia, Latin America and the Middle East, and that Visnews had a dominating role in covering all the regions of the developing countries. But coverage tended to be crisis-coverage. Major clients numbered (1980) over 100 for UPI but 200 for Visnews, which may also have enjoyed a greater measure of financial security given the involvement of several large broadcast organizations in its ownership and management. Vilcek (1979) considered that the film agencies were in competition with the reciprocal broadcasting union exchanges, and because they bought EBU film might actually discourage such exchanges. In response, Curran (1979) argued that the agencies found it useful to buy Eurovision film for sale to parts of the world to which electronic broadcast exchanges did not reach; that if broadcasters did not exchange there would be nothing for the agencies to buy; and that in the case of Visnews, most of the material that it took from Eurovision was in fact Visnews or Visnews-related material injected into the exchange through European centres other than London. Curran also questioned Vilcek's suggestion that the agencies diverted material from Intervision countries that would normally have gone to Eurovision: such material would not normally be filmed in the absence of agency initiative.

Where and in what manner such arrangements were made could depend largely on the personal relationship between agency and other newspaper journalists. There were two considerations which made the personal factor important. First, the journalist of a paper using an agency's communications would naturally be sensitive to the possibility that the contents of his copy, if unfamiliar to the agency, might be 'lifted' and disseminated or in some way used by the agency itself. The second factor was the problem of crisis arrangements: in news emergencies the agencies might well prefer to reserve their communications for their own use. The main advantage of using agency facilities for press users is one of cost, especially in the case of the 'élite' papers, given their more substantial copy flow.

More recently it has become evident that such communication practices have enormous potential for the US agencies inside their own domestic markets, in the handling of the distribution of other syndicated services. Supplementary syndicate services arrange to be distributed at high speed through AP or UPI data networks, choosing either AP or UPI according to which of these the client newspaper subscribes. Only about half of the wordage carried on UPI's US communication networks actually originates with UPI. Such activity will continue to be at least as important with any transfer to satellite distribution, and already makes a substantial contribution to covering the agencies' own communications costs, which represent 20% or more of their respective expenditures. Overseas as well as at home the future attitude of PTTs is an important factor in determining the extent of expansion possible in this sphere. Some PTTs do impose a surcharge for subleasing or for higher than normal usage. If this became common, the agencies might revert to more information-compression technologies. Most PTTs in the late 1970s, however, tacitly allowed the agencies to engage in such activity, while not encouraging excessive practice.

Other 'spin-offs'

The 'Big Four' agencies have engaged in a number of other but smaller-scale activities, which in addition to those already reviewed testify to their continuing search for alternative or complementary means of support to the sometimes financially shaky foundation of daily general news services for media clientele. One of the most curious of these, while short-lived, is interesting as an example of the manner in which agency diversification is constrained by prevailing views as to what constitutes a conflict of interest between an agency's claim to relatively 'objective' news reporting and any other kind of relationship struck between an agency and its news sources.

In the summer of 1963 Senator Fulbright and the Senate Foreign Relations Committee looked into the 'Activities of Nondiplomatic Representatives of Foreign Principals in the United States' – in other words, the public relations and lobbying activities that took place at government level in America at the behest of foreign clients. The committee heard how INS before its takeover by UPI turned over its reporters to commercial clients who paid a fee. Clients would indicate the questions they wanted reporters to pose to certain sources. For additional fees, INS placed clients' material on the news wire. Some Latin-American dictators were prominent amongst the clients. But UPI was involved even more directly than this:

> UPI for at least a generation had had a Special Service Bureau which also made its reporters and photographers available to non-journalistic clients. It has now stopped this. There is no evidence that UPI ever put the client report on its news wire.[15]

Earl Johnson, then editor of UPI, said later that UPI would let reporters and subjects know when inquiry was made for a private client, that it would undertake no tasks for foreign governments and that client material had never been put on the UPI wire and never would be. The public relations operation was transferred to an outside commercial organization after the hearings. UPI Special Service assignments, it emerged, had been undertaken by Washington correspondents on behalf of corporations and publications, both domestic and foreign. Some UPI correspondents did not know of the Special Service bureau's existence until they read about the Fulbright hearings; neither did many senators. In state capitals, UPI Special Services had contracted to ask key state legislators their intentions on banking legislation, on behalf of a non-journalistic client with interests in banking laws. The bureau was found to have taken no responsibility for who the clients were, and reporters did not know who they were working for. Furthermore, two UPI editors were found to be beneficiaries of the sources whose material they put out as part of the UPI service. Sales Director of the UPI Special Service was John Nagel, who had been director of INS Special Services in 1956. UPI had other contracts with public relations agencies taken over from INS, but Earl Johnson said that less than a tenth of one per cent of UPI's money came from this activity.[16]

In a more conventional field, that of book publishing, the agencies have had much less of an impact than might be predicted from organizations with such huge information-gathering facilities. Reuters tried its hand but once with a *Reuters Guide to the New*

Africans in 1967, a data analysis of contemporary politicians and socio-political facts. The experiment was not repeated. In 1978, AP brought to a close its annual production, started in 1964, of a photo-journalistic account of each year's major news events, sold primarily to its newspaper members for resale to newspaper readers. In the US, AP innovated in the educational field by offering its single outlet service to schools and a reading kit known as the 'AP Newspaper Reading Skills Development Programme', offered for sale to client members for local resale. AP also produced an annual sports almanac. Both agencies, AP and UPI, have published major news stories in book form: e.g. UPI published an 'impeachment report' in paperback in conjunction with the New American Library Publishing Co., within 72 hours of the final impeachment vote by the House Judiciary Committee in the final stages of the Watergate saga. It seems very probable that a highly concerted and well organized publishing division in any of the agencies could grow; the danger is that such activity might always seem too peripheral to the top managements. Moreover, publishing might need to be confined to relatively 'neutral' (i.e. non-controversial) and 'public-spirited' areas to avoid tarnishing the agencies' credibility as disinterested reporters.

Diversification

Diversification has been and continues to be an extremely important feature of agency development. It has been most important, perhaps, in the case of Reuters, which, without the post-war expansion of economic services for non-media clients, might well have been unable to survive as a non-government agency. But today that basis of survival is vulnerable to competition from the economic services of other agencies and from bankers and brokers alarmed by the scale of Reuters' success. In this respect, AFP, on the other hand, has diversified least, but at the expense of paying far too high a price, many believe, in dependence on revenues from government clients (an alternative form of diversification). This has had the merit, at least, of rescuing AFP from that particular taint of corruption which had attached to the name of its predecessor, Havas, but suspicion of indirect government influence in the event of highly sensitive domestic stories is difficult for the agency to completely allay. AP has least of all needed to diversify given the size of its domestic US membership. But both US agencies did see the wisdom of moving into radio and later television, even despite the doubts of many print clients, and these services have undoubtedly augmented their revenues. The move into newsphoto was equally inevitable, but in retrospect some believe that the pricing system may have been wrong:

these services were charged as supplementaries, instead of at a realistic long-term economic rate. Reuters did well to expand its resources in a non-media direction. To UP, later UPI, belongs the credit for moving first into many of these fields, ahead of other 'Big Four' agencies: radio, television news, voicecasts, CATV etc. UPI needed to compensate for its second place on the domestic newspaper market. But it has not been able to halt the relentless catching up by AP in all these areas, except in newsfilm, where it has in any case taken second place to Visnews (which was able to capitalize on the prestigious BBC connection) while what was once a joint UPI and ITN operation was temporarily complicated by the curious McGoff involvement. Diversification, therefore, limited by the need to avoid evident professional conflict of interest, has been only a partial solution to the basic problem of agency economics: that the Western media market is not wealthy nor united enough to safely support all four major world-wide agencies. It has provided short-term answers and these have well served media and non-media markets for perhaps as long as anyone could hope. But has it been enough?

Conclusion

So far as there has been a public interest or concern in the 'Big Four' agencies, and in the 1970s it has been represented mainly by news media professionals, Third World politicians and academics, it has tended to concentrate on their role in relation to the Third World; and this role has had a bad press. Recent developments in the pooling of national news agency materials, for instance, have taken place partly in reaction to previous and unwilling over-dependence on 'Big Four' news supply. In this book I have tried to show that while the role of the 'Big Four' in the Third World *is* an important issue, it must be seen in relation to the problem of 'Big Four' viability in the developed world. Furthermore, as much emphasis should be given to the problem of Third World news coverage for the developed world (and of news coverage *generally*) as to Third World news coverage for the Third World itself, and some of the Third World criticisms of 'Big Four' agency operations need to be carefully reconsidered.

For instance, many criticisms focus on the domestic market orientation of the 'Big Four' agencies. This orientation can certainly be demonstrated with respect to a number of variables in the case of at least three of the agencies. But even allowing for the possibility that it leads to a greater content emphasis on domestic market interests even for foreign clients than would otherwise be the case, there may be certain advantages. The sources of imbalance are at least clearly visible, and knowable, and content can be checked or at least reconsidered in the light of this information. Second, given that most agency operations, like most media operations, are nationally based (and news pools are only exchanges between national organizations), it would seem desirable that the world-wide news agencies should at least be based on domestic markets sufficiently affluent to generate the wealth needed to sustain world-wide operations. Moreover such markets generate competitive resources; and competition, while it has some important drawbacks, sharpens professionalism, while the sheer number of professionals helps to establish a recognizable sub-occupational interest with its own independent and informal codes. Finally, the record of press independence in these countries, while not perfect, is very high by comparison with most other countries around the world.

It may be that 'press freedom' is not a very highly trusted concept in many parts of the Third World (or in other parts of the developed world). Of the first generation of independent leaders in the Third World, many came to power partly on the back of nationalist party political newssheets, and their very success has been a constant reminder to them and to their successors of the power of the press. But press restraint is justified by them in terms of the need to adapt media to the requirements of national unity and to developmental objectives. These are possibly laudatory objectives, although it must be said that the actual use of media for 'developmental' purposes is less frequently observed in practice than might be supposed. The question is whether such justifications really do deserve the political weight that is given them. Many Western academics and politicians, in an attempt to demonstrate an urbane sensitivity to Third World problems and thus to minimize the effects of their own cultural and ideological preconceptions, have readily accepted them in the past. Yet even under strictly controlled media conditions, it is not at all self-evident that Third World countries have avoided internal political unrest, civil war and violence, corruption and incompetence, or that these problems would have been any more severe under freer media conditions, or that forces of disunity *should* always be suppressed. In some cases, indeed, a controlled press has very evidently helped to prop up the régimes of unpopular and cruel despots. This is not to say that a 'responsible' press is not unimportant; that journalists should not be as highly educated and as professional as possible; that control of the press by commercial interests is always more acceptable than control by political interests; or that monopoly political sponsorship of the press is not morally acceptable even where the conditions for successful commercial operations are not present. What matters at this stage is that rhetoric be distinguished from realpolitik. Sympathetic Western 'understanding' of the Third World problem has not successfully eschewed the danger of condescension simply by adopting lower standards for non-Western countries. Nor is it sensible to ignore Western interests in as full and as unimpeded a global news flow as possible: people unaware of or unresponsive to their own interests do not necessarily make effective guardians of the interests of other people. And in this case there is by no means a consensus, either among Westerners or in the Third World, that moderately pursued Western interests in news gathering and dissemination would in fact be detrimental to any particular group of countries.

Conclusion

In practice, many countries, including many Third World countries, have shown how easy it is to turn off the 'information' taps, with or without formal censorship policies, with or without a supporting UNESCO-formulated rhetoric, and this ease does to some extent contradict the image of Western-based international news media as all-powerful. The agencies have been more accommodating to the Third World in this respect than many Third World countries find it in their interests to admit to, as the world agencies' developing support for and dependence on Third World national agencies helps to demonstrate. The question of how far such accommodation should be encouraged has not received anything like the public attention it deserves in the Western world.

This is not to say that some Third World criticisms of agency news coverage are not entirely in order. But how the agencies respond to these criticisms should also reflect a more public process of coordinated review of the problems they face in their important developed world markets as well. Should the existing level of diversity be allowed to diminish still further? In the case of the American agencies, a very much weakened UPI might in the long term also weaken AP's credibility at home and abroad by ceding to it a dubious and ultimately demoralizing monopoly power. A positive direction for UPI, in the opinion of this author, would involve the development of an original news media cooperative, one in which press and broadcast media had equal control, perhaps incorporating some of the existing leading supplementaries, and actively involving an international membership. A coordinated review would certainly consider the long-term consequences of a fragmentation of the economic news market among the different agencies, a fragmentation which would threaten, first, to minimize benefits to all the agencies, perhaps to the advantage of non-agency interests, and second, to undermine the main life support for Reuters. Without Reuters the global distribution of news would begin to appear even more top-heavy with American influence and interest than at present, and would generate an even fiercer and more justified process of retaliation and news-protectionism by both European and Third World markets. The long-term solution might be a concerted or coordinated approach to the economic news market, possibly involving cooperative services or shared specialization of services. Whereas Reuters has a creditable record in Third World news, especially from the point of view of the developed world markets, it might perhaps be time for one of the 'Big Four' agencies to become more closely identified with Third World interests, in an attempt to demonstrate the same kind of concern as an agency like Tanjug has already displayed. Although they might not like to think so, the least suitable organizations for this role would be the agencies or media foundations of the Western world's greatest super-power, the US. The power of association is strong, and over long distances it can be sometimes difficult to differentiate between genuine aid and concern and politically-inspired diplomatic manoeuverings. Nor is Reuters ideally qualified for such a role, since its whole commercial thrust since World War Two would not have suited it to engagement in long-term and financially unremunerative tasks of this kind. But AFP not only has a good record on Third World coverage in terms of resource and content distribution, but France is well known for its independent attitude on many international issues. AFP dependence on government subscriptions is widely known and allowed for, though this would inevitably represent a handicap. But the agency has sufficient skills, resources and political credit for some such role. It is indeed a role that it has, in part, already filled in the past, but it could be pursued more assertively. To the French such an operation would lend it considerable prestige in the Third World, while its material interests in the Third World are not so great as to create the same dimension of credibility problem that US interests might risk in assuming such a role. But this factor would again be a handicap. It might be possible to move to a limited system of joint exchanges between the 'Big Four' agencies in the area of Third World news coverage to help compensate for the degree of market specialization that already exists in 'Big Four' coverage of the Third World. All the agencies could certainly consider ways of improving services to the Third World, not only in terms of tailoring services to national requirements, but also in terms of extent and mode of service distribution (where there is choice, and continuing to negotiate for choice where it does not exist), even on a non-profit basis: i.e. doing as much as possible without making a loss. A coordinated review would probably consider patterns of manpower allocation in relation to, first, the agencies' own respective patterns of allocation, and second, the allocation patterns of client media. The purpose would be to identify the underlying rationalities and irrationalities in the consensual news-judgements of Western media, and to seek ways of correcting the irrationalities, perhaps by seeking to establish an overall equalization in distribution of resources between the major world regions. There would be a case for the evaluation of different approaches to resource sharing in foreign news coverage. Such a process might help to 'educate' Western media with respect to the need for a review of practices in international coverage, although such 'education' has arguably been a continuing process in recent decades, throughout the history of the Cold War, the great movement of independence in the Third World, Vietnam and the struggles for power in Africa. It is not a process that can enlighten all dark corners simultaneously; it may not be desirable that it should.

This suggests that the media do have a responsibility to view their labours from a public service angle from time to time; that this may well require general overview exercises, a greater degree of coordination in their distribution of resources and services (possibly even in the light of flexible and regularly monitored and revised common guidelines), and the establishment of professional machinery for systematic and continuing evaluation. One prerequisite to the successful engagement in tasks such as these might be to begin looking at what actually happens as well as at what should or ought to happen, or even what most people commonly *assume* is happening, in news-gathering. This involves a more sociologically grounded approach to the appraisal of what the problems are. Talking about the agencies in terms of history, resources and structure, as I have done, for instance, does inevitably tend to obscure some of the more fragile features of news-gathering in practice. One ex-agency bureau chief[1] has recently shown how some quite important stories are discovered quite fortuitously (e.g. there happened to be agency reporters around at the time in connection with some other, unrelated news story), how easily errors can occur in the process of editing, and how different newsmen react very differently to censorship and sanction. Much more of this kind of discussion is needed, not simply in the anecdotal vein common to journalistic memoirs, no matter how entertaining, but in a more systematic fashion designed to tease out the regularities in situations which may always seem unique to the individuals participating in them, to identify the problems, to review and evaluate different styles of response. To such a process of systematic enquiry I hope this book represents a contribution to a beginning.

Postscript

The offer of limited partnership in UPI was withdrawn in February 1980. The E. W. Scripps Co. had received verbal commitment to 60% of the offer, with 18% of the money actually paid. The reasons why some prospective purchasers had been deterred ranged from legal considerations to the fact that UPI was not a profit centre; some were simply unable to raise the money. The company's president stressed that its goal was still to offer broad participation in UPI, and that other options were being reviewed. UPI's president assured employees that UPI was not going to go out of business. UPI's National Advisory Board expressed its desire in March 1980 that UPI ownership be kept within the US media rather than being sold to a US company with no media connections, and ruled out the possibility of a sale to a foreign-based organization. (*Editor and Publisher*, 2 February 1980 and 29 March 1980.)

By 1980, Reuters' total revenue was the highest of the 'Big Four'. Reuters' clientele now numbered 13,000-plus, of whom half were non-media clients to Monitor services. General news coverage also benefited, as in W. Germany (where local news coverage was increased) or in N. America (where half of the 115 correspondents were primarily general news journalists). Economic services still accounted for around 85% of the entire revenue, in sharp contrast to their 30–50% share in the 1960s. Economic services of other agencies were smaller. But AP-Dow Jones/Telerate was well established in markets such as W. Germany (where it served VWD) or Switzerland (where it was marketed by Telekurs). UNICOM reached well over 200 direct teleprinter clients.

Domestic growth for AFP's economic services was constrained by the news line fed directly from the Paris Bourse to Paris newspapers and by the strength of Reuters-Agefi. Yet half of AFP's total clientele were non-media: mainly governmental or private. The breakdown in 1980 of the partnership between the founder members of Aigles suggested that AFP's domestic security might improve. Foreign and domestic photo sales increased.

In the USA, both US agencies had begun satellite distribution of some services for certain US broadcast and newspaper subscribers, a trend which could do much to stabilize communication costs. Most US agency clients could receive their services by satellite by the mid-1980s or even earlier. UPI's introduction of UPI NewsShare in conjunction with TCA could make UPI newswires available to home computers, while AP's 'A' wire was made available through Mead Data Central's NEXIS service for media, corporations etc. The agencies seemed well placed for the dawning post-newsprint era. But, arguably, the 1970s' revolution in the technology of news-processing and distribution had not yet been matched by an equivalent revolution in resources for and attitudes towards news-gathering requirements.

Notes and references

Introduction

1. DPA (Deutsche Presse Agentur) is very probably the largest of the 'intermediary' agencies of the non-communist world. In 1977 it claimed to maintain bureaux and part-time correspondents in some 80 countries and to serve a total of 144 foreign clients or exchange partners (including 45 agencies) with daily services in German, English, Spanish and Arabic (cf. UNESCO: International Commission for the Study of Communication Problems: Working Papers 14, Monographs (II), pp. 54–69).
2. 'Big Four' agencies and TASS maintain reciprocal subscription or exchange arrangements.
3. These are 1976 UNESCO figures for the total world circulation of daily newspapers (readership would be much higher) and broadcast receivers. The latter figures are underestimates, given the reliance on licence records in some areas, while listener figures would be very considerably higher.
4. Galtung and Ruge (1965)
5. Salamore, B. (1975).
6. Schramm, W. et al (1978).
7. Sparkes, V. M. (1978).
8. Computed from figures supplied in UNESCO's *World Communications*, 1975.
9. Pre-1979 spelling: Hsinhua.
10. MacNeil, R. (1968).
11. Altheide, D. L. and Rasmussen, R. (1973).
12. Braestrup, P. (1977).
13. Adams, B.: *In the News*: BBC TV Channel, 2, 25 Nov. 1974. See also Schlesinger (1978), p. 60.
14. Eurovision survey figures supplied by UPITN.
15. Kleisch (1975). But this decline appeared to have stabilized by 1979 in the case of US news media, and some newspapers were planning an expansion of overseas bureaux (*Editor and Publisher*, 2 June 1979).
16. UNESCO: International Commission for the Study of Communication Problems: Working Papers 15, Monographs (III), p. 135. In the early 1960s the 'Big Four' accounted for 68% of Tanjug's foreign news output. Much of the subsequent decline in the proportion of news they account for is due to the increase in Tanjug's own foreign

correspondents who accounted for an increasing proportion of output from 24% in the late 1960s (cf. Robinson, G., 1970) to 43% in the mid-1970s. Tanjug's general director states that any increase in alternative news sources has not been at the expense of the 'Big Four': '... it is important to emphasize that this better, although still insufficient, balance in sources has accompanied an overall increase in foreign coverage, and has no way been at the expense of the news and information picked up from the international agencies'. Cf. Ivačić, Pero (1978), p. 159.
17. Dickens, M. M. (1978).
18. Shaw, D. L. (1967) has demonstrated a relationship between the rise in the use of news agency material and a decline in partisan coverage of national elections in the US, 1852–1916. Increasing use of news agencies was related to the growth of news agencies; expansion of telegraph; declining relative cost of telegraph; declining cost of newsprint; growing reader demand for telegraph news. (However, Schudson's (1978) thesis suggests the need to examine the broader social context, and in particular the development of a democratic market society, for an understanding of the rise of the notion of objectivity. He distinguishes between 'information' journalism and 'story' journalism, and suggests that by 1900 'information' journalism was sponsored by the economic and social élite. The notion of objectivity as ideology emerged after World War One as an expression of scepticism in a world where 'facts' were no longer seen as trustworthy, in the light of what propaganda and public relations could achieve with 'facts'.) In relation to broadcasting, Schlesinger (1978) suggests a relationship between the authoritativeness as news source acquired by the BBC, and the BBC's complete dependence on news agencies for news bulletins in its formative years. In other words, the BBC's news 'style' was influenced by that of the agencies. Significantly, the strategy of catering for variations in client political leanings by supplying differently nuanced services was not widely adopted by the major agencies, although it has been more common among national agencies. A Germany agency, Hugenberg's Telegraphen-Union before the First World War, for example, put out both a general news service and then differently nuanced services for papers of the political right and for 'neutrals'. Havas, in its earlier years, transmitted a special service that consisted of different political editorials from Paris depending on the political colour of the client. As a strategy for catering for political diversity this approach is wasteful of time and manpower and the sheer cynicism of the exercise might in itself damage an agency's credibility (although it could provide scope for the exercise of greater professional autonomy among employees). In many non-Western countries, communist or simply developing countries, news agencies are expected to be partial in favour of a single ideology or cause – the cause of class solidarity or of national development – and the Western concept of 'impartiality' is itself held to be in the service of material Western interests. And this presents a major problem to the Western

based news agencies. But such communist or developing countries still want a service which is uniformly and consistently partial; not a service that suits different ideological leanings. There are problems with the Western concept of 'impartiality': it is clearly bounded by the shared interests of important media groups and their respective publics. But it is a useful concept as it connotes a certain technique of reporting (e.g. 'balance', direct quotes, who-what-why-when-where etc.) and a valued professional *objective*.

19. Emery, E. (1964).
20. 'Telegraph editors': i.e. those responsible for monitoring news agency wires.
21. Geiber, W. (1956).
22. White, D. M. (1950) and Snider, P. (1966).
23. Liebes, B. H. (1966).
24. Stempel, G. (1959).
25. Schramm, W., et al. (1978).
26. Braestrup, P. (1977), Vol. 1. p. 32.
27. Tuchman, G. (1978), p. 258.
28. Long, Gerald (1975), *News for Whom?*: Seminar at St Antony's College, Oxford, 4 Feb. 1975.
29. Phillips Davison, W. (1974), pp. 175–6.

1 Business begins at home

1. Schwarzlose, R. A. (1965), pp. 115–16.
2. UNESCO: International Commission for the Study of Communication Problems: Working Papers 15, Monographs (III), p. 150.
3. Knight, O. (1966).
4. Senate Judiciary Committee: antitrust and monopoly hearings, 1967.
5. *Editor and Publisher*, 10 Sept. 1978.
6. The agency was given provisional status as a public body in 1944.
7. UNESCO: International Commission for the Study of Communication Problems: Working Papers 13, Monographs (I), p. 19.
8. Righter, R. (1978), p. 64.
9. Ibid.
10. Read, W. H. (1976), p. 108; Schwarzlose (1965) shows that AP foreign service expenditure in 1963 was only 16·5% but that in the period 1953–63, foreign service expenditure had increased faster (74·4%) than domestic expenditure (69·2%).
11. Read, W. H. (1976), p. 113; Righter, R. (1978), p. 64.
12. Righter, R. (1978), p. 64.
13. Ibid.
14. International Press Institute, (1956).
15. Righter, R. (1978).
16. International Press Institute, (1956).
17. IPI Report, June 1978, p. 10.
18. Interview with author, 13 Dec. 1978.

256 Notes and references

19. Righter, R. (1978), p. 65.
20. Meursault, R. (1974).
21. In 1974, for instance, state clients accounted for only 58% of total revenue.
22. *Le Monde*, 16 May 1975.
23. *Editor and Publisher* prints an annual cost-analysis of typical US dailies, from which this figure was taken.
24. Figures obtained by author by request to editors of two Norwegian dailies.
25. Boyd-Barrett, J. O. (1977), p. 29.
26. Read, W. H. (1976), p. 113.
27. Frank Tremaine, Senior Vice-President for UPI, quoted a figure of 50% to the author in an interview, 12 Dec. 1978.
28. Client figures are taken from various agency publications and *Editor and Publisher* reports of annual statements and conventions.
29. UNESCO: International Commission for the Study of Communication Problems: Working Papers 15, Monographs (III), p. 149.
30. Foreign clients accounted for 33% of UP's 1952 total clientele of 3,527.
31. Garin, M. (1966), internal AFP report.
32. UNESCO: International Commission for the Study of Communication Problems: Working Papers 13 and 15, Monographs (I and III).
33. *Reuters News Letter*, Dec. 1969.
34. AFP: *Vie de la Maison*, 1972 (monthly issues provided client details of various regions), 1978.
35. Kleisch (1975).
36. Harris (1977).
37. Boyd-Barrett (1976), pp. 86–7.
38. Ibid.
39. Schwarzlose, R. A. (1965).
40. UNESCO: International Commission for the Study of Communication Problems: Working Papers 15, Monographs (III), p. 153.
41. Weiner, R. (1972).
42. Boyd-Barrett (1976), p. 67.
43. UNESCO: International Commission for the Study of Communication Problems, Working Papers 15, Monographs (III), p. 116.
44. Harris, P. (1977), p. 81.
45. Boyd-Barrett (1976).
46. Elliott, P. and Golding, P. (1974).
47. *Editor and Publisher Yearbook*, (1974), pp. 437–8.
48. UNESCO: International Commission for the Study of Communication Problems: Working Papers 13, Monographs (I), p. 5.
49. US census figures quoted in *Editor and Publisher Yearbook* (1974).
50. National census figures quoted in *Pears Cyclopædia* (1971).
51. Boyd-Barrett (1977).
52. Kleisch (1975). This represented a slight decline from 54% recorded for all full-time correspondents working for US media in an earlier Kleisch study in 1969.
53. Boyd-Barrett (1976), p. 636.

54. Boyd-Barrett (1976), p. 634.
55. Shen, M. E. (1978).
56. Boyd-Barrett (1976), p. 88.
57. UNESCO: International Commission for the Study of Communication Problems: Working Papers 15, Monographs (III), p. 153.
58. Associated Press: APME Red Book (1975), p. 190.
59. *Editor and Publisher*, 11 March 1967.
60. *Editor and Publisher*, 19 May 1969.
61. *Editor and Publisher*, 26 April 1969.
62. Pinch, E. T. (1978).
63. UNESCO (1953).
64. The following researchers give different percentages for international news on AP's trunk wire: Cutlip (1954) – 22·4%; Adams (1964) – 36%; Hester (1971) – 24·7% and Hester (1974) – 33·9%.
65. Read, W. H. (1976), p. 104.
66. International Press Institute (1953).
67. UNESCO (1956).
68. Snider, P. (1968).
69. Bishop, R. L. (1976).
70. Harris, P. (1975).
71. Boyd-Barrett (1976).
72. Hester, A. (1974).
73. Schramm, W. et al. (1978).
74. Boyd-Barrett (1976), Ch. 12.
75. Hester, A. (1974), p. 87.
76. Associated Press: *AP World* (1977), No. 1.
77. Read, W. H. (1976), p. 104.
78. Associated Press: APME *Red Book* (1971), pp. 106–7.
79. Associated Press: APME *Red Book* (1977), p. 187.
80. Associated Press: APME *Red Book* (1977), p. 223.
81. UK *Press Gazette*, 19 May 1974.

2 Structure and process

1. See for instance McQuail, D., Blumler, J. G. and Brown, J. R. (1972).
2. Lewin, Kurt (1952).
3. White, D. M. (1950).
4. See for instance Tunstall (1971), Elliott (1972), Murphy, D. (1976), Schlesinger, P. (1978), Golding, P. (1979).
5. See for instance Miliband, R. (1969).
6. See for instance Murphy, D. (1976).
7. See for instance Halberstam, D. (1965).
8. Pugh, S. S. and Hickson, D. J. (1973).
9. Johnstone, Slawski and Bowman (1976).
10. The 15 completed questionnaires included 3 from Reuters respondents, 3 from UPI, 4 from AFP and 5 from AP: sent out in the pilot

stage of a survey which was not completed in view of agency opposition. The European agencies therefore accounted for 7 and the American agencies for 8. The number of course is only a small percentage of the total number of bureaux, but it does very usefully add to the sum total of information and confirms much of the interview evidence. The countries represented by the questionnaire survey included 2 medium-sized West European countries, 2 Asian countries, 2 Middle Eastern countries, and 3 South American countries. The respondents were bureau chiefs in all but two cases; in one instance a night editor answered the questionnaire, and in another the respondent was a stringer – the only representative of the agency in his country. There were over 50 interviews with UPI personnel, of whom 23 were bureau chiefs, and the rest were mainly editorial executives in New York, London and Washington. Others were bureau correspondents. The total number includes two reinterviews of bureau chiefs who changed their location in the course of the study. There were 57 interviews with Reuters journalists, of which 25 were with bureau chiefs. 12 of the total number of interviews were reinterviews, often with personnel who had changed their location or function in the course of the study. AFP interviews numbered 43, of which 12 were reinterviews. Interviews with AP journalists were in excess of 41, of which 6 were reinterviews, and a total of 20 were bureau chiefs. A further 80 or more interviews were held with newspaper foreign correspondents, national news agency and diplomatic personnel. Further light on agency work was provided in the questionnaire responses to a study published in 1971 (Tunstall), to which the author contributed: 10 correspondents from one agency were involved, in the US and West Germany in the late 1960s.
11. Hester, Al (1974).
12. Tunstall (1971).
13. Woollacott, M. (1975).
14. Schramm, W. et al. (1978).

3 *Wholesale news and market control: Domestic*

1. The major agency histories from which this book draws, especially for Chapters 3 and 4, include: Cooper, K. (1942), Desmond, R. W. (1978), Frédèrix, P. (1959), Gramling, O. (1940), Jones, R. (1951), Kruglak, T. (1962), Morris, J. A. (1957), Palmer, M. (1972, 1974), Schwarzlose, R. A. (1965), Scott, G. (1968), Storey, G. (1951).
2. For full description of the territorial divisions of the cartel or 'ring combination' see Desmond, R. W. (1978).
3. Storey, G. (1951), Ch. 6.
4. Storey, G. (1951), Ch. 13.
5. See for instance an anonymous article entitled 'British News Abroad', in *Round Table*, Vol. 27, 1937, pp. 533–46, which quotes from the Prince of Wales' 1931 speech on the subject of relatively poor circulation of British news in South America.

6. The Post Office Records Library, London, contains interesting documentation of such discussions. See particularly Minute 12742, 1929; Minute 13432, 1930; and Minute 6413, 1931.
7. Scott, G. (1968), Ch. 13.
8. Palmer, M. (1972).
9. Desmond, R. (1978).
10. Gannett, L. (1924).
11. Desmond, R. (1978), p. 137.
12. Denoyer, Pierre quoted in Desmond, R. (1937), p. 57.
13. Laney, Al, quoted in Hohenberg, J. (1964).
14. Lazareffe, P. (1942), *Dernière Edition*, Valiguette, Montreal. p. 90.
15. Weigle, C. (1941).
16. Frédèrix, P. (1959).
17. Weigle, C. (1941), pp. 282–3.
18. Quoted in Palmer, (1972).
19. Becker, T. (1971).
20. Stone, M. (1922), p. 211.
21. Schwarzlose (1965).
22. Californian Newspaper Publishers Association Editors' Conference, reported in *Editor and Publisher*, 29 June 1974.
23. *Editor and Publisher*, 21 Dec. 1974.
24. Knight, O. (1967).
25. Rucker, B. (1968), pp. 71–2.
26. Irwin, W. (1914).
27. Major sources on broadcasting section: Moore, H. (1935), Sanders, K. P. (1967), Rucker, B. (1968), Schwarzlose, R. (1965), pp. 116–9.
28. Schwarzlose (1967).
29. Boyd-Barrett (1976), Ch. 3.
30. *Editor and Publisher*, 28 April 1979.
31. All Scripps-Howard dailies in 1974 subscribed to UPI – of 17 Scripps-Howard papers, 11 took only UPI, and 5 took both AP and UPI. Of 36 Scripps League dailies, 21 took UPI only, 14 took AP, and 1 took both. All 8 Hearst dailies took both AP and UPI (*Editor and Publisher Yearbook*, 1974).
32. *Editor and Publisher*, 31 May 1958.
33. Boyd-Barrett (1976), p. 185.
34. Singletary (1975).
35. Singletary (1975).
36. Boyd-Barrett (1976), p. 184.
37. Schwarzlose, R. A. (1967).
38. Interview, 22 Oct. 1978.
39. Mock, J. R. and Lawson, C. (1939).
40. Hyman, S. (1969).
41. Bernstein V. and Gordon, J. (1967).
42. Ibid.
43. Loory, S. (1974).
44. Schorr, D. (1978), *CJR*, Nov./Dec.
45. The 'cold war' evidence, even in the critical account by Aronson (1970) is mixed. With others, Aronson notes the importance of US

agency journalists in 'exposing' the underlying nature of the Diem regime and US support for Diem. But he also records instances in which the wire services were unwittingly 'used' by the military: e.g. the 'discovery' by AP and UPI correspondents of a 'Vietcong camp' in Cambodia in 1967 which may have been planted. Aronson concluded that 'they were at best unwitting dupes of a clumsy plan to whip up sentiment in the US for an invasion of Cambodia; at worst, they were willing accomplices in the shameful plan'. (Aronson, 1970, p. 243.)

46. Schiller, H. I. (1977).
47. Gunther, J. (1930), p. 646.
48. Gunther, J. (1930), p. 646.
49. Boyd-Barrett (1976), p. 198–9.
50. Johnstone, Slawski and Bowman (1976).
51. Witcover, J. (1973).

4 **Wholesale news and market control: Foreign**

1. See Cohen, B. (1974) for figures on imperial expansion.
2. Ashworth, W. (1962).
3. Aldcroft, D. H. (1968), Ch. 1.
4. Ashworth, W. (1962).
5. Aldcroft, D. H. and Richardson H. W., (1969), Section A, part 3.
6. Gunther, J. (1930).
7. Grossman, M. R. (1947).
8. Kruglak (1975), pp. 15–16.
9. Robinson, G. (1970).
10. UNESCO: International Commission for the Study of Communication Problems: Working Papers 15, Monographs (III), p. 135.
11. Ibid., p. 142.
12. Harris, P. (1977), p. 105.
13. *The Times*, 13 May 1931.
14. Post Office Records Library: Minutes: File 6413, 1933.
15. *Round Table* (1937).
16. Rugeroni, J., Post Office Records Library: Minutes: File 6413, 1938.
17. *Editor and Publisher*, 31 Jan. 1959.
18. Williams, F. (1953).
19. The group originally included 3 Brazilian papers, 2 Chilean, 1 from Colombia, 1 from Ecuador, 1 from Mexico, 2 from Peru and 2 in Venezuela.
20. Rosenblum, Mort (1978), p. 110.
21. Interview with author, 13 Dec. 1978. And in Argentina 1972/3 UPI claimed some 70 news organizations as against AP's 33 newspapers, 12 broadcasters, 16 radiophoto, 11 mail and 42 'casual' or nonregular clients. (Read: 1976, p. 102.) For the next few years the agencies were obliged by the government to distribute through the newly established Noticias Argentinas.

22. Harris, P. (1977), Ch. 3. But see Massing, M.: 'Inside the Wires' Banana Republics', *CJR*, Nov./Dec. 1979, pp. 45-9.
23. However, the establishment of exchange relationships between AP and the Tunisian agency TAP, and the Nigerian agency, NNA, in 1978/9 might have represented a change of attitude.
24. Bishop, R. L. (1976).
25. Hachten, W. (1971).
26. Pinch, E. T. (1977).
27. Shobail, A. (1971).
28. Storey, G. (1951), Ch. 5.
29. Sahni, J. N. (1974).
30. IPI Report, April/May 1978.
31. Jablons, P. H. (1978), pp. 33-36.
32. Government of India: Ministry of Information and Broadcasting: Committee on News Agencies, August 1977.
33. Morris, J. A. (1957).
34. Desmond, R. (1937), p. 341.
35. Nash, V. (1931).
36. Nash, V. (1933), p. 318.
37. Nash, V. (1933).
38. Nafziger, R. (1939).
39. Internal Reuters survey over a three-month period of 1973.
40. Boyd-Barrett (1976), Ch. 5.
41. Lee, J. (1965).
42. IPI (1968).
43. Clayton, C. C., in Lent (1971).

5 *National news agencies: The unstable nexus*

1. Main sources: UNESCO (1953), (1964), (1975), and IOJ (1969).
2. Lennart, Olsson and Lundquist (1971).
3. Snider, P. (1968).
4. UNESCO: International Commission for the Study of Communication Problems: Working Papers 13, Monographs (I), p. 35.
5. Harris, P. (1977), Ch. 6.
6. UNESCO: International Commission for the Study of Communication Problems: Working Papers 15, Monographs (III), p. 135.
7. Interview with Reuters' Shahe Guebenlian, 28 September 1978.
8. IPI Report, Dec. 1978.
9. UNESCO: International Commission for the Study of Communication Problems: Working Papers 15, Monographs (III), p. 107.
10. UK *Press Gazette*: 12 March 1979.
11. MENA was suspended by the Union of Arab News Agencies at its 1978 Beirut Conference for allegedly failing to pay overdue subscriptions: UK *Press Gazette*, 19 Feb. 1979.
12. Ivačić, P. (1978), p. 160.
13. Ibid.

262 Notes and references

14. Pinch, E. T. (1978).
15. For further material on IPS see UNESCO: International Commission for the Study of Communication Problems: Working Papers 14, Monographs (II), pp. 79–89.

6 New markets, new methods, conflict and risk

1. Fleetwood-May, C. (1971).
2. Interview with Reuters' managing director, Gerald Long, 11 March 1973.
3. In the late 1960s there was even talk of the North American division becoming a separate entity. At that time its management was strengthened and placed under the charge of G. Renfrew, who had previously done much to develop Reuters' economic and computer services.
4. Colchester, N. (1978). At the same time it is significant that some national agencies are seeking to supplement revenues through provision of services involving advertising of company information. An IPI report in 1975 indicated that the W. German agency, DDP, was planning to establish a separate operation involving company payments for mention in a companies' service for various media; VWD planned a similar service under the title Complex; DPA had similar plans, involving political rather than commercial news: a separate service would be available for organizations to pay for distribution of information about their activities to various media. (IPI Report, Sept. 1975, No. 9, p. 3.) This was seen as a response to excessive competition in the W. German news market.
5. North, A. (1934).
6. Rosenblum, M. (1978): 'AP and UPI rely heavily on income from photo sales' (p. 108). Rosenblum is possibly generalizing excessively from his Argentinian experience.
7. Stan Swinton, AP vice-president, in interview with author, 13 Dec. 1978. His UPI counterpart, Frank Tremaine, estimated that photos accounted for some 15–16% of UPI revenue (interview 12 Dec. 1978).
8. Stan Swinton, 13 Dec. 1978.
9. Briggs, Asa (1961).
10. Mahoney, J. (1975).
11. Ibid.
12. Eurovision survey figures made available by UPITN.
13. UK *Press Gazette*: 11 June 1979 and 18 June 1979.
14. Eurovision survey figures made available by UPITN.
15. Bagdikian, Ben H. (1963).
16. *Editor and Publisher*: 22 June 1963.

Conclusion

1. Rosenblum, M. (1978, 1979). See also *idem* (1979), *Coups and Earthquakes*, New York, Harper and Row.

Bibliography of major sources

Abu-Lughod, Ibrahim (1962): 'International Affairs in the Arabic Press: A Comparative Analysis', *POQ*, Vol. 26, pp. 600–12.
Adams, John B. (1964): 'A Qualitative Analysis of Domestic and Foreign News on the AP TA Wire', *Gazette*, Vol. 10, Autumn, pp. 285–95.
Aggarwala, N. K. (1978): 'What is Development News?', *Development Forum*.
Aldcroft, D. H. (1968): *The Development of British Industry and Foreign Competition*, London, George Allen and Unwin.
Aldcroft, D. H. and Richardson, H. W. (1969): *The British Economy 1870–1939*, London, Macmillan.
Alisky, M. and Barash, R. (1957): 'Radio News Values of Teletypesetter Copy', *JQ*, Vol. 34, No. 3.
Allen, L. F. (1947): 'Effect of Allied Occupation on the Press of Japan', *JQ*, Vol. 24.
Almaney, Adnan (1970): 'International and Foreign Affairs on Network Television News', *Journal of Broadcasting*, Vol. XIV, No. 4, pp. 499–509.
Altheide, David L. (1976): *Creating Reality: How TV News Distorts Events*, Beverly Hills and London, Sage.
Altheide, David L. and Rasmussen, R. (1973): 'Becoming News', Dept. of Sociology, San Diego, La Jolla, California, April.
Anderson, Russell F. (1950): 'The Disappearing Foreign Correspondent', *The Michigan Alumnus Quarterly Review*, Vol. LVII, No. 10, 9 Dec., pp. 1–12.
Anon (1937): 'AP' *Fortune*, Vol. 15, No. 2, Feb., p. 89.
Anon (1937): 'British News Abroad', *Round Table*, Vol. 27, June, pp. 533–46.
Anon (1942): 'The AP as Monopoly', *New Republic*, Vol. 107, No. 10, 7 Sept.
Arlen, Michael (1969): 'Television and Press in Vietnam', in *Living Room War*, New York, Viking Press, pp. 102–133.
Arnett, Peter (1972): 'Reflections on Vietnam, the Press and America', *Nieman Reports*. Vol. XVI, March.
Aronson, James (1970): *The Press and the Cold War*, New York, Bobbs-Merrill.
Ashworth, William (1962): *A Short History of the International Economy: 1850–1950*, London, Longman.
Bagdikian, Ben H. (1963): 'Journalist Meets Propagandist', *CJR*, Autumn.
Bagdikian, Ben H. (1971): *The Information Machine*, New York, Harper and Row.

264 Bibliography of major sources

Bagdikian, Ben H. (1973): 'Congress and the Media', *CJR*, Vol. XII, Jan/Feb.
Bagdikian, Ben H. (1973): 'Publishing's Quiet Revolution', *CJR*, Vol. XII, May/June.
Baglehole, K. C. (1969): *A Century of Service*, London, Bourehill Press.
Baillie, Hugh (1959): *High Tension*, London, Werner Laurie Ltd.
Barnes, Peter (1964): 'The Wire Services from Latin America', *Nieman Reports*, Vol. XVIII, No. 1.
Barnetson, Sir William (1973): 'Reuters', *The Accountant's Magazine*, June.
Beard, Richard L. and Zoerner II, C. (1969): 'Associated Negro Press: Its Founding, Ascendancy and Demise', *JQ*, Vol. 46, No. 1., pp. 47–52.
Becker, Thomas H. (1971): *The Memphis Commercial Appeal*, Louisiana State University Press.
Bellanger, C. (1962): 'L'AFP Since the Reorganization of 1957', *Gazette*, Vol. VIII, pp. 147–54.
Beltran, Luis R, and Cardona, E. F. (1979): 'Latin America and the United States: Flaws in the Free Flow of Information', in Nordenstreng and Schiller (eds), *National Sovereignty and International Communication*, Norwood, New Jersey, Ablex Publishing Corp, pp. 33–64.
Benet, Stephen, V. (1933): 'The Story of United Press', *Fortune*, May.
Berktau, Fred (1933): 'Tendencies Towards a Financial Concentration in the International Newspaper Field', *JQ*, Vol. X, No. 2.
Bernstein, Victor and Gordon, Jesse (1967): 'The Press and the Bay of Pigs', *Columbia Forum*, Vol. 10, No. 3.
Bishop, Michael (1967): 'An Analysis of How the *New York Times* Gathers and Disseminates International News', *Gazette*, Vol. XIII, No. 4.
Bishop, Robert L. (1975): 'How Reuters and AFP Coverage of Independent Africa Compare', *JQ*, Vol. 52, No. 4, pp. 654–62.
Bogart, Les (1968): 'The Overseas Newsmen: A 1967 Profile Survey', *JQ*, Vol. 45, pp. 293–305.
Borman, Jim (1957): 'How durable is Radio?', *JQ*, Vol. 34, No. 3, pp. 311–16.
Bowers, D. R. (1967): 'A Report on the Activity by Publishers in Directing Newsroom Decisions', *JQ*, Vol. 43, No. 3, pp. 43–52.
Boyd-Barrett, J. O. (1977): 'The Collection of Foreign News in the National Press: Organization and Resources', in Boyd-Barrett, Seymour-Ure and Tunstall: *Studies on the Press*, HMSO, pp. 7–43.
Boyd-Barrett (1976): *The World-Wide News Agencies: Development, Organization, Competition, Markets and Product*, Ph.D. thesis, Open University.
Braestrup, Peter (1977): *Big Story: How the American Press and Television Reported and Interpreted the Crisis of TET 1968 in Vietnam and Washington*, Boulder, Colorado, Westview Press (2 vols).
Briggs, Asa (1961): *History of Broadcasting in the UK*, London, Oxford University Press, Vols. I and II.

Bibliography of major sources

Britton, Rosewall, S. (1934): 'Chinese News Interests', *Pacific Affairs*, Vol. 7., June, pp. 181–93.
Brown, R. (1969): *Telecommunications*, London, Aldis Books.
Browne, Malcolm (1963): 'Vietnam Reporting: Three Years of Crisis', *CJR*, Vol. 2.
Buckalew, James K. (1974): 'The Radio News Gatekeeper and his Sources'; *JQ*, Vol. 51, No. 4, pp. 602–6.
Casey, Ralph D. and Copeland, Thomas H. (1958): 'Use of Foreign News by Minnesota Dailies', *JQ*, Vol. 35, No. 1, pp. 87–9.
Charnley, M. V. (1951): 'The Radio Newsroom', *JQ*, Vol. 28, No. 2.
Chaudhary, Anju, (1974): 'Comparative News Judgement of Indian and American Journalists', *Gazette*, Vol. XX, No. 4.
Cheesman, Robin, (1970): 'Egypt and Israel in European Elite Press', *Psykologiskt Forsvar*, Stockholm.
Cherry, Colin (1971): *World Communication: Threat or Promise?*, New York, Wiley-Interscience.
Chick, J. D. (1967): *The White Press: A Study of the Role of Foreign Owned Newspapers in Ghana, Nigeria and Sierra Leone 1946–1965*, Ph.D. thesis, Manchester University.
Clark, Keith (1931): *International Communications: The American Attitude*, New York, Columbia University Press.
Clayton, Charles C. (1971): 'Hong Kong', in Lent, J. (ed), *The Asian Newspapers' Reluctant Revolution*, Ames, Iowa State University Press.
Cohen, Benjamin, J. (1974): *The Question of Imperialism: The Political Economy of Dominance and Dependence*, London, Macmillan.
Colchester, N. (1978): 'The News Agency Battle for the Market Place', *Financial Times*, 13 Sept.
Cooper, Kent (1942): *Barriers Down*, New York, Farrar and Rinehart.
Cote, Richard J. (1970): 'A Study of Accuracy of Two Wire Services', *JQ*, Vol. 47, No. 4, Winter, pp. 660–6.
Curran, Sir Charles (1979): 'Eurovision and the News Agencies – A Reply.' *EBU Review*, Vol. XXX, No. 6, pp. 30–2.
Cutlip, Scott M. (1954): 'Content and Flow of AP News – From Trunk to TTS to Reader', *JQ*, Vol. 31, pp. 434–46.
Dajoni, Nabil and Donohoe, John (1973): 'Foreign News in the Arab Press; A Content Analysis of Six Arab Dailies', *Gazette*, Vol. XIX, No. 3, pp. 155–65.
Desmond, Robert W. (1937): *The Press and World Affairs*, New York, D. Appleton Century Co.
Desmond, Robert W. (1978): *The Information Process*, Ames, University of Iowa Press.
Dickens, Mary Margaret (1978): 'Transnational News Services: Editors' Views in Sri Lanka and Bangladesh', paper presented at the Transnational Communication Enterprises and National Communication Policies Advanced Summer Seminar, 6–19 Aug., Honolulu.
Eapen, Kenneth E. (1972): 'ZANU: An African News Agency', *Gazette*, Vol. XVIII, pp. 193–207.
Elliott, P. (1972): *The Making of a Television Series*, London, Constable.

Elliott, P. and Golding, P. (1973): 'The News Media and Foreign Affairs', in Boardman, R. and Broom, A. I. R. (eds): *The Management of Britain's External Relations*, London, Macmillan.

Emery, Edwin, (1964): *The Press and America*, N.J., Prentice-Hall.

Eswara, H. S. (1969): 'Flow of News Between India and Africa During Times of Crisis', *Gazette*, Vol. IX, April–June, pp. 15–22.

Fernandez, T. (1964): 'The News Agencies', in Wolsely, Roland E. (ed): *Journalism in Modern India*, New York, Asia Publishing House.

Fernandez, T. (1966): 'Asian News Agency', *Gazette*, Vol. 12, No. 4.

Fett, Roland R. (1949): 'America's Role in International News Exchange: A Study of the AP, UP, INS and "Voice of America" since World War II', Master's thesis, University of Illinois.

Fleetwood-May, Cecil (1971): 'Reuters in the Days of Codes and Pirates', *UK Press Gazette*, 13 Sept.

Frédèrix, Pierre (1959): *Un Siècle de Chasse aux Nouvelles de L'Agence France Presse*, Paris, Flammarion.

Galtung, Johan and Ruge, Mari (1965): 'The Structure of Foreign News', *Journal of Peace Research*, No. 1, pp. 64–90.

Gandhi, D. V. (1972): 'Language News Agencies', *Vidura*, Vol. 9, No. 5, pp. 307 and 331.

Gannett, Lewis (1924): 'The Secret Corruption of the French Press', *The Nation*, Vol. 118.

Gardner, Mary A. (1967): *The Inter-American Press Association*, University of Texas Press.

Garver, Richard A. (1962): 'Content of Korean Language Daily Newspapers', *Gazette*, Vol. VIII.

Geiber, Walter (1956): 'Across the Desk: A Study of 16 Telegraph Editors', *JQ*, Vol. 33, No. 3, pp. 423–32.

Geyn, Mark (1947): 'A Million Words of Poison', *Saturday Evening Post*, 16 June.

Golding, Peter and Elliott, Philip (1979): *Making the News*, London, Longman.

Gould, Stanhope, (1975): 'Coors Brews the News', *CJR*, Vol. XIV.

Gramling, Oliver (1940): AP: *The Story of News*, New York, Farrar and Rinehart Inc.

Grossman, Max R. (1947): 'Some Contemporary Problems of Foreign Correspondence', *JQ*, Vol. 24, No. 1.

Gunther, John (1930): 'Funnelling the European News', *Harpers Monthly*, April, pp. 635–47.

Hachten, William (1971): *Muffled Drums*, Ames, Iowa State University Press.

Halberstam, David (1965): *The Making of a Quagmire*, London, Bodley Head.

Harris, Charles, R. (1957): *Allied Military Administration of Italy, 1943–1945*, London, HMSO.

Harris, Phil (1975): 'International News Media and Underdevelopment', Unpublished M. Phil thesis, Centre for Mass Communication Research, University of Leicester.

Bibliography of major sources

Harris, Phil (1977): 'News Dependence: The Case for a New World Information Order', final report to UNESCO of a study of the international news media.
Hart, Jim A. (1963): 'The Flow of News Between the United States and Canada', *JQ*, Vol. 40, No. 4, pp. 70–4.
Hart, Jim A (1966): 'Foreign News in US and English Daily Newspapers: A Comparison', *JQ*, Vol. 43, No. 3, pp. 443–8.
Haskings, Hack B. (1952): 'Local Broadcasting Practices in Hometown Radio Stations', *JQ*, Vol. 29, No. 4, pp. 443–6.
Hersh, Seymour M. (1969): 'The Story Everyone Ignored', *CJR*, Winter, Vol. VI.
Hester, Al (1971): 'An Analysis of News Flow from Developed and Developing Nations', *Gazette*, Vol. XVII, No. 1/2, pp. 29–43.
Hester, Al (1974): 'The News from Latin America via a World News Agency', *Gazette*, Vol. XX, No. 2, pp. 82–91.
Hicks, G. and Gordon, A. (1974): 'Foreign News Content in Israeli and US Newspapers', *JQ*, Vol. 51, No. 4, pp. 639–49.
Hohenberg, J. (1964): *Foreign Correspondence*, New York, Columbia University Press.
Hohenberg, J. (1967): 'The Flow of News Between Asia and the West', *Nieman Reports*, Vol. XXI, March.
Höhne, Hans Joachim (1976/7): *Report über Nachrichtenagenturen* (2 vols), Baden-Baden, Nomos Verlagsgesellschaft.
Hoopes, Paul R. (1966): 'Content Analysis of News in Three Argentine Dailies', *JQ*, No. 3, Autumn, pp. 534–8.
Hopkins, Albert A (1931): 'Behind the Scenes of News Gathering', *Scientific American*, Vol. 145, No. 4, Oct., pp. 222–6.
Hopkins, Mark W. (1970): *Mass Media in the Soviet Union*, New York, Pegasus.
Horton, Philip (ed) (1978) *The Third World and Press Freedom*, New York, Praeger.
Hyde, G. M. (1931): 'US Journalism in 1931', *JQ*, Vol. VIII, No. 4.
Hyman, Sidney (1969): *The Lives of William Benton*, University of Chicago Press.
International Organization of Journalists (1969): *Handbook of News Agencies*, Prague, IOJ.
International Press Institute (1953): *The Flow of News*, Zurich, IPI.
International Press Institute (1954): *The News from the Middle East*, Zurich, IPI.
International Press Institute (1956): *News in Asia*, Zurich, IPI.
Irwin, Will (1914): 'The United Press', *Harpers Weekly*, 25 April, pp. 6–8.
Ivačić, Pero (1978): 'The Flow of News: Tanjug, the Pool, and the National Agencies', *Journal of Communication*, Autumn, Vol. 28, No. 4, pp. 157–62.
Jablons, Pamela H. (1978): 'India's Press: Can it Become Independent At Last?', *CJR*, Vol. XVII, July/Aug., pp. 33–6.
Johnstone, John W., Slawski, Edward J., and Bowman, W. W. (1976): *The News People*, University of Illinois Press.

Jones, L. R., Troldahl, V. C., Hvistendahl, J. K. (1961): 'News Selection Patterns from a States TTS-Wire', *JQ*, Vol. 38, No. 1, pp. 303–12.
Jones, Roderick (1951): *A Life in Reuters*, London, Hodder and Stoughton.
Karnow, Stanley (1968): 'The Newsmen's War in Vietnam', *Nieman Reports*, Vol. XXII.
Kayser, Jacques (1953): *One Week's News: Comparative Studies of Seventeen Major Dailies for a Seven-Day Period*, Paris, UNESCO.
Kearl, Bryant (1958): 'Effects of Newspaper Competition on Press Service Resources', *JQ*, Vol. 35, No. 4, pp. 56–63.
Kelly, Frank K. (1962): 'The News from Latin America', *CJR*, Fall, Vol. 1.
Khurshid, Abdus Salam (1966): 'Content Analysis of Daily Press in Pakistan', *Gazette*, Vol. VIII, No. 1.
Kieve, J. L. (1973): *Electric Telegraph: A Social and Economic History*, Newton Abbot, David and Charles.
Kitch, Kenneth H. (1938): 'The AP in Kansas: Its Background and Development', PhD Thesis, University of Kansas.
Kleisch, R. (1975): 'A Vanishing Species: The American Newsman Abroad', US *Overseas Press Club Directory*.
Knight, Oliver (ed.) (1966): *Scripps I Protest*, University of Wisconsin Press.
Knightley, Phillip (1975): *The First Casualty*, London, André Deutsch.
Kruglak, Theodore E. (1953): *The Foreign Correspondents*, Paris, Librairie E. Droz.
Kruglak, Theodore E. (1957): 'Foreign News at Wholesale', *The Nation*, Vol. 185, pp. 473–5.
Kruglak, Theodore E. (1958): '"Crash" Coverage of the US Media in Hungary and the Middle East', *JQ*, Vol. 35, No. 1, pp. 15–25.
Kruglak, Theodore E. (1962): *The Two Faces of TASS*, University of Minnesota Press.
Kruglak, Theodore E. (1975): 'The Role and Evolution of Press Agencies in Socialist Countries', *Gazette*, Vol. 21, No. 1, pp. 1–17.
Lambert, Donald (1965): 'Foreign Correspondents Covering the US', *JQ*, Vol. 33, No. 2, Summer, pp. 349–56.
Larson, James F. (1979): 'International Affairs Coverage on US Network Television', *Journal of Communication*, Spring, No. 2., pp. 136–47.
Lee, John (1965): 'International Flow in the Expatriate English-Language Press', *JQ*, Vol. 42, No. 3, pp. 632–8.
Lent, John A. (1968): 'History of the Japanese Press', *Gazette*, Vol. XIV, No. 1.
Lent, John A. (1971): *The Asian Newspapers' Reluctant Revolution*, Ames, Iowa State University Press.
Lent, John A. (1974): 'Mass Media in Laos', *Gazette*, Vol. XX, No. 3, pp. 171–9.
Lent, John A. (1977): *Third World Mass Media and their Search For Modernity. The Case of the Commonwealth Caribbean 1717–1976*, Lewisburg, Bucknell University Press.
Lewin, Kurt (1952): 'Channels of Group Life', *Human Relations*, Vol. 1, No. 2.

Liebes, B. H. (1966): 'Decision-Making by Telegraph Editors – AP or UPI', *JQ*, Vol. 43, No. 3, pp. 434–42.
Lippman, Walter (1922): *Public Opinion*, New York, Harcourt Brace.
Liu, Alan P. (1972): 'Ideology and Information: Correspondents of the New China News Agency and Chinese Foreign Policy Making', *Journal of International Affairs*, Vol. 26, No. 2, pp. 131–44.
Loory, Stuart H. (1974): 'The CIA and its Use of the Press', *CJR*, Vol. XII.
McCartney, James (1968): 'Can the Media Cover Guerilla Wars?', *CJR*, Vol. VI.
McCleary, W. T. (1937): 'Mastering the Second Fiddle', *JQ*, Vol. XIV, No. 3, Autumn, pp. 244–8.
McFadder, Tom J. (1953): 'News Agencies and Propaganda in Five Arab States', *JQ*, Vol. 30, No. 3, Fall, pp. 482–91.
MacFarquhar, Roderick (1973): 'A Visit to the Chinese Press', *China Quarterly*, No. 53, pp. 144–51.
MacNeil, Robert (1968): 'The News on TV and How it is Unmade', *Harpers Magazine*, Vol. 237, Oct.
McNelly, John T. (1979): 'International News for Latin America', *Journal of Communication*, Vol. 29, Spring, No. 2, pp. 156–163.
McQuail, D., Blumler, J. G., Brown, J. R. (1972): 'The Television Audience: A Revised Perspective', in McQuail, D. (ed): *Sociology of Mass Communications*, Harmondsworth, Penguin.
Maddox, Brenda (1972): *Beyond Babel*, London, André Deutsch.
Mahoney, John (1975): 'The News Exchange: The Agency Dimension', *EBU Review*, Vol. XXVI, No. 3, pp. 32–4.
Marchetti, Victor and Marks, J. D. (1974): *The CIA and the Cult of Intelligence*, London, Jonathan Cape.
Markham, J. (1961): 'Foreign News in the United States and South American Press', *POQ*, Vol. 25, No. 2, pp. 249–62.
Marsan, Claude (1973): *L'Agence France Presse*, Paris, Presse Actualité.
Martin, Leslie, J. (1960): 'The Rise and Development of AFP', *JQ*, Vol. 37, No. 1.
Matta, Fernando, R. (1979): 'The Latin American Concept of News', *Journal of Communication*, Vol. 29, Spring, No. 2.
Mayer, Henry L. (1964): *The Press in Australia*, London, Angus & Robertson.
Meursault, R. (1974): *L'Agence Reuter*, Paris, Presse Actualité.
Mishra, V. M. (1979) 'From the Middle East to US Media', *JQ*, Vol. 56, Summer, pp. 375–8.
Mitchell, John D. (1965): 'Thailand's Unexamined Media: Non-Daily Newspapers and Radio-TV', *JQ*, Vol. 42, No. 1.
Mock, J. R. and Lawson, C. (1939): 'Activities of the Mexico Section of the Creel Committee 1917–1918', *JQ*, Vol. XVI, No. 2.
Modig, Jan-Otto (1963): 'Scandinavian News Agencies', *Gazette*, Vol. IX, No. 1, pp. 142, 148.
Moore, Herbert (1935): 'The News War in the Air', *JQ*, Vol. XII, March, pp. 43–53.

Morris, Gilbert (1939): 'From Usually Reliable Sources', *Harper's*, Vol. 179, Sept., pp. 385–96.

Morris, Joe A. (1957): *Deadline Every Minute: The Story of United Press*, New York, Doubleday.

Moung, Tim (1947): 'Contemporary Burmese Press Undergoing an Evolution', *JQ*, Vol. 24, No. 2.

Murphy, David (1976): *The Silent Watchdog: The Press in Local Politics*, London, Constable.

Nafziger, Ralph O. (1937): 'World War Correspondents and Censorship of the Belligerents', *JQ*, Vol. XIV, No. 3.

Nash, Vernon (1931): 'Chinese Journalism', *JQ*, Vol. 8, No. 4, pp. 316–22.

Nash, Vernon (1933): 'Chinese Journalism', *JQ*, Vol. 10, No. 4, pp. 446–52.

Nichols, John S. (1975): 'Latin Latin-American Regional News Agency', *Gazette*, Vol. XXI, No. 3.

North, Anthony (1934): 'No, But I Saw the Pictures', *New Outlook*, Vol. 163, No. 6, June.

Oiseth, Howard (1938): 'News Agency Practices in Scandinavia', *JQ*, Vol. 15, March, pp. 12–18.

Olsson, Claes-Olaf and Weibull, Lennart (1973): 'The Reporting of News in Scandinavian Countries', *Scandinavian Political Studies*, Vol. 8, pp. 141–67.

Ostgaard, Einar (1965): 'Factors Influencing Flow of News', *Journal of Peace Research*, No. 1, pp. 41–63.

Palmer, Michael, (1972): 'Some Aspects of the French Press During the Rise of the Popular French Daily, circa 1860–90', D. Phil. Thesis, Bodleian, Oxford.

Palmer, Michael (1974): *News and Propaganda in Press: The French State News Agency under Vichy, 1940–44*, Strasbourg, European Consortium for Political Research Workshop.

Phillips Davison, W. (1974), 'News Media and International Negotiation', *POQ*, Summer.

Pinch, Edward T. (1977): 'The Third World and the Fourth Estate: A Look at the Non-Aligned News Agencies' Pool', 19th session of the Senior Seminar in Foreign Policy, US Dept. of State.

Pinch, Edward T. (1978): 'The Flow of News: An Assessment of the Non-Aligned News Agencies Pool', *Journal of Communication*, Autumn, Vol. 28, No. 4, pp. 163–71.

Political and Economic Planning (1938): *Report on the British Press*, London, PEP.

Powers, Ron and Oppenheim, J. (1973): 'The Failed Promise of All-News Radio', *CJR*, Vol. XII, No. 3, Sept/Oct., pp. 21–8.

Read, William H. (1976): *America's Mass Media Merchants*, Baltimore, Johns Hopkins University Press.

Resch, F. A. (1943): 'Photo Coverage of the War by the "Still Pictures Pool"', *JQ*, Vol. 20, No. 4.

Richstead, Tom and McMillan, Michael (1974): 'The Pacific Islands Press', *JQ*, Vol. 51, No. 3, Autumn, pp. 470–97.

Righter, R. (1978): *Whose News?*, London, André Deutsch.
Robinson, Gertrude (1970): 'Foreign News Selection is Non-Linear in Yugoslavia's Tanjug Agency', *JQ*, Vol. 47, No. 2, pp. 340–51.
Robinson, Gertrude (1977): *Tito's Maverick Media: The Politics of Mass Communications in Yugoslavia*, Urbana, University of Chicago Press.
Rogers, Walter S. (1925): 'Electrical Communications in the Pacific', *Annals of the American Academy of Political and Social Sciences*, Vol. 122, pp. 78–81.
Rollin, Leon (1948): 'Lag in Economic Recovery Reflected in French Press', *JQ*, Vol. 25, No. 1.
Rosenblum, Mort (1978): 'Western Wire Services', in Horton, Philip (ed) (1978), op. cit., pp. 104–26.
Rosenblum, Mort (1979): 'Reporting from the Third World', in Nordenstreng, K. and Schiller, H. I.: *National Sovereignty and International Communication*, Norwood, New Jersey, Ablex Publishing Corp.
Rubin, Ronald I. (1973): 'A New Voice for America', *Gazette*, Vol. XIX, No. 4, pp. 213–21.
Rucker, Byrce (1960): 'News Services' Crowd Reporting in the 1956 Presidential Campaign', *JQ*, Vol. 37, No. 1, pp. 195–8.
Rucker, Bryce (1968): *The First Freedom*, Southern Illinois University Press, Ch. 5, pp. 60–79.
Sahni, J. N. (1974): *Truth About the Indian Press*, Bombay, Allied Publishers.
Saint Louis Journalism Review (1973): 'Now, the Hourly Plagiarism', *CJR*, Vol. X11.
Salamore, Barbara A. (1975): 'Reporting of External Behaviours in the World's Press: A Comparison of Regional Sources', paper presented at Annual Meeting of the International Studies Association, Washington, D.C., 19–22 Feb.
Sanders, Keith P. (1967): 'The Collapse of the Press-Radio News Bureau', *JQ*, Vol. 44, Vol. 3, pp. 549–51.
Schiller, Herbert I (1977): 'Genesis of the Free Flow of Information Principle: The Imposition of Communications Domination', Instant Research on Peace and Violence, Tampere, part 2, pp. 75–89.
Schlesinger, Philip (1978): *Putting Reality Together*, London, Constable.
Schramm, W. et al (1978): *International News Wires and Third World News in Asia. A Preliminary Report*, The Centre for Communication Studies, Chinese University of Hong Kong.
Schudson, M. (1978): *Discovering the News: A Social History of the News*, New York, Basic Books Inc.
Schwarzlose, Richard A. (1965): 'The American Wire Services: A Study of their Development as Social Institutions', Ph. D. Thesis, University of Illinois.
Schwarzlose, Richard A. (1966): 'Trends in Newspapers' Wire Service Resources 1934–66', *JQ*, Vol. 43, No. 4, pp. 627–38.
Schwarzlose, Richard A. (1968): 'Harbor News Association: The Formal Origins of the AP', *JQ*, Vol. 45, No. 2, Summer, pp. 253–60.

Schwarzlose, Richard A. (1974): 'Early Telegraphic News Dispatches: Forerunner of the AP', *JQ*, Vol. 51, No. 4.
Scott, George (1968): *Reporter Anonymous*, London, Hutchinson.
Scott, J. M. (1972): *Extel 100*, London, Ernest Benn.
Shaw, Donald L. (1967): 'News Bias and the Telegraph', *JQ*, Vol. 44, No. 1, pp. 3–12.
Sherman, Charles E. and Ruby, John (1974): 'The Eurovision News Exchange', *JQ*, Vol. 51, No. 3, pp. 478–85.
Shobail, Abdulrahman S. (1971): 'An Historical and Analytical Study of Broadcasting and the Press in Saudi Arabia', Unpublished Ph.D. Thesis, Ohio State University.
Singletary, Michael W. (1975): 'Newspaper Use of Supplemental Services, 1969–73', *JQ*, Vol. 52, No. 4, pp. 748–51.
Slattery, William J. (1970): 'Who Now Dow Jones?', *Esquire*, Oct.
Smith, Raymond F. (1969): 'On the Structure of Foreign News: A Comparison of the *New York Times* and the Indian White Papers', *Journal of Peace Research*, Vol. 6, No. 1, pp. 23–36.
Snider, Paul B. (1966): 'The Route of International News to the Press of Afghanistan through Bakhtar, the Afghan National News Agency', *Gazette*, Vol. XIV.
Snider, Paul B. (1967): '"Mr. Gates" Revisited: A 1966 Version of the 1949 Case Study', *JQ*, Vol. 44, No. 3, pp. 419–27.
Sparkes, Vernon M. (1978): 'The Flow of News Between Canada and the United States', *Gazette*, Vol. 55, No. 2, pp. 260–8.
Starck, Kenneth (1968): 'The Handling of Foreign News in Finland's Daily Newspapers', *JQ*, Vol. 45, No. 3, pp. 516–21.
Stempel, Guido H. (1959): 'Uniformity of Wire Content of Six Michigan Dailies', *JQ*, Vol. 36, No. 1, pp. 45–8.
Stillman, Don (1970): 'Tonkin: What Should Have Been Asked', *CJR*, Vol. IX.
Stone, Melville E. (1922): *Fifty Years a Journalist*, New York, Heinemann.
Sunwoo Nam (1970): 'The Flow of International News into Korea', *Gazette*, Vol. 16, No. 1.
Swett, Herbert E. (1970): 'AP Coverage of the Lincoln Assassination', *JQ*, Vol. 47, pp. 157–9.
Swindler, William F. (1946): 'The AP Anti-Trust Case in Historical Perspective', *JQ*, Vol. 23, No. 1, Spring.
Takaishi, Shingoro (1936–7): 'The Domei Press Agency Makes Its Bow', *Contemporary Japan*, pp. 245–53.
Thompson, R. L. (1947): *Wiring a Continent*, Princeton, N. J., Princeton University Press.
Thoren, Stig (1968): 'The Flow of Foreign News Into the Swedish Press', *JQ*, Vol. 45, No. 3, Autumn, pp. 521–4.
Trayes, E. J. (1972): 'News/Features Services by Circulation Group Use', *JQ*, Vol. 49, Spring, pp. 133–6.
Tuchman, G. (1978): 'The News Net', *Social Research*, Vol. 45, No. 2, Summer, pp. 253–76.

Tunstall, J. (1971): *Journalists at Work*, London, Constable.
Tunstall, J. (1977): *The Media are American*, London, Constable.
Turnbull, George S. (1957): 'Reporting of the War in Indochina', *JQ*, Vol. 34. pp. 87–9.
UNESCO (1950): *World Communications*, Paris, UNESCO.
UNESCO (1960): 'Developing Mass Media in Asia', Reports and Papers on Mass Communications, No. 30, Paris, UNESCO.
UNESCO (1964): *World Press: Newspapers and News Agencies*, Paris, UNESCO.
UNESCO (1975): *World Communications*, London, Gower Press.
UNESCO (1977/8): International Commission for the Study of Communication Problems: Working Papers: Nos. 13, 14 and 15 (Monographs I–II–III).
Van Horn, George (1952): 'Analysis of AP News on Trunk and Wisconsin State Wires', *JQ.*, Vol. 29, No. 3., Fall.
Varis, Tapio (1973): *International Inventory of Television Programme Structure and the Flow of TV Programmes Between Nations*, University of Tampere.
Varis, Tapio (1977): 'European Broadcasting and the New International Order', in Varis, T., Salinas, R., and Jokelin, R. (eds) (1977).
Varis, T. Salinas, R., and Jokelin, R. (eds) (1977): *International News and the New Information Order*, Institute of Journalism and Mass Communication, University of Tampere.
Vilcek, Miroslav (1979): 'Eurovision is More than Meets the Eye', *EBU Review*, Vol. XXX, No. 3. pp. 42–5.
Weibull, Lennart, Olsson, Claes-Olaf and Lundquist, Lars-Anders (1971): *Nordisk Nyhetsformedling*, Statsvetenskapliga Institutionen, Göteborgs Universitet.
Weigle, Clifford (1942): 'The Rise and Fall of the Havas News Agency', *JQ*, Vol. 19, Sept., pp. 277–86.
White, David M. (1950): 'The Gate-Keeper: A Case Study in the Selection of News', *JQ*, Vol. 27, No. 3, Autumn, pp. 383–90.
Whitehead, R. and Ziff, Howard (1974): 'Statehouse Coverage: Lobbyists Outlasts Journalists', *CJR*, Vol. XII, No. 5, pp. 11–12.
Wickham-Steed, H. (1938): *The Press*, London, Penguin.
Wilcox, D. (1975): *Mass Media in Black Africa*, New York, Praeger.
Wiley, Malcolm M. and Rice, Stuart A. (1933): *Communication Agencies and Social Life*, New York, McGraw Hill.
Williams, Francis (1953): *Transmitting World News*, UNESCO.
Wilson, Clifton E. (1953): 'Impact of Teletypesetter on Publishing Media', *JQ*, Vol. 30, No. 3.
Windhal, Sven (1972): *Kommunikations-Modeller*, Studentlitteratur, Lund, Sweden.
Witcover, Jules (1969): 'Washington: The Workhorse Wire Services', *CJR*, Vol. VIII.
Wolfe, Wayne (1964): 'Images of the United States in the Latin American Press', *JQ*, Vol. 41, No. 1, pp. 79–86.
Woodward, Julian L. (1968): *Foreign News in American Morning Newspapers*, New York, AMS Press.

Woollacott, Martin (1975): 'Where No News is Bad News', *Guardian*, 27 August.

Journal Abbreviations

CJR: Columbia Journalism Review.
JQ: Journalism Quarterly.
POQ: Public Opinion Quarterly.
UKPG: United Kingdom Press Gazette.

Index

ACACAN (Central American Agency), 175, 194, 201
ACME, photo agency, 234
ACP agency, France, 61
Adams, John B., 104, 106
ADN agency, East Germany, 14, 163
Adolph Coors Company, Golden, Colorado, 239
advertising, 219, 220, 223; Havas, 123, 124, 125, 128, 218, 220
AFA, 127
Afghan news agency, 63
Africa, 152, 153, 197; agency expansion, 177–80; agency news content, 105, 106, 108; national news agencies, 193–4; newsfilm, 242; regional news agencies, 212–13; regionalization, 63, 65; world agency promotion of new satellites, 201–2
Agefi (Agence Economique et Financière), 126, 226
L'Agence Centrale Parisienne de Presse (ACP), 128–9
L'Agence Continentale, 126
L'Agence Ewig, 126
L'Agence Fournier, 126, 158, 200
L'Agence Française Indépendante, 127, 174
L'Agence France Presse (AFP), 14, 16, 23, 24, 25, 98, 121, 122, 143, 161, 195, 201, 218, 245, 250; administrative and higher councils, 34, 35; in Asia, 182, 187, 188, 189; client relations with, 42, 71–2; competition, 128–9; distribution, 54–5, 56, 58; domestic market, 122, 127–30; editorial centralization, 80, 84; financial commission, 34–5; in Francophone Africa, 177, 178, 201; Jean Marin appointed director-general, 127; in Latin America, 174, 175; location of bureaux, 154; and manpower, 44, 45, 46–7; in Middle East, 180; news content, 104, 105, 106–7, 108; ownership and control, 34–6, 127; Paris HQ, 80, 84; photo distribution, 235; political influence, 35–6; range of services, 51; regionalization, 60, 63, 64, 66; revenue and expenditure, 36, 39–40, 128, 154; in USA, 165, 171; in Vienna, 47, 164
Agencia JB (AJB), Brazil, 57, 58
agency scheduling, 74–6
Aigles (French agency), 129
AIR (India's b/casting service), 183
Albania, 163, 165
Allende, Salvador, 62
Allied Newspapers, Inc., 32
American Press Association (APA), 134–5
L'Ami du Peuple, 124
ANETA, Dutch national agency, 227
ANGOP, Angola, 194
ANPA, 72, 141
ANSA, Italy, 57, 205, 228
Antara agency, Indonesia, 58
AP–Dow Jones economic news, 17, 36, 52, 81, 121, 170, 231–4; *see also* Dow Jones
APS agency, Senegal, 195
Arab-Israeli conflict, 179
Arab News Agency (ANA), 179
Arabic news services, 55, 65, 80, 179
Argentina, 62, 128, 154, 174, 176n, 194
Aronson, James, 109, 110
Asia, 20–1, 83–4; agency development, 180–91; and agencies' news content, 106; bureaux, 153–4; national news agencies, 193, 194; newsfilm, 240, 241; regionalization, 62–3, 64, 65; Telecom Highway

Index

Asia—*cont.*
satellite, 213; vernacular press, 189-90
Asian News Agency (ANS), 216, 217
ASIN (Action by National Information Systems), 14, 213
Associated Press (AP), 14, 16, 17, 23, 25, 61, 81, 98, 200; A and B national trunk wires, 50, 60; in Africa, 177, 178; A.M. and P.M., 134-7; in Asia, 182-3, 184, 185, 186, 187, 189; book publishing, 245; broadcasting and, 137-9, 236-7, 238, 245; clients, 41, 68, 69, 140-1; DataFeature, 147; Datastream, 50; distribution, 55, 56, 57, 58; diversification, 218, 245-6; in Eastern Europe, 162, 163; editorial centralization, 79, 80; electronic darkroom, 54; enterprise reporting, 52; European cartel and, 132, 159, 209-11; exclusivity, 133-4; expansion in Europe, 158-61; foreign language services, 57, 128; hub bureaux, 46, 50, 133; laserphoto, 54; leased communication facilities, 243; location of bureaux, 153-5; *Log* reports, 69; manpower and bureaux, 43, 44-5, 46; market trends, 139-44; the metropolitan interest, 131-3; in Middle East, 179-80; national news agencies and, 195, 203; news content, 104, 106, 107-8, 110; newsfilm distribution, 238; newsphoto service, 17, 90, 234, 235, 245; news service in France, 128; non-routine client servicing, 68; ownership and control, 31-2; political factor, 148-51; range of services, 50, 51, 52; regionalization, 62, 64, 66; Reuters' relations with, 117, 132, 166-8; revenue and expenditure, 43, 44-5, 46; rivalry between NYAP and WAP, 131-2; sales to non-aligned countries, 55, 56; special assignments team, 51-2; in South America, 171, 172, 173, 175-6 &n, 210; structured channels for client influence, 69-70; supplementary agencies and, 144-8
Associated Press Editors' Association (APME), 51, 69, 70, 71, 133
Associated Press of India (API), 181, 182
audio 'voicecasts', 17, 236-7
Australia and New Zealand, 33-4, 119, 180, 182, 211, 222, 228, 229, 234, 238, 239, 240
Australian Press Association, 33-4, 119
Austria, 46, 57, 163, 164-5, 214, 234
Austria Presse Agentur (APA), 164-5
Automatic Data Exchange (ADX), 81, 82

Bakhtar agency, Afghanistan, 195
Bangladesh, 18-19, 58, 102
Bassi, Michel, 129
BBC, 18, 138, 237, 254n; Visnews and, 238, 239, 240
BCINA, 238
Beaverbrook, Lord, 118
Beirut, 82, 89, 153, 179
Belgium, 153, 161, 214
Beltran, Luis R., 176n
Bernstein, Victor, 108-9
Beuve-Monde, Hubert, 35
Bishop, Robert L., 105, 107, 108
Blum, Léon, 124
Boersen-Daten-Zentrale (BDZ), W. Germany, 227
Bolivian news coverage, 109
Bombay Times, 181
book publishing, 244-5
Bouzinac, Robert, 35
Boyd-Barrett, J. O., 105, 106, 107, 139, 146
Braestrup, Peter, 109-10
Brazil, 56, 57, 58, 154, 171, 172, 194, 235
British Commercial Bank, 223
British United Press (BUP), 120, 159
broadcast media, 17, 50, 51; agency services to, 236-8; national news agencies v., 205, 206; newsfilm agencies and, 238-42; print and, 137-9, 220
Brussels, 66, 82, 83, 153
BSS of Bangladesh, 58
Buchan, John, 118
Buenos Aires, 88, 152, 172, 173, 217
Bulgaria, 163, 164, 165, 199, 214
Bunker-Ramo, 234
bureaux, 85-95; AP's hub, 46, 50, 133; at work: in the office, 95-6; chiefs, 49, 76, 87-8, 92-3, 94, 95;

Index

domestic, 44–5; East European, 163, 164; factors determining location of major, 152–5; managers, 49, 88; manpower and, 43–9; markets, 97–8; news-gathering, 84–5; news sources, 96–7; regional message switching, 66; scope, size and composition, 88–95; travel, 96; in Vienna, 164–5; with multi-national responsibility, 88, 89; wordage, 97
Bush, George, 149

Cable News, 131
Cairo, 80, 89, 179–80
Cambodia, 228, 260n
CANA (Caribbean News Agency), 14, 18, 55, 194, 202, 213
Canada, 16, 61–2, 167, 194, 211, 229, 238, 239
Canadian Press (CP), 61
Capen, Richard, 141
Capitol Hill News Service, 146
Cardona, E. F., 176n
cartel, European (Reuters-Havas-Wolff), 116–17, 122, 125, 132, 133, 157, 158, 162, 163, 166, 167, 196–8, 218; AP's relations with, 132, 159, 209–11; 'joint purse' arrangement, 196, 197; promotion of new satellites by, 201–3; satellite agencies, 198–201
CATV, 17, 61, 140, 169, 170–1, 227, 237
CBS, 138
CBS Newsfilm Syndication, 238
censorship, 72, 212, 249
Central News, London, 114, 116, 120, 132, 138, 158
Central News Agency, China, 184–5, 189, 200
Chancellor, Sir Christopher, 174
Chiang Kai-Shek, 185
Chicago: Reuters' bureau in, 168, 169, 229; UPI's radio centres in, 236
Chicago Daily News/Chicago Sun-Times, 146
Chicago Tribune-New York Daily News Service (CT-NYN), 145, 146
China, 16, 183–5, 186, 212
client-agency relationships, 40–3, 47, 67–72; agenda-setting role of agencies, 19–22; contractual basis of, 25; distribution, 59; monitoring of client consumption, 69, 71; non-media services, 218–20; non-routine services to clients, 67–8; structured channels for client influence, 68, 69–72
client media participation, 25–6
coding, direct source-client, 66
Colby, William, 149
Cold War, 109, 110, 149, 204, 250, 259n
Colombia, 194, 195
commentary journalism, 26
Commercial Appeal, Memphis, 131
Commodity News Service (CNS), 52, 169, 232
Commonwealth Press Association, 119
communications, agencies' leased facilities, 242–3
communications technology, 28, 52–4, 65, 76, 207, 220, 225
computer technology, 60, 81, 82, 226, 227, 230
Comtel economic agency, 168, 225, 226
Comtelsa, Spain, 228
'continuous deadline', 74–5
Cooper, Kent, 135, 209, 210
copy-tasters, 78, 81, 177n
Corrbureau, 163
Cosmo, Switzerland, 227
Costa Rica Intergovernmental Conference, 108n
Coty, François, 124
Crispi, Francesco, 197
Crosse, Patrick, 178
CTK agency, Czechoslovakia, 199
Cuba, 22, 57, 109, 148–9, 203
Curran, Sir Charles, 242n
Customprice, 227
Cutlip, Scott M., 104, 110
Czechoslovakia, 163, 164, 165, 199, 214, 235

Daily Telegraph, 160, 242
Dalamar, Alexander and Herman, 199
Dalziel's agency, 115, 116, 120, 126
DataFeature, 147
'day books' of agencies, 21
DDP agency, Germany, 55, 262n
Deferre, Gaston, 129

Index

Degandt, John, 127
Dentsu Tsushin (or Nippon Dentsu), Japan, 186, 187
Depth News service, 19, 217
Desmond, R., 123, 125
Deutsches Nachrichtenbüro (DNB), 163, 186, 211
digital transmission systems, 220, 230, 242
diplomatic correspondents, 52
Disraeli, Benjamin, 197
distribution, direct and indirect, 54–9
diversification, 26, 29, 218–46
Domei agency, Japan, 186–7, 211
domestic markets, 24, 72, 247; AP and UPI, 130–51; clients, 40–1, 42; decentralization, 84; Havas/AFP, 122–30; manpower and bureaux, 44–5, 46; non-routine services to clients, 68; range of services, 50, 51–2; regionalization, 60; Reuters, 112–22; as revenue sources, 36, 39, 40; wholesale news and market control, 112–51
Dow Jones, 81, 168, 169–70, 186, 229, 231; *see also* AP-Dow Jones
DPA (Deutsche Presse Agentur), 14, 55, 61, 98, 142, 160, 195, 201, 205, 208, 209, 253n, 262n; Reuters' joint operation with, 225

East Germany, 163, 164, 214
Eastern Europe, 106, 155, 161–5, 204
Eastern News Agency, India, 199
economic (financial) news services, 16–17, 22, 50, 52, 81–2, 104, 105, 116, 128, 161, 168, 169–70, 218–19; AP–Dow Jones, 231–4; Reuters, 221–31; stock-exchange prices, 126; UPI–CNS, 232, 234
Edicon conferences, 33, 70–1
Editor and Publisher Yearbooks, 139, 143, 144, 167
editorial controls, 74–9; centralization of, 79–85
EFE agency, Spain, 14, 58, 175
Egypt, 179–80, 197, 213–14, 223, 228
electronic darkroom, 54, 235
elimination process, editorial, 77, 78–9
Elliott, Philip, 241n
ENA agency, Bangladesh, 58
Englander, Sigismund, 222
enterprise reporting, 52

Estlow, Edward W., 141
European Alliance (Group 39), 214
Eurovision news, 18, 239, 241–2 &n
Extel, 115–16, 120, 126, 158, 200, 227

Fabra agency, Spain, 171, 175, 198
Fenby, Jonathan, 230
Financial Times, 242
firefighters, 85, 86–7
Focus Service (Extel's), 227
foreign correspondents, 43–4, 47, 49, 52, 100–2, 116, 192, 193
foreign language services, 55–6, 57, 59–60, 80
foreign markets, 152–91
foreign radio stations, monitoring, 208
forward planning, 99
France, 15, 24, 55–6, 57, 61, 153, 160, 214, 228; *see also* Agence France Presse; Havas
Frédèrix, Pierre, 124
Free Press of India, 181–2
French language services, 55–6, 57, 61, 82, 128
Fuller, Keith, 37–8, 65

Gallagher, Wes, 51, 149
Gandhi, Mrs Indira, 54, 183
Gannett News Service, 147, 148
Geiber, W., 19
Gemini news service, 217
Geringer, Alfred, 225
German language service, 56, 57
Ghana news agency, 195, 206, 212–13
Golding, Peter, 241n
Gordon, Jesse, 108–9
government, 22, 24–5; AP and UPI's relations with, 148–51; control of national agencies by, 193, 202, 203, 219; Havas/AFP's relations with, 24, 122, 123, 125, 128, 218; as non-media client of agencies, 219–20; Reuters and, 24, 117–18
Government Information Services, Hong Kong, 188
Grey, Anthony, 185
Grossman, Max, 161
Gunther, John, 150

Handelsblatt, 233
Harris, Phil, 43, 44, 105, 106, 107, 108

Index

Havas, Charles, 125, 221
Havas agency, 23, 36, 115, 119, 129, 156, 159, 162, 166, 167, 180, 200, 223, 245, 254n; advertising activities, 123, 124, 125, 126, 128, 218, 220; cartel agreement with Reuters and Wolff's, 116, 122, 125, 157, 196–7; in China, 184; competition, 125–6; domestic market, 122–6; early expansion, 156, 157, 158; in Eastern Europe, 163; financial service provided by, 221; in Japan, 186; in Middle East, 179; in North Africa, 177; resistance to, 211; satellite agencies, 198, 199; in South America, 156, 157, 159, 171–2, 173, 174, 177, 210; Spanish-language service, 173; *see also* Agence France Presse
Hearst, William Randolph, 136
Hearst newspapers, 32, 142, 143, 234
Hersh, Seymour, 51
Hester, Al, 91, 104, 105, 106
high-speed news delivery services, 50, 54
Hirsch bureau, Berlin, 158
Höhne, Hans, 158n
Holland, 46, 161, 214, 227
Hong Kong, 65, 153, 154, 185, 188, 237, 240; Reuters in, 82, 188, 228, 229; UPI's message-switching centre in, 66, 83; vernacular papers, 190
Houssaye, Henri, 126
Howard, Roy, 159
Hsin Hua (Red China News Agency), 185, 212
Hungary, 163, 164, 165, 199, 214, 234, 235

Imperial Bank of Persia, 222
INA agency, Iraq, 217
Independent Television News (ITN), 238–9, 240
India, 16, 49, 58, 62, 102, 104, 199, 222, 228; agency expansion in, 181–3
Indian News Agency, 181
Indian News Service, 182
Indochina, 180, 189
Indonesia, 58, 152, 194, 228
Information Distribution and Retrieval (IDR), 230–1
Interbureau (IB), 50

intermediate news agencies, 14, 18, 208
International Commission for the Study of Communications Problems (UNESCO), 13, 43, 45, 64
international intermediate news agencies, 14, 201
International News Association, 136
International News Service (INS), 23, 32, 104, 125, 136, 138, 142–3, 175, 184, 244
International Press Institute, 72, 104
International Press Telecommunications Council, 72
Inter Press Service (IPS), 201, 216–17
Investors Management Services (IMS), 227
Israel, 180
Italy, 46, 57, 152, 153, 160, 214, 228

Japan, 16, 37, 47, 58, 60, 153–4, 159, 169, 185–8, 194, 199, 211, 228, 233, 234
Jiji agency, Japan, 187, 188, 194
Johnson, Earl, 244
Jones, Sir Roderick, 117–18 &n, 119, 178, 223–4, 237

Kenya, 16, 108
Kleisch, R., 43, 44
KNI agency, Indonesia, 58
Knight Newspapers, 146
Knudson, Jerry, 109
Kokusai agency, Japan, 186, 199
Korrespondenz-Bureau, Vienna, 197, 198–9
Kyodo (Japanese national agency), 14, 16, 58, 187–8, 194, 209, 233

Lafitte, Mathieu, 123, 125, 126
Lanka Puwarth, 194
Laserphoto, 54, 235
Latin News Agency, 55, 174–5, 201, 202
Lazareff, Pierre, 124
Lebanon, 16, 153, 179
Leser, Lawrence A., 33
Lewin, Kurt, 73
Liebes, B. H., 20
Long, Gerald, 174, 225
Los Angeles Times-Washington Post (LAT–WP) News Service, 144, 145, 146, 147, 148, 171

Index

McArthur, General, 187
McGoff, John P., 240, 246
MacKay's Postal Telegraph Company, 131
Mahoney, John, 238
Malta, Fernando, 110
manpower, 43–9, 89–95; foreign locally recruited, 49, 85–6, 90, 91–4, 100, 101, 102; *see also* bureaux
Marin, Jean, director-general of AFP, 35, 127
Massing, M., 176–7n
May, Fleetwood, 224
M'Bow, Amadou Mahtar, 13
Mecham, Evan, 134
MENA agency, Egypt, 213–14
message-switching centres (MSCS), 66, 82, 83, 230
Mexico, 167, 173, 235
Middle East, 55, 106, 143n, 153, 182; national agencies, 193–4, 202; newsfilm, 240, 241, 242; regional news agencies, 213–14; Western agency expansion, 178–80
Miller, Paul, AP President, 51–2, 147
Le Monde, 35, 40
Moore, Herbert, 138
Morning Standard, London, 115
Morris, Joe A., 183
Moscow, 152, 162, 163, 164
MTI agency, Hungary, 199
Multinational News Agency (MNA), 213
multiplexing, 53, 65

La Nación, Buenos Aires, 172, 210
Nagel, John, 244
NANA news pool, 18–19, 147, 213
Nash, Vernon, 184
national news agencies, 14–15, 51, 53, 61, 72, 192–217; broadcast media v., 205; as clients of world agencies, 207; distribution via, 54–9, 192; foreign correspondents employed by, 192, 193; growth and resource distribution, 193–5; journalists, 207; news flow as news exchange, 195–8; resistance and alternatives, 209–11; satellite agencies, 198–201; shifting centre of resistance, 211–17; as source of national news, 205–6; world agency promotion of new satellites, 201–3

national trunk wire services, 50, 60
NBC, 17, 138, 239, 240
New China News Agency (NCNA), 60, 212
New York, 186; AP in, 80, 130–3; European agencies in, 154, 166, 168, 169, 171
New York Daily News, 136
New York Times News Service (NYTNS), 18, 144, 145, 146, 147, 148
New Zealand Press Association, 33–4, 119
news content, 16; agency, 103–10; newsfilm, 241–2 &n
news exchange, 18, 195–8, 218, 227–8
newsfilm agencies, 238–42
Newspaper Advisory Board (NAB), 71
Newspaper Enterprises Association (NEA), 145, 146, 147, 150
Newspaper Proprietors' Association (NPA), 33, 119
newsphoto services, 15, 17, 51, 56, 57, 58, 129, 183, 234–5, 236; automatic transmission, 50, 220; Electronic Darkroom, 54, 235; Laserphoto, 54, 235; on-screen editing, 220; radiophoto, 234; wirephoto, 234–5
news selection, 73–4; criteria, 99–100; elimination process, 77–9; 'gatekeeper' approach, 73
Nicholas II, Czar, 162
Nigeria, 17n, 177, 178, 241–2n
Nigerian News Agency (NNA), 57, 178, 194, 203, 213
Nihon Keizai Shimbun, Japan, 227
Nixon, Richard, 185
Nkrumah, Kwame, 212
Non-Aligned News Agencies Pool, 13, 14, 130, 213, 214–15
Non-Aligned Summits, 13, 214
non-media markets/clients, 218–20; advertising, 219, 220; financial, 219, 220, 221–31; governments, 219–20; 'private' clients, 219, 220
Norderney Cable, Reuters' sale of, 223
Norsk Press Service, 57
North Africa, 129, 177, 204
Norway, 15, 16, 40, 57
NYAP (New York Associated Press), 131–2

Office Français d'Information (OFI), 127

Index

on-screen editing, 220
Ottoman Telegraph Agency, 199
ownership and control of world agencies, 31–7, 49, 127

Panax Corporation, 240
Paramount Picture Corporation, 239, 240
Paz, Gainza, 175
People's Republic of the Congo, 195
Peron, President, 62, 174
Le Petit Parisien, 124
Petrograd (St Petersburg) Telegraph Agency, 162
Philadelphia AP 'hub' bureau, 46
photographs *see* newsphotos
photographers, 46, 90, 92
Pigeat, Henri, 35
Pinch, E. T., 55, 56, 57
Poland, 163, 165, 214, 234
Portugal, 57, 214, 234
Portuguese-language service, 56, 57, 175
La Prensa, Buenos Aires, 159, 174, 175
Prensa Latina, Cuba, 57, 203, 217
Press Association (PA), Britain, 16, 31, 33, 58, 122, 200, 205; AP's service to, 120–1; centralization, 84; Extel's relations with, 116, 120; Reuters' special relationship with, 38, 112–14, 115, 116, 119, 224
Press Foundation of Asia, 19
Press-Radio Bureau, 138, 167
Press Trust of India (PTI), 58, 119, 182–3, 194
pricing policies of agencies, 28–9
product similarity, 26–7
Psychological War Branch, 160
public relations and lobbying, 244

Radicor, 228
Radio News Association, 138
radio news programmes, 17, 137, 141, 236–7
radiophoto, 234
radio-telegraph, 172
radio-teletype, 53
Rank Organization, 238, 239
Red China News Agency, 185, 212
regional news agencies/alliances, 14, 15, 18, 52, 212–15, 229
Regional News Service (RNS), 179
regionalization of news services, 60–7, 81, 179

Rengo agency, Japan, 186, 187, 211
Renier, Léon, 124
Reuter, Baron Julius, 166, 221, 222–3
Reuter-Agefi, Europe, 226
Reuter Commodity Report, 226
Reuters, 14, 16, 17, 22, 23, 24, 25, 31, 98, 125, 126, 127, 128, 129, 138, 142, 143 &n, 157, 158, 160, 161; ADX system, 81, 230; in Africa, 177–8, 201–2, 206; American Markets Service, 168; AP's relations with, 132, 166–8; Arabic-language news service, 55, 65; Audio service, 170; broadcast wire services, 237–8; cartel agreement with Havas and Wolff's, 116–17, 157, 196–7; Central Desk (later World Desk), 80–1; in China, 183–4, 185; client relations, 42, 71–2; competition, 114–17, 120–1, 231–4; computer services, 170, 226, 227, 228, 230; distribution, 55, 56, 57, 58; domestic market, 112–22; early expansion, 155–7; in Eastern Europe, 162, 163; editorial centralization, 79–82; in Hong Kong, Singapore and Thailand, 188–9; and in India, 181–2; and in Japan, 186, 187, 188; leased communication facilities, 242; location of bureaux, 153, 154–5; manpower and bureaux, 43–4, 45, 88, 94–5; in Middle East, 179, 180; national news agencies and, 195, 205, 206; news content, 104, 105, 106, 107, 108; non-media diversification, 218–19, 220–1, 246; in North America, 155, 165–71, 228, 229; ownership and control, 33–4, 119–20; PA's special relationship with, 33, 112–14, 115, 116; photo distribution, 235; private telegram and telegraph remittance service, 222, 223, 224; Quotation Retrieval Service, 175; regionalization, 61, 63, 64, 65, 66–7; relations with Establishment, 117–18; resistance to, 211; revenue and expenditure, 36, 38–9, 40, 154; Roderick Jones' purchase of, 117–18; sales to non-aligned countries, 55, 56; satellite agencies, 198, 199, 200–2; in South America, 167,

Index

Reuters—*cont.*
171, 172-5, 202, 222; Stockmaster, 226, 227; Times Tower electronic news ticker, 171; TV newsfilm service, 17, 238, 239, 240; US national news coverage by, 61; Videomaster, 170, 226, 227; *see also* RES
Reuters Advertisement Branch, 223
Reuters Economic Services (RES), 17, 38, 39, 61, 80, 108, 168, 169-70, 186, 188, 218-19, 221-31, 245; AP-DJ and other competition to, 231-4; changing relations between general news services and, 229-30; concentration of activities in developed markets, 228-9; exchange agreements, 227-8; research and development orientation, 230-1
Reuters Financial Publicity Department, 223
Reuters Guide to the New Africans, 244-5
Reuters Monitor Services, 22, 170, 226-7, 233
Reuters World Services, 18, 80, 229, 230
revenue and expenditure, 36-40, 154
Rio de Janeiro, 172, 175, 222
Ritzhaus agency, Denmark, 199
Robinson, Gertrude, 109n, 165n
ROSTA, 162
Roussel, Claude, 35
roving correspondents, 52, 85, 86, 87
Roy, K. G., 181
Rumania, 163, 164, 165, 199, 235
Russia (Soviet Union), 106, 155, 161-4, 197-8, 214, 234; *see also* TASS

Sacramento Union Corporation, 240
Sadanand, S., 181
Sahni, J. N., 181
Salinas, Raquel, 108n
San Francisco, 163, 168
sanctions, 100, 101
satellite agencies, 198-201; world agency promotion of new, 201-3
satellite transmission, 53, 65, 236-7, 240
Saudi Arabian broadcasting, 180
Scandinavia, 55, 104, 161, 195, 199, 214, 228

Schlesinger, Philip, 254n
Schramm, W., 20, 21, 105, 106, 107
Schudson, M., 254n
Schwarzlose, Richard A., 132, 139
Scripps-Howard Newspaper Alliance (SHNA), 146, 147
Scripps-Howard Newspapers (E. W. Scripps Co.), 32-3, 132, 133, 135, 138, 141, 142, 146, 150, 234
Scripps League Service, 133
services, 50-60; communications technology, 52-4; direct and indirect distribution, 54-9; languages, 59-60; range, 50-2
Shanghai, 183, 184
Shaw, D. L., 254n
Singapore, 65, 80, 81, 84, 88, 153, 154, 188-9, 190, 228, 229, 240
Singletary, Michael, 139, 146
Snider, P., 63
South Africa, 39, 63, 105, 106, 107, 182; 'Muldergate' scandal, 240; Reuters in, 177-8, 199, 211, 228
South African Press Agency (SAPA), 178, 199, 211
South/Latin America, 37, 39, 49, 80, 81, 83, 112, 128, 130; agency expansion, 171-6, 177; AP in, 171, 172, 173, 175-6 &n, 210; bureaux in, 88, 91, 98, 154, 155; distribution, 54, 55, 56-7; freedom to report, 102; Havas/AFP in, 156, 157, 159, 171, 172, 173, 174, 175, 177, 210; Inter Press Service, 216-17; Latin agency in, 174-5; national news agencies, 194, 202; news content of agencies, 104-5, 106, 107-8, 110; newsfilm, 240, 241, 242; regional news agencies, 213; and regionalization, 62, 64, 65; Reuters in, 167, 171, 172-5, 202, 222, 225
South Vietnam, 153, 154, 228
Southern Television (UK), 239
Spain, 57-8, 159, 171, 198, 214, 228, 234, 235
Spanish-language services, 56, 57, 173, 175, 217
special assignment coverage, 51-2
special correspondents, 116
special-relevance news, 62, 66
sports news, 15, 52, 90, 105, 116, 120, 136, 175, 241
spot news, 26, 27, 28, 87, 97, 126, 143

Index

Sri Lanka, 19, 194
staffers, 43, 46, 47, 86, 165
States News Service, 146
Stefani agency, Italy, 197, 198
Stempel, G., 20, 21
Sterling Newspapers Ltd, 62
Stockmaster, 226, 227, 229
Stone, Melville, 162, 210
Storey, G., 167, 180, 223
stringers, 44, 47, 85, 86, 88, 90, 92, 94, 165, 207
Sweden, 56, 161
Swinton, Stan, 38, 62, 176, 237
Swiss Bourse ticker, 226
Switzerland, 57, 161, 199, 214, 228, 234
syndicated services, 15, 50, 243

Taiwan, 93, 185, 189
Tanjug agency, Yugoslavia, 14, 18, 19, 109n, 130, 163–4, 195, 214–15, 216–17, 249, 253–4n
TAP agency, Tunisia, 57, 203, 217
TASS, 14, 60, 162, 163, 164, 198, 212; in Africa, 178; news service in USA, 162, 163; use of 'Big Four' agency reports by, 16
'team reporting', 70
technology, 52–4, 65, 75, 76, 207, 220, 225, 236; computer, 60, 81, 82, 226, 227, 230; newsfilm operations, 240–1; photo distribution, 234–5
Telam agency, Argentina, 128
Telecom Highway satellite, 213
telegraph companies, 122–3, 131, 135, 223
Telekurs, Zurich, 234
teleprinter services, 17, 220, 226–7, 233
Telerate, USA, 234
Television News (USA), 239–40
television newsfilm (or video), 17, 50, 140, 220, 236; newsfilm agencies, 238–42
Third World, 16, 20–1, 28, 53, 112, 130; national news agencies, 192, 194, 201, 203, 206; news content of agencies, 105, 106, 110; newsfilm and, 241; political control of agency operations, 162; press freedom, 102, 248–9; regional news agencies, 212–15; regionalization, 62–4, 67; resistance to world agencies, 212–17; revenue importance for agencies, 37–8, 39; role of 'Big Four', 247, 248–50; world agency promotion of new satellites, 201–2, 203; *see also* Africa; Asia; South America
The Times of India, 181, 182
The Times of London, 115, 160, 222, 242
Tokyo, 169, 182, 186, 187, 188, 190
Toronto Star Publishing Group, 61
Trade Telegraph Agency (TTA), 162
translation services, 55, 56, 58, 59, 65–6, 81, 82
Trans-Ocean agency, 158n, 184, 200, 211
Transradio Press Service, 138–9
Trayes, E. J., 139
Tremaine, Frank, 71
TT agency, Sweden, 56
Tu agency, Germany, *158*, 159
Tuchman, G., 21
Tunisia, 57, 177, 203
Turkey, 163, 194, 197, 199, 214, 228

Ultra Prensa, Colombia, 195
Ultronics, 170, 234; Reuters' deal with, 225–6, 227, 231
UNESCO, 13, 43, 45, 62, 64, 102, 108
United Features Syndicate, 146, 147
United Kingdom *see* Reuters; Press Association
United Media Enterprises, Inc. (UME), 32, 146–7
United News, India (UNI), 58, 182, 183
United Press International (UPI), 14, 16, 17, 20, 23, 25, 79, 80, 117, 120, 125, 128, 200, 204, 249; in Africa, 177, 178; A.M. and P.M. press, 135–7; in Asia, 182–3, 184, 185, 186, 187, 189; book publishing by, 245; broadcast news and, 138, 139, 236–7, 238, 245; bureaux, 88, 92, 153–5; centralization, 82–3, 84; clients, 41, 42, 140–1; DataNews, 50; distribution, 55–7, 58; diversification, 218, 245–6; in Eastern Europe, 162, 163, 164; economic reporting, 52; exclusivity, 133–4; expansion in Europe, 158–61; foreign language services, 55–6, 57; leased communications facilities, 243; manpower and

United Press International—*cont.*
bureaux, 43, 44, 45–6, 49; market trends, 139–44; in Middle East, 179, 180; MSC system, 66, 82, 83; news content, 104, 105, 106, 107–8, 110; newspaper Advisory Board, 71; newsphoto service, 17, 90, 234, 235, 245; New York influence, 132; non-routine client servicing, 68; organization for client influence, 70–1, 72; ownership and control, 32–3; political factor, 148–51; range of services, 50, 52; regionalization, 61–2, 64, 65, 66; *Reporter*, 69; revenue and expenditure, 37–8; sales to non-aligned countries, 55, 56; in South America, 172, 173, 174, 175–6 &n, 210; Special Service Bureau, 175, 244; supplementary agencies and, 144–8; TV newsfilm service, 17, 238–9, 240
United Press Movietone Television (UPMT), 238
United Press of India, 182
United States *see* Associated Press; United Press International
Universal News Services (UNS), 225
UP (United Press), 131, 132, 133, 135, 137, 162, 167
UPI Broadcast Advisory Board, 33
UPI–CNS commodity news service, 232, 234
UPI National Advisory Board, 144, 147
UPI Newsfilm, Inc., 238
UPI Newspaper Advisory Board, 33, 141
UPITN, 17, 18, 140, 237, 238–9, 240
US Mutual Broadcasting Corporation, 170
US Senate Foreign Relations Committee, 244

Venezuela, 194, 217
Vereinigte Wirtschaftsdienst (VWD), 225, 227, 233 &n, 234
video-display editing terminals, 83, 231
Videomaster, 170, 226, 227, 228
video technology, 240
Vienna, 47, 56, 164–5, 197, 204
Vietnam War, 18, 109, 150, 153

Vilcek, Miroslav, 242n
Visnews, 17 &n, 18, 238, 239–40, 241, 242n, 246
voicecasts, 17, 50, 220, 236–7

Wall Street Journal, 141–2, 169, 231, 232, 233n
WAP (Western Associated Press), 131, 132, 135
Washington, 148, 151, 154, 168, 171
Washington Star, 240
Weibull, Lennart, 104, 106, 107
West Germany, 14, 55, 57, 61, 153, 160, 214, 225, 233–4
Western Europe/Europe (*see also* East Germany): agency news content, 105, 106, 107; cartel (Reuters-Havas-Wolff), 116–17, 122, 125, 132, 133, 157–8, 162, 167, 196–8, 209–11; early expansion of Havas and Wolff, 156; Eurovision news, 18, 239, 241–2 &n; foreign correspondents, 47, 49; and foreign-language services, 55–6, 57 location of bureaux, 153, 154; satellite agencies, 198–9; US agency expansion, 155, 158–61
Western Union, 131, 135
White, David Manning, 73
Wirephoto, 234–5
Wolff, Dr Bernhard, 221
Wolff's (Continental) agency (WTB), 23, 125, 163, 166, 200, 211; alliance between Korrespondenz-Bureau of Vienna and, 198–9; cartel with Reuters and Havas, 116, 125, 157, 196, 197, 198; commercial news service, 221; early expansion, 156, 157, 158 &n; news supply to Russia, 162
Woollacott, Martin, 102
World War I, 117–18, 148, 159, 162, 172
World War II, 119, 127, 160, 163, 173–4, 237

Xinhua (Chinese news agency), 16

Yugoslavia, 163, 164, 165n, 214–15; *see also* Tanjug

Zaire news agency, 206